30p

I N S I D E R 'S
PORTUGAL
G   U   I   D   E

THE INSIDER'S GUIDES

AUSTRALIA • BALI • CALIFORNIA • CHINA • EASTERN CANADA • FLORIDA • HAWAII •
HONG KONG • INDIA • INDONESIA • JAPAN • KENYA • KOREA • NEPAL • NEW ENGLAND • NEW
ZEALAND • MALAYSIA AND SINGAPORE • MEDITERRANEAN FRANCE • MEXICO • PORTUGAL •
RUSSIA • SPAIN • THAILAND • TURKEY • VIETNAM, LAOS AND CAMBODIA • WESTERN CANADA

The Insider's Guide to Portugal

© 1995 Novo Editions, S.A.

Moorland Publishing Co Ltd
Moor Farm Road, Airfield Estate, Ashbourne, DE61HD, England
published by arrangement with Novo Editions SA
53 rue Beaudouin, 27700 Les Andelys, France
Telefax: (33) 32 54 54 50

ISBN: 0-86190-284-X

Created, edited and produced by Novo Editions, S.A.
Editor in Chief: Allan Amsel
Original design concept: Hon Bing-wah/Kinggraphic
Picture editor and designer: Michelle Chan
Text and artwork composed and information updated
using Ventura Publisher software

Printed by Samhwa Printing Co Ltd, Seoul, Korea

INSIDER'S
PORTUGAL
GUIDE

by Mikhael Khorian

Photographed by
Bruno Barbier and Nik Wheeler

MPC

Contents

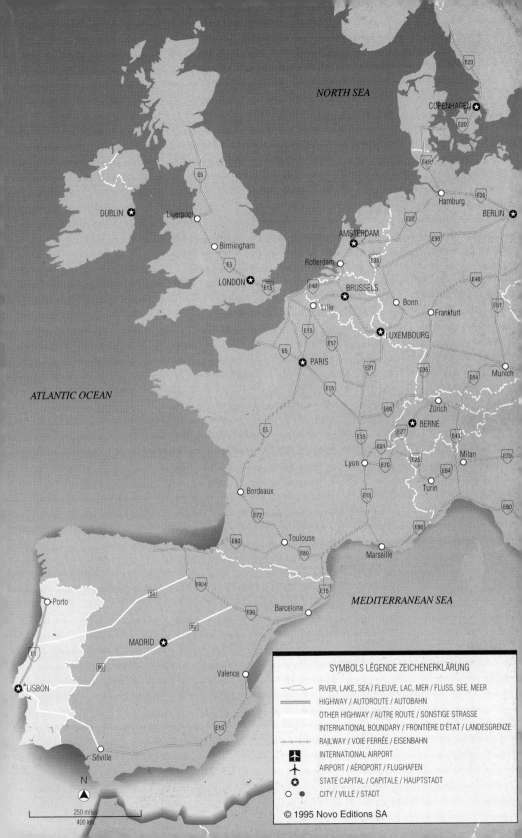

TOP SPOTS

Dabble in the Douro

THE RIO DOURO ("RIVER OF GOLD") IS THE GRANDEST RIVER IN PORTUGAL, wriggling east for some 200 km (125 miles) from Porto to Barca d'Alva on the Spanish border. You won't find any river in the world more tipsy than this: all along the upper reaches are the country's famous port wine vineyards, covering the steep surrounding hillsides and creeping right down to the water's edge. Occasionally you may spot a bright white *quinta* among the serried ranks of vines — a farm house belonging to a wine farmer or one of the port wine companies, many of which have been in operation for centuries.

There's nothing more delightful than to take a cruise from Porto into the heart of the port wine country at Pinhão, sipping a little port as you go. Endouro Turismo in

Porto (((02) 324236) organize regular day-long outings. There are shorter 50-minute jaunts, cruising beneath the city's four bridges, but though these give you a little taste of Douro delight the river's real drama — deep gorges and expansive calm stretches between a series of dams — only starts in earnest further inland.

Organized cruises aren't your only option: if you want to go it alone, you can take the train (two hours and 30 minutes) to Peso de Régua, a center for the port wine industry with a couple of port wine lodges you can visit, the Casa do Douro and Ramos Pinto. Even better if you've got the time is to take the train all the way to the end of its river-hugging route at Pocinho (four hours and 30 minutes from Porto). You won't find much here except the very best that the Douro offers: a sound of chuckling water and a sweet aroma of wine.

Dream to *Fado*

IF THERE IS ONE UNIQUELY PORTUGUESE ART FORM IT IS THE STYLE OF SINGING CALLED FADO (literally meaning fate). No visit to Portugal is complete without an evening spent listening to this haunting music. Intensely nostalgic songs are sung by soberly dressed men or women swathed in black shawls, apparently in mourning for the first famous *fadista*, a gypsy girl called Maria Severa. The songs tend to

Jerónimos monastery OPPOSITE in Lisbon, the jewel in the crown of Manueline architecture. ABOVE: Iron bridge over the river Douro at Pinhão, a main center of the port wine trade.

resolve around the themes of home-sickness, lost love and death, and the *fadista's* voice is powerful, usually accompanied by 12-string guitars. Frankly, this music is an acquired taste, but enthusiasts will not hear a word said against it.

The style originated in the Alfama district of Lisbon in the eighteenth century, and there is a slightly different variety in Coimbra. Unfortunately, much of the *fado* you're likely to find in Lisbon clubs today is geared for the tourists (with a minimum entrance fee of around 2500$00 escudos), but if you stick to the smaller clubs you'll stand a better chance of hearing the real thing. My Lisbon friends all recommend **Adega do Ribatejo**, Rua Diário Notícias N° 23, ((01) 346-8343 in the city's Barro Alto district; and in Coimbra you can grow misty-eyed and dream the evening away at the **Diligencia Bar**, Rua Nova N° 30, ((039) 27667, which is a popular haunt for both experienced and up-and-coming *fadistas*.

well as fascinating photos of Porto from the good old days when trams ruled the road.

Trundle on the Trams

IF YOU'RE A TRAM FAN YOU'LL BE IN SEVENTH HEAVEN IN LISBON AND PORTO: although they're gradually being replaced by buses, ancient trams (called *electricos*) still trundle along the seashore in Porto and tackle some of Lisbon's steepest streets. You won't get anywhere very fast but who needs speed when you've got a vehicle of such character, with gleaming wooden and brass interiors?

In Lisbon, **tram number 28** is the best one to sample. It starts from the central Rua Conceicão and clatters up into the old quarter. But I find the best tram delights are often unplanned: hop onto any tram you see (it only costs 140$00 escudos a ticket) and simply enjoy the ride. The central Praça do Comercio is a good place to take your pick. In Porto, don't miss **tram number 1** which starts near the waterfront Ribeira and potters along the coast to Foz. En route, you can stop at the recently-opened **Tram Museum** at Cais do Bicalho which displays dozens of restored trams dating from the turn of the century to the 1970s as

Sleep in a Private Palace

FANCY SOMETHING A LITTLE DIFFERENT FOR YOUR NIGHT IN THE COUNTRY? How about a seventeenth century manor house where a king once slept, or a baronial mansion where your host is a count? It's all possible in Portugal, and not for outrageous prices, either. Thanks to a scheme called Turismo de Habitação or TURIHAB (see ACCOMMODATION in TRAVELER'S TIPS), dozens of select private houses now offer some of the best accommodation you can find in Europe from about US$50 a night.

TURIHAB was established by the owners of the houses themselves with the idea of providing an unique service: you're not just a casual "hotel" visitor, but a personal guest. The owners can give you an unique insight to the surroundings, too — their personal tips on sights to see and anecdotes on local history (one countess I met delighted in telling me about the scandalous

A tram OPPOSITE trundles past Lisbon's cathedral. Valença do Minho ABOVE faces Spain across the river Minho at Portugal's northern tip.

goings-on of her ancestors!), while your room is likely to be lavishly furnished with the family's antiques, perhaps dating back to the sixteenth century. Not all TURIHAB's accommodation is in this kind of baronial league: you can choose a simple *casa rustica* (country cottage) if it's more to your taste or a rambling farmhouse or *quinta* (manor house). Contact the main TURIHAB organization at Praça da República, 4990 Ponte de Lima, ℭ (058) 741-672 for their full brochure.

Marvel at the Manueline

EVEN IF YOU'RE NOT AN ARCHITECTURE BUFF, YOU CAN'T FAIL TO MARVEL AT PORTUGAL'S INCREDIBLY ORNATE MANUELINE STYLE OF ARCHITECTURE. It takes its name from King Manuel who reigned during Portugal's fifteenth to sixteenth century heyday — the Age of the Discoveries when Portugal's seafaring explorers discovered the sea route to India, making Portugal one of the most powerful trading countries in the world.

The resulting wealth and confidence gave rise to magnificent cathedrals, monasteries and churches — all embellished with the unique Manueline touch: exuberant stonework of knots and globes and seafaring motifs. The flagship of the era is the **Jerónimos Monastery** at Belém near Lisbon but other stunning examples worth going out of your way to see are the chapter house window in Tomar's Convento de Cristo and the Unfinished Chapels of Batalha.

Celebrate with Leeks!

NO-ONE ENJOYS A FESTIVAL MORE THAN THE PORTUGUESE. Despite the rapid changes now affecting traditional life and the growing influences from abroad, the Portuguese are still passionate supporters of their own unique folk culture. Throughout the year — and especially during spring and summer — you can find a festival (*festa*), fair (*feira*) or religious event in honor of a patron saint (*romária*) going on somewhere every weekend.

Every town or village still has its own dance group — men and women, girls and boys — who perform in beautifully-embroidered traditional costume at regional events. And every village can boast its own female singer who takes

immense pride in performing the songs with the required ear-splitting screech.

There's no better place to be to soak up the local atmosphere than at one of these festivals. The larger events feature everything from orderly religious processions to fireworks and intricate floral displays but you can find simple song-and-dance events in even the smallest country village. One of my favorite small festivals takes place on May lst in the Algarve, at Alte, where ribbon-adorned donkeys are part of each team and dancers twirl in the narrow streets. The local tourist offices can always tell you where to find a festival like this going on.

Among the biggest and best is the Holy Week festival in Braga, with its colourful processions of penitents and devotees; and the outrageously lively **St John's Festival**, held around the 23rd and 24th of June in Porto. The whole town seems to be out partying on those nights, with singing, dancing and riotous merrymaking. Don't ask me why (I've never been given a sensible explanation) but there's a strange little ritual to this particular festival which entails bashing anyone you meet with a leek!

Walk Medieval Walls

SCATTERED ALL OVER PORTUGAL IS EVIDENCE OF THE COUNTRY'S PLUCKY PAST: DOZENS OF HILLTOP FORTS AND CASTLES which were Portugal's frontline of defence against the Moors, and later, the Spanish and French. Many of the forts have been rebuilt several times; others used right up until the nineteenth century. Linked to many of them is the name of Dom Dinis, the "fortress King" of Portugal, who during his reign from 1279 to 1325 built or rebuilt over 50 castles, particularly along the strategic eastern frontier with Spain.

Walking the walls is a great way to glimpse Portugal's past and see some of the most picturesque corners of its present landscape. Hugging the safety of the castle are often old villages, many little changed

Religious procession at Barqueiros OPPOSITE in the Minho, Portugal's most strongly Catholic province. Ancient ruins RIGHT at the Citânia de Briteiros.

from the days of Dinis himself. Arguably the prettiest and most romantic walled town is **Óbidos** (which Dinis gave his fiancee as a bridal gift) while **Elvas**, just 13 km (eight miles) from the Spanish border, still ranks as one of the best-fortified towns in Europe.

Don't miss **Castelo de Vide** and nearby **Marvão**, either — the latter perched so high on a rocky hilltop it's a wonder it was ever defeated. Stay the night if you can when you visit these fortified villages and in the windswept silence of the narrow lanes you'll catch a real sense of Portugal's indomitable spirit which helped preserve her independence for centuries.

Catch a Country Market

PORTUGAL STILL KNOWS HOW TO HOLD A PROPER OUTDOOR COUNTRY MARKET — the sort where you can find everything from clucking hens and squealing pigs to hand-made ceramics, baskets and carved wooden ox yokes. You'll catch some of the best markets in the country's northern Minho district, especially at **Barcelos** on a Thursday. This huge country fair, held in the town's central square, is a microcosm of Portuguese rural life: smallholders with little piles of fruit or vegetables for sale, potters displaying their brightly-coloured wares, gypsy women selling clothes and shoes. This is the place to pick up your typical Portuguese gifts and souvenirs, or simply mingle with the locals.

Other good markets to take in on your tour include the Saturday fair at **Estremoz** in the Alentejo (great for terracotta dishes and water jugs as well as fine little home-made wooden toys) and the daily market at **Caldas da Rainha** in Estremadura, which is famous for its whimsical cabbage-leaf ceramics (a national ceramics' fair is held here in early July).

Take a Bite of *Bacalhau*

IT'S GREY, DULL AND SALTY. DRIED, IT KEEPS FOR MONTHS — A STAPLE FOOD FOR VILLAGERS ALL OVER THE COUNTRY. IT'S PORTUGAL'S MOST POPULAR DISH, with a reputed 365 recipes to its name — but it doesn't even come from the country.

Bacalhau, dried cod, isn't the most attractive fish you could find, cooked or uncooked, but if you want an unique taste of Portugal, this is it. The Portuguese first fell in love with *bacalhau* when their fishing fleets returned from forays in Newfoundland in the early fifteenth

century. Now the favored fish is imported from Norway and Iceland.

One of the tastiest ways to eat it is in a dish called **bacalhau à Gomes de Sa** (perhaps because it's mixed up well with black olives and slices of hard-boiled egg) but my fondest memory of the fish is from a trip I once made into the mountains near Coimbra. The little village where I finally stopped, Piodão, had no guesthouse and no restaurant, but a villager took me under her wing and offered me a bed for the night and a meal. Within minutes she had dug up fresh potatoes from her garden, sliced off a piece of dried cod hanging from her kitchen ceiling, and cooked me the standard dish of the country: boiled potatoes and *bacalhau*, drowning in rich olive oil. It couldn't have been simpler, but I never tasted a meal so good.

Hunt for the Best *Azulejos*

STEP INTO ALMOST ANY CHURCH OR PALACE IN PORTUGAL AND YOU'LL NOTICE ONE RECURRENT FEATURE — THE EXTRAVAGANT USE YOUR CHOICE

OF AZULEJOS, *BLUE AND WHITE OR POLYCHROME WALL TILES.*

The Portuguese have been refining the art for over 500 years, starting with mainly blue (*azul*) tiles after the Moors originally introduced a geometric style of *azulejos* into the country.

Some of the most striking *azulejos* are in places where they're least expected — as in the São Bento train station at Porto, for instance. But undoubtedly the best are found in churches such as **Almancil's Church of São Lourenço** in the Algarve and Évora's Loios Church in the Alentejo. And for one of the finest museums in Lisbon, you can't beat the **Museu dos Azulejos** within the Madre de Deus church and cloisters which boasts a 37 m- (120 ft)-long panorama of Lisbon, all in *azulejos*, and completed in the eighteenth century.

Open air market OPPOSITE BOTTOM at Viana do Castelo in the Minho. *Azulejo* tiles ABOVE adorn Portugal's public buildings.

YOUR CHOICE

The Great Outdoors

With so much attention given to Portugal's splendid architectural sights and well-developed southern seaside resorts, the country's great outdoor attractions further north are often overlooked. But if you're a walker or nature-lover you'll find Portugal has some of the best-kept outdoor secrets in Europe, ranging from rambling forests and gardens to rugged mountain ranges.

On the wild side, there are 21 officially protected areas, including the Peneda-Gerês National Park in the north and some 15 *parques naturais* and *reservas naturais* scattered all over the country. You can pick up information on these from the National Parks Services' headquarters in Lisbon at Rua Ferreira Lapa, Nº 29, ((01) 352-3317.

The highest mountain range in the country is the north-eastern **Serra da Estrêla** which features Portugal's tallest peak, the 1,991 m (4,800 ft) Torre. With its superbly varied landscape, from deep ravines to lush forests, this is the area to head for if you're after some challenging hiking. Penhas de Saúde, near Covilhã, is a good spot to base yourself — in winter you can even ski here. There are several major trails in the Serra da Estrêla Natural Park, with guidebooks and maps available from the information offices in Manteigas, Covilhã or Seia. Alternatively, you can contact the Club Nacional de Montanhismo, ((075) 323364 to find out about organized weekend expeditions.

Less demanding trails are found in the popular **Peneda-Gerês National Park** in the far north of the country, though here, too, there are plenty of tough hikes for those who want them. The sleepy spa town of Caldas do Gerês is the park's main base with a good range of accommodation available and a park office which sells maps detailing roads and major trails.

You can do easy day-trip walks into the hills from here — one of my favorites is to follow the old Roman road (complete with Roman milestones) past the Vilarinho das Furnas reservoir. Further afield, trails through the forests lead to the simple hamlets of Ermida and Cabril, and on again to the mountain village of Paradela.

The basilica of Santa Luzia OPPOSITE on top of Viana do Castelo, affords expansive vistas up and down the Minho coast. ABOVE: Costa da Caparica.

This last 23-km (14-mile) section is part of an official long-distance footpath which is slowly being established in the park, mostly following traditional routes.

If you'd rather someone else showed you the way, contact Trote-Gerês in Cabril, ((053) 659343 for information on organized walks, horse-riding and canoeing in the area. Two UK-based organizations, Explore Worldwide, ((44-1252) 319448 and Ramblers Holidays, ((44-1707) 331133, also organise walking holidays in Portugal, including in the Peneda-Gerês region.

Down from the mountainous north, you can enjoy some wonderfully relaxing rambles in the verdant hills of Sintra near Lisbon and in the 480-acre (1,185-hectare) Buçaco Forest near Coimbra. **Sintra**'s charms were frequently praised by British poets and travellers of the eighteenth century, most famously by Byron, who used "Cintra's glorious Eden" as an opening setting for his poem, "Childe Harold". Today, the town center's Royal Palace and hilltop Pena Palace attract coach-loads of tourists daily but it's easy to find your own Byronic Eden in the romantically unkempt Monserrate Gardens or Pena Palace Park. Nearby Colares makes another fine base for walkers, and as everywhere in Portugal you'll find several good campsites nearby. The helpful Sintra tourist office can provide information on these and other types of accommodation in the area.

Buçaco Forest is rather more special: Benedictine monks built a hermitage here as long ago as the sixth century, establishing a religious presence which was protected by a papal bull in 1622 forbidding women to enter the forest and another in 1643 threatening anyone who damaged the trees with excommunication. Carmelite monks who settled here in the seventeenth century built boundary walls and planted new varieties of trees including Mexican cedars and Austrian oaks. They remained in the forest right up until 1834 when religious orders were abolished throughout Portugal.

The Forest is now open to anyone, its rich variety of over 700 different types of trees making it an extraordinarily lush little haven. At the heart of the Forest are the remains

of the Carmelite monastery with its cork-clad cells, and the more eye-catching pseudo-Manueline Royal Palace Hotel, once a royal hunting lodge. But the Forest's best attractions are its trees. Easy-to-follow paths meander among them and lead to panoramic summits past tiny chapels and crosses, waterfalls and streams. At weekends the Forest can be packed with local picnickers, but linger here on a weekday and you'll capture some of Buçaco's special quality of tranquillity and reverence.

Sporting Spree

Wherever you go in Portugal — whether it's the sparkling south or the

mountainous north — you'll find plenty of challenging sports to keep your adrenalin pumping. Your best destination if you're a golf or tennis fan is the southern Algarve region, which has long been famous for its superb **golf** courses. There are now 33 to choose from, many designed by international experts such as Henry Cotton, Frank Pennink and Robert Trent-Jones. All of them are complemented by fabulous settings of pines, lakes and flowers against a turquoise backdrop of sea and sky. The creme de la creme? The Quinta do Lago course, built on a 2,000-acre (800-hectare) luxury estate.

Serious golfers who want to be sure of enjoying their golf should consider booking a package which includes green fees and pre-booked tee-off times —

dozens of UK-based operators offer these specialized holidays, such as Golf Holidays International, ((44-1480) 433000; Longshot Golf Holidays, ((44-1730) 268621; and Sovereign Golf, ((44-1293) 599911.

In July and August you may find the Algarve too hot for golf (many courses reduce their fees at this time) but that's when **tennis** becomes the most popular sport. You can find excellent tennis centers in the Algarve at Vilamoura, Vale de Lobo and Carvoeiro — and if you're heading for Lisbon, check out the highly sophisticated Estoril Tennis Club

Fighting bulls are bred on the plains of the Ribatejo. Unlike in Spain, the beasts are not killed in the ring.

nearby where you can enjoy complete tennis holidays.

Package tennis holidays to the Algarve including coaching by international professionals are good value: try the UK-based Roger Taylor Tennis Holidays, ((44-081) 947-9272, or The Travel Club of Upminster ((44-1708) 223000 which can also arrange mixed sporting weeks of tennis, golf and riding.

Watersports, of course, are another Algarve specialty: water-skiing, scuba diving, sailing and big game fishing are all available through the major resorts here, though serious wind-surfers should head north, to Praia do Guincho (near Cascais) for some really awesome Atlantic rollers (World Championships have been held here).

Canoeing and fishing is delightful on Portugal's northern rivers. Once you've got your **fishing** license (available from Instituto Florestal, Avenida João Crisostomo, 26, Lisbon) you can fish on any of Portugal's rivers. In the north, the Minho, Mouro, Castro and Douro rivers are particularly good for salmon, trout and barbel.

But if the fish aren't biting, you can always have a day **canoeing** instead. When you're in Coimbra, contact O Pioneiro do Mondego, ((039) 478385 for a paddle on the Mondego River. Even further north, in the mountainous Peneda-Gerês National Park, Trote-Gerês, ((053) 659343 can set you canoeing on the tranquil River Cavado. They also have **horse-riding** facilities — another popular sport in

Portugal which you can find almost everywhere (ask at the local tourist offices for contacts), with horses ranging from Anglo-Arab to the famous Lusitano variety, known as the "Royal Horse of Europe."

The extensive plains of the Alentejo province are particularly enjoyable for horse-riders. In Évora, Mendes & Murteira, ((066) 23616 can make arrangements for horse-riding excursions as well as for fishing, **walking** and **bicycling** tours in the region. And how about an aerial ride in a hot-air balloon while you're here? Or an off-road drive-yourself **jeep safari**? Contact Mendes & Murteira or TurAventur, ((066) 743134 for these novel ways of looking at the countryside.

Mountain-biking is catching on fast in Portugal, though you'd be advised to bring a bag of spares if you're bringing your own machine as supply shops are few and far between. If you just want to rent a bike for a day, ask at the local tourist office — a few resorts, mostly in the Algarve, have a bike rental outfit. Or for an organized cycling holiday, try Cicle Portugal, ((01) 486-2044, based near Lisbon.

And if you've still got energy to burn, you might fancy a weekend's **canyoning** (tackling a river canyon on foot: a combination of swimming, abseiling and rock climbing) or **hydrospeed** (a form of white-water rafting using individual floats — and crash helmets!). These are action-packed, high-thrills adventure sports, offering a real hands-on experience of the country. I think I'll stick to walking myself, but for those who are game, these are the people to contact: Turnatur, in Lisbon, ((01) 207-6886; and Trilhos, in Porto, ((02) 520740.

SPECTATOR SPORT

Soccer is Portugal's national obsession: in fact, perhaps it would have been better to put it under the heading entitled religion. When the football season is on, people talk about little else: televisions in cafés and bars are on during important matches, and rapt attention holds the faces of the lounge-lizards. Don't interrupt!

The other sport associated with Portugal is **bull-fighting**. The main center is the province of Ribatejo where the bulls are bred, although there are rings throughout the country. The season lasts from April to October and bullfights take place mainly on Sundays. Costumes are elaborate, and the whole affair has an extraordinary atmosphere. Everyone will tell you how much more humane it is here than in Spain, but until I hear it from the bull's own mouth, I reserve my decision: while they are not killed in the ring, they still have a pretty rotten time and are finished off after the spectacle, anyway.

Motor racing is also popular in Portugal, the major races taking place at the *autodromo* in Estoril, attracting huge crowds. There is also the Rallye de Portugal do Vinho de Porto, held for a week each March on country roads: it begins and ends at Estoril as well.

The Open Road

There's no better way to explore the real Portugal than by meandering by car or by foot in the countryside. Leave the *auto-estrada* highways (especially those along the Algarve and between Lisbon and Oporto) to the Portuguese kamikaze drivers and follow

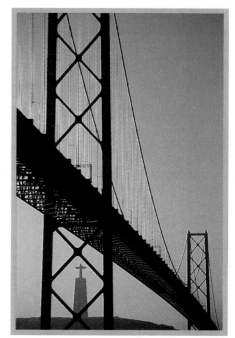

the minor roads wherever possible. The Michelin 1:400,000 map of Portugal is the best guide for this kind of touring.

Unless you're trying to see as much of the country as possible you'll probably find it more enjoyable to stick to one region and make day-trips from a long-term base than worry about finding new accommodation every night. If you're intent on driving far afield don't be fooled by Portugal's small size: distances may look easy to accomplish in a day but you'll find minor roads in the boondocks are often charmingly unkempt, with traffic of donkeys and ox-carts to hold you up. Distractions are frequent, too — ruined forts or deserted beaches, meadows of wild flowers or a good wine at lunch. The trick is to keep your plans flexible and stop whenever the fancy takes you. Even in high season you should be able to find a place to stay in a small town or village without booking ahead (the local tourist offices can always help). Take your pick from the following suggestions for some of the best scenic discoveries of Portugal.

The golf courses of the Algarve OPPOSITE TOP are famed for their manicured greens. Fishing boats OPPOSITE BOTTOM are drawn up on the sand at the Algarve's resort village of Albufeira. The 25th April bridge ABOVE spans the Tagus at Lisbon.

The obvious attraction in the **Algarve** is the coastline and its fabulous beaches but if you're after something a little less crowded and more unusual, head inland, to the foothills of the Serra de Monchique. If you're based in or near Faro, it's worth following a route that takes in the ruins of Estoi Palace, the historic town of Loulé and the picturesque riverside castle-town of Silves, on the N269. A perfect place for a lunch-stop, Silves is just 21 km (13 miles) from your goal at Monchique, but leave time to stop first at Caldas de Monchique, an atmospheric little spa deep within a dingle. Monchique itself is a lively market town, with accommodation if you fancy staying the night, and a panoramic view of the whole Algarve coastline from nearby Foia.

Heading out of the Algarve, into the **Alentejo** plains, the easiest route is to follow the main IP2 to Beja and on to Évora. But for lovers of wiggly country roads and rich doses of atmosphere I can heartily recommend the minor N122 which hugs the Spanish border from Castro Marim to Métola. The first part of this route, with a little side-trip to Alcoutim and its 14th century castle, is one of the most dramatic in the Algarve, following the River Guadiana past villages right on the water's edge. The old walled town of Métola, perched high above the Guadiana, makes a wonderful stopover, with its remote and mysterious air. The atmosphere lingers long after you leave, especially if you continue on the back-roads N265 and N255, meandering through classic Alentejo scenery, to the attractive towns of Serpa and Moura. From here you're about 70 km (44 miles) from the spectacular walled hilltop village of Monsaraz: the route from Mourão, 12 km (seven miles) south provides a magical approach, through fields of wild flowers, cork and olive trees (keep a look-out, too, for hoopoee birds). A night's stopover here could well be a highlight of your Alentejo tour, a dreamy interlude before you reach Évora some 82 km (51 miles) to the northwest.

There are several excellent day-trips possible from Évora. The most obvious is to head for the beautiful marble town of Estremoz, 46 km (28 miles) to the northeast, stopping at the hilltop fort of Évoramonte en route. Coming back, you can take a different route via Arraiolos, famous since the 17th century for its carpets. A day-trip to Monsaraz is also a must if you haven't already seen it.

But my favorite Évora excursions are those in search of dolmens. There are over a dozen megalithic sites in the area, dating from around 3000 BC. Pick up the special *Guide to Megalithic Monuments* from the Évora tourist office and you could find yourself happily pottering around in the countryside for days on the hunt for standing stones and circles. The nearest are about 14 km (eight miles) away, near Guadalupe, off the N114 to Montemor, and also southwest of Évora, near Valverde, off the N380. The strangest is the huge dolmen-cum-chapel at Pavia, 29 km (18 miles) north of Arraiolos, on the N370. These dolmen hunts make ideal day-trips for bikers, too.

It's hard to beat the Alentejo for dreamy touring. From **Lisbon to Porto** (317 km, or 197 miles) you'll inevitably find roads more crowded. But the coastal route between these cities is splendid, becoming quieter the further north you go, and ideal in many places for seaside stopovers. From Sintra, stick to the minor N247 and you'll find the beach calling all the way to Peniche, a fine place to base yourself and less touristy than Nazaré further north, though the Pinhal de Leiria pine forest near Nazaré is also tempting for stopovers, with its excellent beaches and campsites. From here you can skirt the coast, avoiding major roads nearly all the way to Aveiro, though an inland diversion to Coimbra is highly recommended if you've got the time. The nearby Forest of Buçaco is a worthwhile day-trip from Coimbra, too (see THE GREAT OUTDOORS). But if it's sea-breezes you're after, the Praia de Mira 29 km (18 miles) to the south of Aveiro offers some great stretches of sand. Furadouro, near Ovar, 25 km (16 miles) north of Aveiro is another pleasant little spot for a beach stopover before you hit the traffic mayhem of Porto.

The most scenic tour from **Porto** is along the River Douro, following the river-hugging and extremely wriggly N108 north of the river, or the even prettier N222 to the

south. The glossy *Rio Douro* map (available in Porto bookshops) makes a good companion for this tour, with detailed notes about places of interest en route.

The provincial town and port wine center of Peso de Régua, 100 km (62 miles) east makes a good first night's stop — or two nights if you have time for a day's sight-seeing trip to the attractive town of Lamego nine kilometers (five miles) south. Filling a day's excursion itself in the vicinity of Lamego are a trio of curious, half-forgotten treasures: the twelfth century São

João de Tarouca Cistercian Monastery; the medieval fortified bridge of Ucanha; and the derelict Cistercian monastery of Salzedas.

Back on the **Douro**, the further east you go the deeper you find yourself in port wine country (see TOP SPOTS) and the wilder the N222 seems to become. Roller-coaster fans will love the dramatic crossing of the Douro east of Pinhão at São João de Pesqueira where the road plunges down and up again so steeply your ears pop. Faithfully, the N222 sticks to within sight of the river almost to the very end — the timid border town of Barca d'Alva, where you can hear Spanish sheep bleating from across the frontier while the river chuckles onwards. A night spent in nearby Freixo de Espada a Cinta is a memorable

Azulejos ABOVE TOP adorn a Braga facade. A slug of wine for Alentejo farm laborers ABOVE. Roof top scenes at Viana do Castelo RIGHT. Barcelos OPPOSITE is home to the Minho's largest weekly market.

experience in remoteness. From here, you're at the back-door to Trás-os-Montes, the least-known region of Portugal, worth days of desultory rambling.

Another touring alternative from Porto is to leave your car behind and take the train on the Douro line to Peso de Régua. From here you can make a day's excursion to Vila Real on the spectacular Corgo line before continuing eastwards to Pinhão from where the narrow-gauge Tua line (one of the last of its kind in Portugal) meanders up to Mirandela. The Douro line itself ends at Pocinho, about as isolated a place as you'll find on the river. From Porto direct to Pocinho by train takes about four-and-a-half hours.

The northern **Minho** district is a perfect place to potter. As long as you're not after any great nightlife or shopping facilities, the little town of Ponte de Lima, 23 km (14 miles) east of Viana do Castelo, could make an ideal base, conveniently close both to the coast at Viana and to inland places of interest such as Braga, Barcelos and Valença do Minho, on the northern Spanish border. From Braga you can strike up into the Serra do Gerês mountains and base yourself at Caldas do Gerês for a few days' hiking in the hills (see THE GREAT OUTDOORS).

Finally, for the adventurous explorer who's after the unknown, there's the vast, remote **Trás-os-Montes** region. Montalegre, Chaves, Braganæa and Miranda do Douro are recommended for stopovers but be prepared for long, isolated drives and frequent distractions: I found myself delayed even before I reached Chaves by the extraordinarily remote villages around Montalegre, little changed for centuries. Even the Portuguese themselves know little about this area. Linger here too long and you may lose all sense of time.

Backpacking

Despite rising prices, Portugal remains one of the cheapest places to travel in Western Europe. Living frugally by using trains and buses, staying in campsites or youth hostels and self-catering, you could get by on about US$35 a day. Moving up a

notch, staying in cheap *pensões* and enjoying reasonably-priced restaurant meals will cost you about US$50 to $60 a day. If you're a student you can also take advantage of discounts on admission prices to museums as well as on long-distance bus and train fares. Off-season, you'll find accommodation prices drop considerably — and even in high season it's always worth asking at the reception desk for cheaper rooms (for example, without bathroom or windows) since these are often not mentioned initially.

There are dozens of authorised campsites in Portugal — the *Roteiro Campista* booklet available in Portuguese bookshops gives full details, or you can ask at the local tourist offices. Another good bargain is the chain of 20 youth hostels, although the most popular ones (for instance, in Lisbon and Lagos) quickly get booked up in high season. For advance reservations or further details, contact Movijovem, Central de Reservas, Av. Duque de Avila, Nº 137, Lisbon. ((01) 355-9081.

Some of the best budget accommodation are rooms (*quartos* or *dormidas*) in private houses let out by the owners. Similar to the bed-and-breakfast system (although breakfast is rarely included in the price, or even available), the rooms are invariably immaculate (frilly bed-covers and lace curtains are popular), and at around US$25 a double in high season are good value. You can find these rooms either through the local tourist office, or more likely, they'll find you: *dormidas* owners often accost customers at bus or train stations in the more popular resorts (the harridans of Nazaré are particularly memorable!). And don't be alarmed if your host speaks nothing but Portuguese: you'll generally find they understand you anyway, and make charming hosts.

Traveling solo works out as more expensive if you use anything other than a youth hostel. Single room rates are more than half the double room rate. Traveling in a pair you can afford to splash out on the occasional *pensão* (see TRAVELERS' TIPS: ACCOMMODATION) or two-star hotel. It's worth considering that in winter prices often drop so low you could stay in a palace hotel for the price of a summertime *pensão!*

Getting around Portugal by public transport isn't going to break the bank, either. Trains are generally cheaper than buses but slower, and they don't delve into the countryside as well as buses. You can get pretty much anywhere in Portugal by bus as long as you've got the time. Hitching is perfectly acceptable, too, though in remote areas you're likely to find your driver is only going to the next farmhouse. Bringing your own bike is a great alternative, as long as you avoid the sweltering Alentejo summers and the mountainous north. Bikes are allowed on trains and buses (certain services only) for a small fee — and several hours' lugubrious paperwork at the station.

The lively Algarve resorts of Lagos and Albufeira are popular starting places for many young budget travelers — many don't go any further! Lisbon, of course, is another magnet but its expensive and

Colorful washing OPPOSITE hangs to dry above the narrow streets of Lisbon's Alfama district. Aveiro BELOW, the "Venice of Portugal".

crowded accommodation scene soon drives backpackers westwards to Cascais or Sintra or north to Coimbra (another major university town) and Porto. The Serra da Estrêla and Peneda-Gerês mountain ranges are where the energetic ones head for, leaving their backpacks to hike across the hills or taking them with them to camp in the wilderness.

Living it Up

The Portuguese aren't shy of living it up: most bars and discos in Lisbon, Porto and the major Algarve resorts stay open until at least 2 am and there's always some new in-places to discover. You can party away your whole holiday if you like, at no great expense, or splurge out for dinner or accommodation in some of Europe's most opulent restaurants and hotels.

You'll have no trouble pinpointing the **Algarve**'s hottest night spots in Lagos and Albufeira — the bars and clubs regularly advertise special-price drinks or events with fliers and posters around town. Reliably lively bars in Lagos are Mullens, Rua Candido dos Reis Nº 86 and Phoenix at Rua 5 de Outubro Nº 11; while in Albufeira you can start the evening on high decibels at Classic Bar, Rua Candido dos Reis Nº 10. Casinos, for those with money to burn, can be found at Alvor, Monte Gordo, Vilamoura and Albufeira (and, beyond the Algarve, at Figueira da Foz, Póvoa de Varzim and Estoril).

The Algarve's smartest restaurants and hotels are mostly found in the coastal resorts, concentrating in the deluxe resort complexes of Quinta do Lago and Vale do Lobo. Finding your own exclusive patch is more fun: La Reserve restaurant and Hotel near Estoi (snobbishly just far enough away from the seaside resorts) is a well-established favorite, while Faro's little Cidade Velha restaurant is a romantic hideaway for special celebrations. Far to the west, on a windswept clifftop near Sagres, the Fortaleza do Beliche *pousada*

The Four Season Hotel in Vilamoura, a massive Algarve holiday complex with four golf courses and capacity for more than 50,000 tourists.

annexe (with just four rooms) is as close to the sea and wind of this rugged end of Portugal as you could get while still enjoying luxurious accommodation.

Traveling north through Portugal you'll find that these goverment-run *pousadas* offer some of the country's most sophisticated accommodation. Throughout Portugal, but particularly in the northern Douro and Minho regions you can also indulge in the comforts of exquisite private manor-houses under the scheme called Turismo de Habitação oTURIHAB (see TOP SPOTS: SLEEP IN A PRIVATE PALACE, and TRAVELERS' TIPS: ACCOMMODATION) —a more personal approach to deluxe living, with the owner-host treating you as a private guest.

The best of the *pousadas* — restored castles, keeps and palaces stuffed with antiques, such as the *pousadas* of Évora, Estremoz, Óbidos and Guimarães — require bookings months ahead. If you're out of luck with a *pousada*, ask at the local tourist office about Turismo de Habitação villas or mansions in the region. I've found few places more enchanting than the Quinta da Capela, a seventeenth-century manor house overlooking the lush Monserrate Gardens near Sintra; and the tiny four-room Casa do Poço in Óbidos, both TURIHAB properties.

In **Lisbon**, of course, your most sophisticated hotels are big and brash, like the Ritz Intercontinental and Meridien. But richer in atmosphere by far is very posh Palácio dos Seteais in nearby Sintra or within Lisbon itself the more modest but quite unique York House, a former sixteenth-century monastery with rooms around a courtyard. It makes an eccentric contrast to late nights on the town — and you'll have plenty of those in Lisbon if you want to savor some of the best restaurants and clubs in the country.

One of the city's favorite plush restaurants (reservations are essential) is Avis, at Rua Serpa Pinto Nº 12, ℓ (01) 342-8391. The turn-of-the-century setting is so ornate you're liable to forget the food. Not so at Solmar, Rua das Portas de Santo Antão Nº 108, ℓ (01) 346-0010, which serves fantastic seafood amidst a flamboyant 50s decor including a vast marine-life mural.

The nightlife highlights are even harder to choose: Lisbon rocks, bops and drinks hard all night, though you can swoon to traditional *fado* (see TOP SPOTS) if that's more your scene. The **Bairro Alto** area is the traditional center of all nightlife activity with dozens of bars, old and new — nose around here and you'll soon find something to suit your taste. Favorite rendezvous are the Procopio bar near Largo do Rato, the live jazz venue Hot Clube de Portugal in Praça da Alegria, and Pintai, a lively Brazilian bar at Largo Trinidade Coelho, Nº 22. Newest on the Lisbon scene are a rash of designer bars in the Alcantara docks area and along the nearby Avenida 24 Julho (the velvet-decor XXIV Julho and Alcantara Cafe are the trendiest). For discos, try the popular Skylab at Rua Artilharia 1, Nº 69-B, which keeps bopping until 4 am.

Not to be outdone, **Porto** boasts its own brand of opulence on the hotel and restaurant front: Hotel Infante de Sagres, Praça Dona Filipa de Lencestre, Nº 652 has the most luxurious restaurant and rooms in the city, though the exclusive lunchtime restaurant in Taylor Fladgate & Yeatman's port wine lodge, Rua do Choupelo Nº 250, Vila Nova de Gaia has surely the finest view of the city and river Douro. Sophisticated soirées sipping port wine is best done in the Solar do Vinho do Porto, Rua Entre Quintas, Jardim do Palácio de Cristal, a civilised setting where you're offered a choice of over 150 varieties of port.

Nightlife in Porto revolves around the riverside Ribeira area: the trendy Gremyo at Rua de São João Nº 76 has some of the city's best live music while Meia Cave at Praça da Ribeira Nº 6 is a current favorite, attracting a well-dressed set. Across the river at Rua Rei Ramiro Nº228 , Vila Nova de Gaia, Rocks is worth visiting for its atmospheric setting of old port cellars and lively rock music, while the best disco in town, Swing, is across town in the other direction, at the Centro Comercial Brasilia, Avenida da Boavista.

Beyond Porto, luxurious accommodation is best found through the TURIHAB scheme — top of the line are the flagship Paço de Calheiros in Ponte de Lima, the elegant family home of TURIHAB's president, Count Francisco de Calheiros (the "Paço" indicates a King once stayed here), and the Casa de Sezim near Guimarães, an active wine-producing property which has been in the same family since 1376. For Manueline extravagance and architecture you have to see to believe, head for the Forest of Buçaco near Coimbra where you can wine, dine and stay the night in the Palace Hotel at the very heart of this ancient Forest.

Family Fun

You won't have to worry about keeping the kids happy in Portugal: there's an abundance of outdoor activities to hand and a happy-go-lucky atmosphere that infects even the mums and dads. The Portuguese are child-friendly, welcoming kids in hotels and restaurants, cooing over chubby babies and, given the slightest excuse, handing out sweets or gooey cakes.

The most suitable family accommodation is in simple pensions which are used to coping with young children. Campsites and youth hostels (see BACKPACKING) are great rendezvous for kids of all nationalities and good value if you've got a large family. And at some of the larger resorts in the Algarve, there are several special children's clubs for three to eleven-year-olds which you can book through British tour operators such as Martyn Holidays (see TAKING A TOUR), Thomson Holidays and Caravela Tours.

You'll probably find the best family fun in the **Algarve**, with its fine beaches, plentiful supply of simple cafés and restaurants and wide choice of watersports. If the children are old enough, you might fancy doing some family day-trips by bicycle (rental outfits are available in Lagos, Quarteira and Tavira), a good option almost everywhere in Portugal.

Lisbon and Porto pose more problems because their major sights — churches and museums — aren't exactly a kid's idea of a jolly time. But some of the museums could go down very well, such as **Lisbon**'s Maritime Museum with its fantastic displays of ships

and sea-faring paraphernalia; and the Ethnological Museum which combines displays from Portugal's former African colonies with an imaginative use of audio-visuals. Both these museums are on Lisbon's outskirts (in Belém) — the journey there by tram is fun in itself. Lisbon's other quaint forms of transport — the Gloria funicular and Santa Justa elevator — are so popular I know some families end up riding them several times a day!

Trams are a highlight in **Porto**, too, including the Tram Museum (See TOP SPOTS) but an aquatic alternative popular with children is the little jaunt down river by boat (trips leave regularly from the Ribeira waterfront). Throughout the summer the lively *Fieria do Porto* funfair is held nightly at the Palácio Cristal.

If the kids start to get restless in Lisbon, you can hop on a train to the lively seaside resort of Cascais for the day, or have a break in nearby **Sintra**. Forget the serious tour of Sintra's Royal Palace, and head for the hilltop Pena Palace and castle instead — the energetic can clamber up to the castle from the town center in about an hour.

Children parade in fancy dress at *festas* held on saints days throughout the country.

Portugal's castles are brilliant for families: you can walk the walls, play hide and seek in the old keeps, and picnic in the shadow of history. The best fun are those of Silves, Óbidos, Castelo de Vide, Marvão, Valença do Minho and Elvas. Most of these have accommodation facilities right within the walls which gives you a chance for some atmospheric evening explorations.

Even miniature castles provide entertainment: in the northern town of **Coimbra** there's the Portugal dos Pequenitos Park, where Portugal's most famous monuments (including some from the former colonies) have been recreated in miniature. The kids scramble in, on and over them to their hearts' content. Older children would probably prefer canoeing down the river instead (see SPORTING SPREE for details) or horse-riding in the nearby park (call the Coimbra Riding Centre on (039) 37695).

Horse-riding is an increasingly popular family activity in Portugal, particularly in the Algarve, Alentejo and Peneda-Gerês National Park. The local tourist offices have contact numbers for stables that offer both training sessions and guided hacks into the countryside.

For the family with seriously active teenagers you might consider throwing yourselves into a weekend of canyoning or hydrospeed (see SPORTING SPREE), or sending off the kids for their own adventure holiday with a week's

potholing or rafting organized by Movijovem (the youth hostel head office, at Avenida Duque d'Alvila, Nº 137, Lisbon). A less dramatic action-packed option is to base yourselves at a place like Cabril in the **Peneda-Gerês National Park** and take advantage of the horse-riding, canoeing and hiking possibilities in the area. Nearby Rio Caldo, on the edge of the Caniçada reservoir, is another attractive base, with wind-surfing, motorboats, canoes and pedal boats available.

Cultural Kicks

The great thing about Portugal's cultural attractions are their variety. Churches, palaces and museums may be the obvious highlights but just as memorable and not to be missed on your cultural itinerary are medieval hilltop castles, railway stations "wall-papered" with *azulejos* and even the eccentric art deco cafés and their customers.

So what's the pick of the best? For **museums**, the giant towering over all is the Gulbenkian in Lisbon, a minimum two-day indulgence if you want to do it properly. Others that are worth going out of your way to visit are the Machado de Castro in Coimbra, the Alberto Sampaio in Guimarães and Évora's Municipal Museum. Évora itself is one huge open-air museum, arguably the most cultured city in the country with everything from a Roman-era temple to beautiful seventeenth-century piazzas and mansions.

But architecturally, you must move nearer Lisbon to find Portugal's greatest **monuments**: the Alcobaça Cistercian Monastery which represents the finest creation of Portuguese Gothic architecture; the nearby Batalha Monastery, a stunning achievement of Manueline design; and, above all, the Jerónimos Monastery in Belém, the country's undisputed Manueline masterpiece. See these

Penitents marvel at baroque fountains and balustrades ABOVE as they make their pilgrimage up to Bom Jesus sanctuary. Ornamental lakes, intricate granite stonework and *azulejos* OPPOSITE are features of many country homes.

three and you can go home feeling architecturally fulfilled.

That still leaves a few notable holes in the cultural itinerary, however: uniquely Portuguese are the *azulejo*-decorated stairway at Bom Jesus, near Braga, and São Bento railway station in Porto as well as the superb *azulejo*-rich churches of Almancil, Évora and Barcelos. Staggering examples of the country's heavily gilded chapels are those of São Roque in Lisbon and Santo António in Lagos. And who would want to miss the historic walled towns of Óbidos, Monsaraz and Marvão? Or the extravagant palaces of Queluz and Pena?

More immediately threatened by urban development are Portugal's wonderful **art deco cafés** such as Nicola and A Brasileira do Chiado in Lisbon; Cafe

Aliança in Faro; Cafe Brasileira in Braga; and Cafe Majestic in Porto. Catch them while you can for these fragile cultural relics of an elegant past may not last forever.

Shop till you Drop

In Portugal every region has its specialties, best bought where they are made.

The northwestern province of **Minho** is famous for its beautiful traditional costumes. The port lodges of Vila Nova de Gaia, in **Porto**, are the best places to shop for port wine, Portugal's most famous product. In the northeast province of **Trás-os-Montes**, woven goods, tapestries, black pottery, wrought-ironwork, and painted furniture are all good buys. In the neighboring provinces of Beira Alta and Beira Baixa, black pottery and wrought-ironwork remain favorites, with the **Serra da Estrêla** region famous for the excellent cheese called *queijo de Serra*, and Castelo Branco, also a cheese producer, noted for embroidered bedspreads.

The coastal province of **Beira Litoral** makes some of the most attractive Portuguese pottery, and the famous old porcelain factory of Vista Alegre near **Aveiro** produces the expensive and sought-after dinner services and figurines sold in shops at Lisbon, Porto, and worldwide. The fishing towns here and throughout the country sell traditional clothing, and are usually good for lace, particularly at **Peniche** where the delicate bone lace is displayed outside the houses. In inland **Estremadura** the town of Caldas da Rainha is famous for its quirky bright green pottery made in the shape of cabbage leaves, vegetables, fruits, and animals, and is seen in shops throughout the world. Lisbon is a showcase for regional craftwork from all around the country and has some good bargains in gold and silver filigree jewelry.

Embroidered head scarves ABOVE are a Viana do Castelo specialty. Crude Barcelos cocks LEFT are sold as souvenirs throughout Portugal. Open air market OPPOSITE TOP in Viana do Castelo. Spaniards cross the frontier to shop at Valença do Minho OPPOSITE BOTTOM.

The southern province of the **Alentejo** sells all sorts of goods made of cork that won't pose too much of a problem in baggage weight. Good buys are generally goatskin goods, peasant-style clothing, woolen capes, wickerwork, and copperware, with the area around Évora particularly noted for its painted furniture. Most precious of all are the rugs from Arraiolos that the town has been producing since the seventeenth century.

In the **Algarve**, one of the most distinctive features of the houses is the latticed chimney pots which are sometimes sold as souvenirs. I'm not convinced that these wouldn't come in the category of purchases that were nice when you bought them, but what do you do with them when you get home? Unless, of course, you want to grow rhubarb in one, or don't mind it sticking out like a sore thumb on your roof. One rather useful item is the copper *cataplana*, the Moorish invention for steaming food that is both practical and good to look at. Copper and brass ware is generally a good buy here, as is palm and wicker work.

Non-European Union residents are entitled to VAT refunds on certain goods purchased in Portugal. Europe Tax-free Shopping now operates a tax refund system that does the bulk of the paperwork for you, so look for the Tax Free for Tourists sign in shop windows, and when making your purchase ask for a tax-free shopping cheque. When you leave you can take the cheques to the Tax-Free counter in the airport transit hall where you will be given a refund. You will need to carry your purchases in your hand luggage as customs officials will want to see the goods. For further information call (01) 418-8703 in Lisbon.

Short Breaks

Short-stay trips are perfect for Portugal: within a few days you can soak up enough sun and atmosphere, culture and good times to make you feel you've lingered for weeks.

Lisbon and Sintra make an ideal pair: after a few days in the big city seeing the sights, you'll find nearby Sintra a pleasantly relaxing rural retreat. Walking in the hills or through the rambling Monserrate Gardens gives you a fine taste of Portuguese countryside, while the Pena Palace and Capuchos Monastery provide the touch of eccentric culture for which Sintra is famous.

Porto and the Douro Valley is another obvious city-country combination. Lively Porto and its port wine center of Vila Nova de Gaia have depended for centuries on the Douro River which runs by its doorstep. Cruising the Douro (or taking the train — see TOP SPOTS) is a trip through the country's port wine history and an ideal way to see one of the most scenic parts of Portugal. If you have the time you may want to stop en route to explore Lamego, Amarante or the area around Pinhão: Porto by train is never far away.

That's the great joy of short break holidays in Portugal: the country is so small you can whizz from south to north in a couple of days if you really want to, though it's hardly advisable. Instead, why not dally in the Algarve for the first few days and then take an express bus (four to five hours) to Lisbon? Porto is only another three-hour express bus ride away, making it quite feasible to include in a one-week itinerary which covers much of the country.

Alternatively you may want to stick to the Lisbon area, visiting Sintra, Óbidos, Nazaré and Batalha to give you a culturally-varied experience of some of the country's highlights, with a seaside resort (Nazaré) thrown in for good measure.

A more unusual but attractive option for hikers would be a trip from Porto to the Peneda-Gerês National Park, basing yourself at Caldas do Gerês for a few days and stopping on the way back at Braga for a dose of culture.

Festive Flings

Portugal, particularly in the summer months, is a procession of colorful and

flamboyant festivals. Every city, town, and village holds a festival to honor a patron saint or the Holy Virgin. The larger the place, the longer or bigger the celebrations. These festivals are in part religious, in part simply celebrations with song, dance, fireworks, traditional costumes, eating, and drinking. They are wonderfully colorful occasions and you should try to see one if you can. Country fairs (*feiras*) selling handicrafts and local produce are held as part of the festivities.

Here is a selection of some of the more interesting festivals, but it is by no means a complete list. The Instituo de Promoção Turistica or I.P.T. (see page 76 for addresses) publishes a booklet giving exact dates and details of fairs, festivals,

and folk pilgrimages: you should pick up a copy before you leave for Portugal so that you can try to fit one or two into your itinerary.

March and April
Holy Week (the week before Easter): Holy Week Festival in Braga.
Easter Sunday: Romária da Senhora da Piedade or Mãe Soberana in Loulé.

May
3 May: Festas das Cruzes in Barcelos.
First Sunday in May: Festas das Cruzes or Festa do Castelo at Monsanto.
First or second weekend: Festas da Senhora das Rosas in Vila Franca do Lima.

June
First weekend: Romária de São Gonçalo de Amarante in Amarante.
12–29 June: Festas dos Santos Populares in Lisbon.
23–24 June: Festas de São João in Vila do Conde, in Braga, and in Porto.
28–29 June: Festas de São Pedro in Póvoa de Varzim; the Feira Grande de São Pedro in Sintra.

July
First weekend: Tabuleiros Festival in Tomar (even years only).

Traditional Minho costume OPPOSITE is worn at *festas*. A folkloric festival ABOVE LEFT at Barqueiros in the Minho. Bishops come young ABOVE RIGHT at *festa* time.

1–5 July: Festas da Rainha Santa in Coimbra (even years only).
Late July–early August: Feira de Santiago in Setúbal.

August
First week: Festival of Meadela in Meadela.
First weekend: Festas Gualterianas in Guimarães.
Third week: Festival of the Assumption of Our Lady in Póvoa de Varzim; Festas da Senhora da Agonia in Viana do Castelo.
Third weekend: Festas de Santa Bárbara in Miranda do Douro.

September
Second week: Romária da Senhora da Nazaré in Nazaré; Algarve Folk Music and Dance Festival in Praia da Rocha and various other localities.

HOLIDAYS
1 JANUARY: New Year's Day
25 APRIL: Liberation Day
1 MAY: May Day
10 JUNE: Camões Day
15 AUGUST: Assumption Day
5 OCTOBER: Republic Day
1 NOVEMBER: All Saints' Day
1 DECEMBER: Independence Day
8 DECEMBER: Immaculate Conception
25 DECEMBER: Christmas Day

MOVABLE HOLIDAYS
Shrove Tuesday (February or March),

Good Friday and Easter Sunday (March or April), Corpus Christi (June)

REGIONAL HOLIDAYS
In Lisbon 13 JUNE is St. Anthony's Day; in Porto 24 JUNE is St. John's Day

Galloping Gourmets

A culinary tour of Portugal is like taking little tastes of the country's history, from the time of the Romans and their love of wine to the days of the Moors and their fondness for sweets. But above all, it's the Age of Discoveries and the country's colonial experience which have provided most of the flavor of Portuguese cuisine. In your travels round the country you'll soon notice the Portuguese love of spices, most being of Asian and African provenance: cinnamon, chilli, nutmeg, cloves and so forth.

Onions, garlic and olive oil are paramount, as they are in all Mediterranean cooking. While good Portuguese food is delicious, the whole tradition is provincial: tastes are strong, quantities will make you wonder whether you should have ordered an ambulance to get home, and if you like bland, insipid food, it's not for you. If you have an adventurous palate, you are sure to derive pleasure from this cuisine, especially if you enjoy seafood.

You'll find good seafood almost everywhere in Portugal, though inevitably the coastal areas boast the best variety. When you're in the **Algarve** or **Alentejo**, don't miss trying the regions' famous *cataplana* dish — shellfish or fish cooked with ham, tomatoes, peppers and onions (servings are usually for a minimum of two people). The name *cataplana* actually refers to the kind of saucepan in which the dish is cooked: the forerunner of the pressure cooker, it's a Moorish contraption used for cooking casseroles and still favored by the Portuguese.

Seafood forms the basis of many local dishes. Freshly caught sardines, *sardinhas*, are excellent, as is swordfish, *espada*: the latter can be smoked in the Sesimbra fashion, or eaten raw with a little olive oil

and vinegar, once a popular dish in Mozambique. Octopus (*polvo*) and spider crab (*sapateiro*) are often served stuffed, as are fresh-water fish such as salmon, lamprey and trout (*salmão, lampreía* and *truta*) while around Lisbon and in the north eel (*enguia*) is considered a delicacy.

With all these delightful creatures waiting to make you happy, it seems strange that the most popular dish of all is dried, salted cod (*bacalhau*), once a staple for the poor, now rather more pricey. Every restaurant carries this commonest of fish, though there are said to be 365 ways of preparing it. Try **bacalhau à Brás**, in which flakes of cod are fried in olive oil with garlic and vegetables, or **bacalhau à Gomes de Sá**, a casseroled version topped

with black olives and egg slices. As an hors d'œuvre try **bolinhos de bacalhau**, little balls of cod mixed with potato and fried.

Another popular fishy dish is **caldeira**, a fish stew which can be eaten as a very filling soup. Portuguese soups like these are good news for hungry travelers on a budget: you can dine well for very little if you snack on **caldo verde**, a dark green potato soup with shredded cabbage and a slice of spiced sausage; or *sopa alentejana*, a garlic bread soup. Bread itself — usually white bread (*pão*) served with butter at every meal — is one of the

Fiddler OPPOSITE at Barqueiros folkloric festival. Nightlife ABOVE at Albufeira.

culinary stakes: the local specialty here is tripe! But set aside your prejudices and try the admirable *tripas à modo do Porto*, tripe with haricot beans and belly pork; this way of preparing it (one of many) is particularly delicious, and will give you a new perspective on tripe.

Turning to deserts, these vary by region, but most tend to be very sweet. Try *pudim de flan*, a kind of caramel custard, and *arroz doce*, a rich, cinnamon-flavored rice pudding. There are also egg-rich sweets, collectively known as *doces de ovos*, often incorporating fruit or almonds. Some originated in convent kitchens and have tongue-in-cheek names, such as *toucinho de céu* (bacon from heaven) and *barrigas de freiras* (nun's bellies.)

There are some interesting cheeses to sample, mainly made of goat's or ewe's milk and sometimes served as an appetizer. The most famous is probably *Queijo da Serra*, a soft but slightly firm and quite strong cheese produced from ewe's milk from the Serra da Estrêla. Made between October and May it should be eaten young, but an aged variety called *Serra Velho*, considerably more pungent, is also available.

WINE AND OTHER BEVERAGES

Wine connoisseurs will be in for a pleasant surprise as they travel round Portugal: whites, reds, rosés and fortified wines are all produced here and are of such high standards that they are winning growing recognition abroad. Within Portugal itself, you'll soon notice how enthusiastic the locals are about their wine: it's as much a part of the daily lunch and dinner menu as bread or *bacalhau*. In fact, the Portuguese have one of Europe's largest consumptions of wine per head, not surprising when you consider how important viticulture has been to the economy for hundreds of years. With the prices of most wines so reasonable and the choice so wide you can have the happy temptation of sampling a regional wine wherever you go. Even the cheapest and humblest *vinho da casa* is usually very agreeable.

The wines here are generally reasonably priced, and fall into two

simple pleasures of eating in Portugal. In your travels round the country you'll come across several other types of bread, such as rye bread (*pão de centeio*), or the rougher-textured breads often served in the north.

Pork is the staple red meat, and can be excellent. Recommended is *presunto*, cured ham, available almost everywhere but particularly good in Lamego (it makes a great picnic sandwich together with the local sparkling wine). Spiced and smoked sausages such as *chouriço* or *linguica* are also well worth trying. They're ofen served as appetizers or to add flavor to soups, omelettes and sandwiches. And in your **Alentejo** wanderings, be sure to try the *carne de porco à alentejana*, pork marinated in wine and herbs, then cooked with baby clams. *Borrego*, lamb, is another Alentejan specialty — you'll find the restaurants of Évora all feature a *borrego* dish or two (my favorite is the *feijoada à alentejana* a very filling lamb and bean stew).

When you reach **Porto**, however, you'll face a rather tougher challenge on the

Pastries ABOVE are a tradition in Lisbon. Stone-carved arches OPPOSITE are a feature of Minho towns.

categories: table wines and fortified wines.

To control production and quality there are 10 demarcated regions in continental Portugal designated by the National Wine Council. The wines produced there must conform to certain specifications regarding the variety of grape, the alcohol content and the length of time they are aged: these carry the *selo de garantia*, a seal of approval rather like the French *Appelation d'Origine Contrôlée*.

Vinho Verde accounts for a quarter of Portugal's production, and is made from grapes grown in the northeast of the country, mainly Minho; *verde* (green) refers to the youth of the wine, not its color. Most produced is in fact red, although the international market tends to favor white. The latter is light and refreshing with a low alcohol content, and should be drunk young: it does not travel well. They are the best known Portuguese table wines, together with two **rosés**, Mateus Rosé and Lancers, both of which are light and have become popular exports over the last few years.

Further south, the Dão Valley in the Viseu area of central Portugal is the home of the **Dão wines**. These are largely full-bodied reds, matured for a minimum of 18 months in the cask; the whites are drier and matured for a shorter period. Near the coast, the Bairrada region around Coimbra produces some excellent fruity reds which age well, and some sparkling white wines.

Near Lisbon are four old demarcated regions which are much reduced in size because of urban development, and several new ones. In the Trancão Valley north of Lisbon the small Bucelas region produces **whites** under the Caves Velhas label, and in the Colares region west of Sintra the vines planted in sand produce rare and distinctive red wine which is at its best after years of maturing.

South of the Tejo the Setúbal region is the origin of Moscatel de Setúbal, one of the best **muscat** wines in the world.

Turning to fortified wines, the country's most famous product is, of course, **port**, made by adding brandy to wine in order to arrest the fermentation of the sugar: the effect is to raise the alcohol content to between 18 and 20 percent by volume while retaining the sweetness. While you can find port all over Portugal, the best place to sample it is in its "home town", Porto, and across the river in Vila Nova de Gaia where the wines are matured in casks in the famous port lodges. This area was once the province of English shippers. Port became so popular in England it became an English institution, as the brand names still testify: Sandeman, Dow, Cockburn and Croft. If you're a port novice (and even if you're not) you should pop in to one of the lodges while you're in Porto for a free port-tasting tour — one of the best ways to find out briefly how port is produced and how best to drink it. There are really four categories of port: top of the list is Vintage port, followed by Late Bottled Vintage, then Ruby and Tawny ports, and finally White port.

Vintage port is made from the wines of especially good years and the grapes of one harvest only, matured for two years in the vat and then at least ten in the bottle. It improves as it gets older and is the most expensive, being drunk as an after-dinner wine.

Late Bottled Vintage is made from grapes of a good year — usually not vintage years — and matured for about five years in the cask to speed up the process. Once bottled it is ready to drink and requires no decanting; the result is a lighter, sharper wine.

The remaining ports are all aged in the cask and are ready to drink when bottled; Vintage Dated Tawny comes from a single year, with a minimum of seven years in the cask, while others are known by their age, 10, 20, 30 or over 40 years old, and are blended with different vintages. Ruby port matures for three years in the cask and is the most widely drunk of all the ports.

White port, finally, lacks the body of the others but is usually dry and served chilled as an apéritif.

A wide range of **brandies** is also made, called *aguardente* or *aguardente de vinho*, the older ones being *aguardente velhas*.

Beware of *aguardente de bagaceira*, a ferocious spirit made from grape skins, pips and stalks, which has nothing to do with brandy.

Some interesting **liqueurs** are made: Brandymel, a mixture of brandy and honey, Amênoa Amargandoa, made from almonds, and Medronha, made from arbutus berries. If wine or port isn't to your taste, you can always stick with Sagres, the most popular local **beer** (*cerveja*). It's produced by a state-run brewery which also makes two stronger brews called Superbock and Cristal. Similar to English lager, these beers are served cold. There's a low-alcohol lager, too, but you may have trouble finding it beyond the major cities.

Common everywhere are Portugal's excellent brands of **mineral water** (either still, *sem gas*, or carbonated, *com gas*). And if you're a coffee freak you'll be very happy: the ubiquitous cafés and *pastelarias* serve excellent coffee day and night. Similar in flavor to the French or Italian beverage, Portuguese **coffee** can be consumed in a variety of ways. If you want a small strong cup, like an espresso, ask for *uma bica*. A popular breakfast brew of hot milk with a *bica* tipped in and,

half-water served in a glass is called *um galão*, while a small milky coffee is *um meia de leite*. Fancy an iced coffee? That's *um café gelado*. Simplest of all is *um café*, an ordinary black coffee. If you want milk with it, ask for *um café com leite*.

Tea, *cha*, is also widely drunk; you can have it with milk (*com leite*) or a slice of lemon (*com uma rodela de limao*). And for an elegant ambience in which to drink your afternoon tea, keep an eye out for the lovely old *casas de cha* scattered across the country.

Special Interests

RELIGIOUS SIGHTS
On May 13th, 1917, three young shepherd children aged 10, nine and seven, saw the Virgin Mary while tending their flocks of sheep near Fátima. The apparitions recurred five times, all on the 13th of the month, but only one of the children could converse with the Virgin and hear her warnings against sinful living and her entreaties for prayer to ensure world peace. By October

Theatrical costumes at Santo António processions in Lisbon's Alfama district.

13th, some 70,000 people had gathered to witness — or refute — the miracle, which was accompanied this time by strange celestial distractions.

Fátima is now the most important religious place in Portugal, the ultimate goal if you are interested in making a tour of the country's most notable religious sites. Like every Roman Catholic country, Portugal is rich in magnificent churches, cathedrals and monasteries (see CULTURAL KICKS for the architectural highlights) and it would be easy to drift from town to town discovering impressive religious art and devotion wherever you go.

But there are several other specific pilgrimage points worth visiting en route to Fátima: **Bom Jesus do Monte** near Braga and **Nossa Senhora dos Remedios** at Lamego are dazzling black-and-white baroque stairways zigzagging up hills and culminating in churches at the top. The most fervent penitents climb the stairways on their knees, pausing to pray at little chapels on their way up. Visit Bom Jesus at Pentecost and Nossa Senhora dos Remedios in early September if you're interested in seeing their largest pilgrimages.

Braga at Easter is also a must for witnessing serious religious fervor. The climax is the **Ecce Homo** procession on Easter Thursday night which features hundreds of barefoot penitents carrying torches. Easter Sunday witnesses processions and pilgrimages at dozens of places in Portugal, most famously at Braga and at Loulé in the Algarve.

Even in the farthest corner of the country — at Mirando do Douro in Trás-os-Montes — there's an annual pilgrimage (in early September) to Our Lady of Nazo at Póvoa. But the Fátima pilgrimages to commemorate those first apparitions are still the largest and most impressive: tens of thousands of pilgrims converge on Fátima on the 12th and 13th of every month and up to 100,000 pilgrims in the months of May and October. Many of them literally crawl on bended knee towards the great white neo-classical basilica which dominates the vast esplanade below. If you're simply a curious traveler, these are crowds and

dates to avoid. But for a fellow pilgrim, there's no better time to be in Portugal.

GARDENS

Gardens in Portugal come in two verdant varieties: romantic and rambling or formal and trim. And you don't have to go far even from the center of Lisbon to find both. The city's **Estufa Fria** (Cool House), a botanic garden in the Parque Eduardo VII, is a delightful place to start a garden tour of Portugal. Established over 60 years ago, there's an abundance of exotic plants, ferns and flowers tumbling under canopies of wicker and glass as well as an **Estufa Quente** (Hot House) for orchids and cacti.

Less exotic but equally enjoyable as a respite from city traffic is the **Jardim Botanico** whose paths meander through corridors of royal palms. And for some of Portugal's most imaginative formal gardens don't miss the privately-owned **Quinta do Marques de Fronteira** on Lisbon's northwestern outskirts. With a design dating from the seventeenth century, the gardens are arranged around astrological and geometric themes, and feature 365 box trees interspersed with azulejo panels representing the planets, signs of the zodiac and months of the year.

Leaving Lisbon, a garden-lover's first port of call should be **Queluz**, whose elegant eighteenth-century palace is complemented by an inspired formal garden, cascading with bougainvillea and fountains and peppered with statues. Allow plenty of time to meander for there's more here than at first meets the eye.

Rambles become even more enchanting in the **Monserrate Gardens** of Sintra. The abandoned *quinta* here was originally built for an Englishman, Sir Francis Cook, in the 1860s but the garden and a previous gothic house had already attracted several notable English visitors: the eccentric gay author, William Beckford (who fled England in the wake of a scandal) lived at Monserrate from 1794 to 1808 and even imported a flock of sheep to meander among the English landscaped garden. A year after Beckford's departure, the poet Byron popped in, creating a fashion for visiting the place.

But the garden's present attractions — fabulous Himalayan rhododendrons, plants from Australasia and Mexico — are due to the efforts of a painter, William Stockdale, who planted this ambitious botanic collection in the 1850s. Today, after decades of neglect, it's mostly a magical shambles, where you can lose yourself for hours, though pathways and flower beds in the immediate vicinity of the *quinta* are well-maintained.

Moving further north, tree-lovers should be sure to take in the ancient **Buçaco Forest** near Coimbra (see THE GREAT OUTDOORS) before heading for Vila Real and the nearby Solar de Mateus. Built in 1743, this flamboyant little palace is recognised the world over from the picture represented on bottles of Mateus Rosé wine, now made by the Sogrape company down the road. The tour of the palace can be disappointing, but the formal gardens behind are a joy, with prim little statues guarding tiny box hedges, and a perfectly trimmed tunnel of trees, cool, dark and inviting.

These are the highlights — all easily accessible to any traveler — but if you're a serious garden explorer you may like to join a specialized tour organized by UK companies such as Cox & Kings (℅ (44-071)

873-5002) whose Portugal Garden Tour includes visits to palaces, manor houses and gardens, accompanied by expert lecturers. Prospect (℅ (44-081) 995-2151) also organizes a guided gardens tour from Lisbon and Porto.

WINES AND PORTS

Wine buffs and port-lovers have two tasty options in Portugal: wander at random, sampling local wines as you go, or make for the famous *quintas* and wine estates for some serious wine-tasting.

The obvious choice when it comes to **port** is the Douro Valley, home of the port wine estates. The best place to start a Douro Valley tour is in Porto: across the river is Vila Nova de Gaia where the valley's port wine is stored and matured in the lodges' huge cellars. A dozen of the lodges offer free port-tasting tours: it's worth visiting one of the smaller, more personal lodges such as the old British firm, Taylor Fladgate & Yeatman, as well as the larger more obvious crowd-pullers

Botanical curiosities OPPOSITE in Lisbon's garden of Estrêla. Exquisite eighteenth century formal gardens ABOVE in the grounds of Braga's Casa dos Biscainhos Museum.

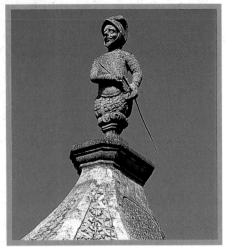

which welcomes visitors. For **rosés**, of course, you should head for the Solar de Mateus near Vila Real and the nearby Sogrape modern winery which now produces the famous brew. You can also visit the wineries of Lancer's rosé operation at Vila Nogueira de Azeitão near Lisbon.

But one of the excitements for a wine-lover in Portugal is discovering lesser-known names as you travel round the country. The smooth, full-bodied red **Dão** wines of the Beira Alta region are some of the country's best — though still largely unknown abroad. The sparkling Raposeira wine of Lamego near Peso de Régua is a delight (you can visit the factory for tours and tastings). And in the eastern part of the Alentejo, Portugal's most recently Demarcated Region is now producing some very tasty reds.

such as Sandeman (now owned by Seagrams, an American company).

Taking the train (or a cruise — see TOP SPOTS) up the Douro, you'll reach Peso de Régua, a major transport center for the Douro Valley's wine industry through which the wines pass on their way to Porto. There are two lodges here you can visit without prior appointment — Casa do Douro and Ramos Pinto — both of which offer excellent tours.

But Pinhão, further east, is the real heart of the port wine estates. If you base yourself at the lovely seventeenth-century Casa de Casal de Loivos, or the Casa das Pontes, you'll be right at the heart of port wine activity: both these mansions (part of the Turismo de Habitação scheme) are on active port wine estates near Pinhão. The tourist office in Porto can provide details for reservations — essential months ahead if you want to visit during the lively harvest season (mid-September to mid-October). This is a far better time for a visit than the summer months when the Douro Valley can experience scorchingly hot temperatures.

When it comes to discovering Portugal's table wine districts, you've got a far wider choice of regions. Best known are the *vinho verde* wines of the northern Minho area, a fine place for touring. One of the best of the cooperatives' *vinho verdes* is the Alvarinho of Monção but more famous abroad are those of Aveleda at Penafiel, east of Porto, a major operation

Lastly, for something quite unique, you might like to try the *vinho dos mortos*, "Wine of the Dead." Produced by villagers of Boticas, an unremarkable little village near Chaves, in Trás-os-Montes, this is wine that has literally been buried for a year or two. The custom dates from 1809 when villagers concealed their wine underground from the invading French and discovered afterwards that the taste had improved. The Cafe de Armindo near the main street usually has some *vinho dos mortos* to hand, but don't be surprised if it tastes a little gritty.

Several UK operators organize special wine tours if you're interested in learning more about Portugal's wineries. Arblaster & Clark (℃ (44-1730) 266883) often organize visits to Porto combined with a weekend at Taylor's port school. Blackheath Wine Trails (℃ (44-081) 463-0012) can arrange trips in September harvest season touring the *vinho verde* wineries of the Minho.

Taking a Tour

Thanks to the popularity of the Algarve among British holiday-makers, package tours offered by British tour

A stone figure ABOVE stands sentinel over the treasures of Casa dos Biscainhos. OPPOSITE: needs checking. Is this Barcelos?

agencies to Algarve resorts provide some of the best holiday deals available. You can find a wide range of tours from reliable companies such as Martyn Holidays (℃ (44-161) 745-7000), Thomson Holidays (℃ (44-081) 200-8733) or Caravela Tours (℃ (44-071) 630-9223) offering return flight and one week's accommodation (in beachside villas or hotels) from around U$350 to $400 per person in high season. There are also fly-drive and self-catering packages as well as car rental deals. In low season you'll find even better bargains.

Increasingly popular, too, are the more specialized package holidays to Portugal, such as fly-drive programmes to the Costa Verde or northern Portugal with accommodation in manor houses or *pousadas*. Sunvil Holidays (℃ (44-081) 568-4499), Unicorn Holidays (℃ (44-1582) 834400) and Vintage Portugal (℃ (44-1954) 261431) are just three of many reputable companies which can arrange this.

Specializing in luxury one-week cruises along the Douro River is Voyages Jules Verne (℃ (44-071) 723-5066), while Inspirations (℃ (44-1293) 820207) offers an unusual combination of excursions in the Algarve including river cruises and trips to the Monchique Mountains.

Serious golfers and tennis-players can take advantage of several good package tour offers (see SPORTING SPREE), while crafts enthusiasts might enjoy the northern Portugal tours organized by The Travel Alternative (℃ (44-1865) 791636) which includes visits to textile cooperatives as well as several historic sites in the area.

Short breaks (two or three nights) to Lisbon and Porto from the UK are also becoming very popular. Travelscene (℃ (44-081) 427-4445), Time Off (℃ (44-071) 235-8070), British Airways Holidays (℃ (44-1293) 615353) and Crystal Premier Cities (℃ (44-081) 390-9900) all offer flight-and-accommodation packages for reasonable prices, some including pre-bookable excursions to nearby places of interest such as Mafra and Sintra. Car rental can also be included if required.

Any major travel agency should be able to provide information on these and other package tours to Portugal. For a full listing of companies, including those catering to more specialized holidays, contact the Portuguese National Tourist Office for a copy of their *Tour Operators Guide*.

Creaking wheels BELOW announce the arrival of bullock carts. still used in Minho agriculture. OPPOSITE: Relaxing at Albufeira in the Algarve.

Welcome
to Portugal

SMALL AS IT IS even by European standards and devoid of the ancient pedigrees of Egypt and Greece, no nation has had a more profound effect in changing the course of modern history, no people braver and more adventurous in exploring the unknown.

Perhaps what will strike you most about this country and its people is their generosity of spirit: the cities are human in scale, where most sights of interest can be reached on foot. Wherever you go you will find cafés, small restaurants, wine bars, little hotels, and public gardens where you can stop and rest. There is no shortage of style and elegance either, but even the grandest hotels and restaurants are on a scale which engenders warmth, not intimidation. Similarly, the churches and public buildings were built with sensible dimensions, (although there are one or two glaring exceptions, as you will discover later in this book) but even the smallest structures never reflect meanness or parsimoniousness on the part of the designer.

The Portuguese are justly proud of their illustrious history, and with diversity here comes regional loyalty; much of what you see will be of interest and perhaps curious, but for the natives of these parts it is their history, a milestone in the continuum of which they themselves are part.

Although Portugal always did have a certain following as a tourist destination, in days gone by it was less accessible than the south of France, the Swiss mountain resorts or the great Italian cities. Part of the reason was that it lies right at the end of Europe: it was off the beaten track, and until the advent of high speed air travel, getting there took too long. For decades its tough, dictatorial political system did little to help, but things have changed: cheap air travel has made it possible to be in Portugal in no more time than it takes to get to Rome, Monte Carlo or Geneva, and the peaceful transfer to a more socially-acceptable government in 1974 brought a rush of outside ideas and influences with astonishing speed.

In many ways this is an extraordinary country; you will be hard put to find such artistic and architectural wealth in an area as small elsewhere, or such diversity in landscape with its opportunities for recreation.

Somehow Portugal has always preserved the monuments of past greatness. Its natural beauty, warm and balmy climate, forests, rivers and beaches, all confined in a relatively small area, make it easy to understand why people have wanted to be here. A strategic position at the extreme southwest of Europe, guarding access to the Mediterranean Sea made it politically and militarily desirable. Waves of invaders came in succession, leaving splendid relics of their vanished civilizations: the whole country is filled with prehistoric dolmens, Roman

aqueducts and castles, Visigoth churches, Moorish palaces and fortresses, and English mansions. The Portuguese have surpassed them all in manifesting their rich and varied architectural tradition.

The avalanche of concrete, chrome and glass which has swept away much of Western Europe's charm missed Portugal, where buildings, cobbled roads, a way of life, manners and a kind of sleepy elegance lie undisturbed. The lingering impression is one of warmth from a people who have known better times, of quiet good taste which is

OPPOSITE: Newlyweds pose on a promontary overlooking the River Cávado at Barcelos in the Minho. ABOVE: A tempting display of local food and wine on offer in Viana da Castello.

often a little faded, and of style without ostentation.

This book has been arranged in geographical sequence, starting in Lisbon in the southwest, moving north through the provinces of Estremadura, Ribatejo and the three Beiras to the Douro and Minho, before turning away from the Atlantic to the mountainous northeast and Trás-os-Montes; the journey continues southwards through Alentejo, and ends in the Algarve on the Mediterranean coast. At the end is a chapter entitled TRAVELERS' TIPS with some practical advice to assist you arrange your journey and make the best of your stay.

The information is set out in a way that can be of help in deciding the kind of holiday to choose in Portugal; much will depend on your tastes, the time of the year you plan to be there, the number of people traveling, and your budget. As always, you will get more out of your holiday if you arrive with a reasonably clear idea of what you would like to see and do, making it possible to select suitable accommodation, especially with regard to transport requirements.

For example, if your interest is in architecture and the cultural aspects of Portugal centered in the towns and cities, you will do well to avoid traffic and parking problems by using the cheap and excellent public transport. For visits to places further afield excursions are often available, or you can negotiate a deal with a taxi driver. In the urban centers there is usually a wide choice of accommodation: grand old hotels in the traditional style, modern international establishments, *pousadas*, or simple but charming bed and breakfast places. Although the choice may be more restricted out of town, there are small hotels, stately houses which offer rooms, and even farms which take guests, all of which can be arranged by specialist agencies.

A wide range of options is also available for the kind of holiday you want; all arrangements can be made in advance through an agent or directly with the hotels and transport companies of your choice; alternatively, you may simply prefer to book hotels to serve as a base, allowing your plans to unfold as you go. The opposite extreme is also possible: to take one of the many excellent package

holidays offered by an experienced operator, where every aspect of your trip is taken care of. Many agencies will tailor a holiday specially around the places you want to see and the time you intend to spend there.

If you are more interested in visiting archaeological sites off the beaten track, it makes sense to drive because remote areas in the countryside are not well served by trains and buses. An alternative is to hire a car for a specific trip, making it unnecessary to bring your own from elsewhere. Bear in mind that while the roads are quite usable, they are often sinuous and cluttered with slow-moving vehicles which in rural areas are frequently animal-drawn. What is more, you will discover very quickly that the Portuguese are not Driving Miss Daisy: the

accident rate is appalling, and the worst in Europe.

It could be that you have simply come to relax in the sun of the Algarve or Alentejo for a summer break; if so, independent movement may not be of much importance in your plans as many resort areas are self-contained, in walking distance of the beaches, restaurants and night-spots. They will have their own arrangements for connections to the nearest airport or railway station.

There are wonderful forests and mountains to explore on foot, especially in the northern areas of the country. Invariably you will be able to find somewhere welcoming to stay, although in the high season it is important to book well in advance and not rely on luck. In this case, it makes sense to

have your own transport, not only for access but also to be independent. Often where country districts are served by buses or trains, their schedules will be unsuitable and may restrict you.

Whatever your choice, this is a land where natural beauty, artistic and architectural marvels, history, intimacy and an abundance of facilities are there to make your vacation memorable and rewarding.

Most prices here compare favorably with those for comparable services in other parts of Europe: in other words, excellent value for money.

Misty morning haze on the tranquil lagoon (*ria*) which is the focus of the Parque Natural da Ria de Aveiro near Coimbra.

The Country and Its People

PORTUGAL LIES IN A narrow strip at the western edge of the Iberian Peninsula, overshadowed in some respects by its larger neighbor, Spain. The two countries share more than their peoples care to admit: their histories are intertwined, and the very existence of Portugal as a separate entity could be described as an accident, rather than the result of uniqueness in culture, race, language or experience. For better or for worse, the Portuguese found themselves in an area of geographical importance in the westernmost part of Europe, the gateway to the Mediterranean Sea, Africa, the lands beyond the Atlantic and the route to northern Europe. Having the only good natural harbors on the Iberian Peninsula, perhaps it was appropriate that the young Kingdom's destiny should have been to turn Europe's face to the future and a new world, discovering and charting routes to far-off places known to exist but shrouded in the mists of legend. The spirit of adventure, then, is one thread that runs through the Portuguese character, tempered by other realities.

As the spearhead of European exploration and conquest in the New World, Africa and Asia, little Portugal had to defend herself against larger and more powerful nations who resented her success and new-found wealth. She had to accept unfavorable political alliances, to learn to accommodate double standards in ethical matters, and to tread the tightrope of peaceful coexistence with her powerful, predatory neighbor, Spain. Descended from successive waves of prehistoric migrants from Europe and Africa, the Portuguese national consciousness has known invasion and subjugation by the Moors, the Spanish, the French and the English, engendering a certain fatalism in their psyche.

Their country has seen great riches at times, but much longer periods of poverty. When there was wealth it rarely benefited anyone but the aristocracy, the Roman Catholic Church, the royal family and a few merchants: most lived in penury, eking out a meager existence from the inhospitable soil on tiny plots of land in the north, and as tenants or hired labor on the great estates of the south. Nevertheless, they have a kind of collective memory of the days of imperial greatness and also a deep iden-

tification with the Roman Catholic Church, in spite of their suffering at its hands. A curious nostalgia, an almost Slavic melancholy called *saudade* sometimes manifests itself in their character, not only in sadness but also pleasure in being sad.

In some intangible way, people who live close to the land mirror its qualities: Portugal is small, but diverse in topography and climate, with green, rolling hills, harsh, rocky mountains, scorched plains, hot Mediterranean-like regions and cold, wet mountains typical of the Atlantic seaboard. Few countries are so

richly endowed with architectural treasures of such splendor: castles, monasteries, fortified towns and villages, palaces, formal gardens and great country houses. Thus the Portuguese are a people of obvious warmth, brave and stoical; their unpretentious formality is not only courteous, but implies a wish not to encroach on your privacy, a breath of fresh air after the nastiness of institutionalized Anglo-Saxon familiarity. No people work harder anywhere, and yet none manage to do so with such indolence or insouciance. There is a timeless aspect to

Seaweed ABOVE is dried on beaches of Afife in the Minho for use as fertilizer. The shrine of Fátima OPPOSITE is one of the Catholic world's most important pilgrimage destinations.

their way of life, which anyone who has visited Macau, or who in happier times knew Lourenço Marques or Luanda and their dozy cafés and prawn restaurants, their elegant but rather down-at-heel houses set in well-tended gardens will recognize in Portugal, making him feel at home and amongst friends.

THE MISTY PAST

In the Stone Age the territory which is now

Portugal was inhabited, even though we know little about those early hunters and farmers. They did leave us some megalithic burial sites, mysterious and silent. They grew cereals of a sort, kept animals which they had tamed or were the ancestors of our domestic varieties, and fished in the sea. They made bone carvings and rough earthenware pottery. The relationship between pottery and bronze casting implies a knowledge of ceramics to make the molds, pottery invariably being a precursor to the making of bronze weapons and vessels. So it was with these ancestors of the Portuguese, who still make pottery to this day.

In time, successive waves of immigrants came into the area: the people known as the

Iberians crossed the Mediterranean from Africa and gave their name to the Iberian Peninsula, settling mainly in the south and what is now eastern Spain. The Ligurians came overland from Italy and settled largely in the north of the Peninsula, as did the Celts who came by boat from northern France and Britain. Excavations have uncovered settlements dating from those times; the best example in Portugal is the Citânia de Briteiros just outside Braga.

Over a thousand years before the birth of Christ the Phoenicians arrived, traders, metalworkers and sailors who left the Portuguese a tradition of nautical exploration and commerce.

Three hundred years later they were followed by the Greeks, who established harbors on the Mediterranean coast of the Peninsula and introduced the vine and the olive. The Carthaginians also came; each added something, and each left tangible evidence of its presence. All paled into insignificance when the Romans arrived in about 200 BC.

THE ROMANS

After their conquest of Carthage and its territories, the Romans turned their attention to the rest of the Iberian Peninsula in 201 BC. Between the Tagus and Douro rivers they encountered a tribe known as the Lusitani. These Lusitanians, the ancestors of today's Portuguese, were what could best be described as a whole heap of trouble: it took the greatest military power in the world, their finest generals and a hundred years to conquer them. The job was finally done by Julius Caesar, and the Romans set about colonizing that region and elsewhere in the Peninsula. They brought magnificent architecture; they engaged in enormous hydraulic engineering projects, to transport water across the country and provide it in the cities; they introduced a new and sophisticated artistic taste in gardens, the use of mosaics and the sculpting of tombs. Perhaps their most important contributions were a legal system, the Romanizing of the language and — without intending it — Christianity. Around that time it was Roman policy to resettle the troublesome Jews in far-flung corners of the empire, so many were exiled to Iberia; in later centuries the consequences were to have a profound effect on both the Jews and their hosts .

The Romans used a system of municipal governments to administer the territory, minting their own coins and operating a complex code of financial and urban law which defined both rights and obligations; slavery was introduced, a technique the Portuguese were later to use in their own colonies and which lasted until the eighteenth century. Gold, copper, lead and iron were

trymen began attacking the disintegrating Roman Empire. A tribe called the Suevi conquered parts of Iberia, as did the Alans and the rapacious Vandals; the Visigoths followed, but differed from the others in that they adopted Christianity and many Roman customs and ways, administering much as the Romans themselves had. They got rid of the Byzantines and Suevi and introduced Arianism for a time, a heretical Christian doctrine which held that Jesus was more man than God and not of the same essence, contrary to Orthodox scripture. In time they

mined: marble was quarried, and great farms flourished, producing cereals, fruit and olives, where magnificent horses were bred. Fish was harvested from the sea and estuaries along the coast, textiles were woven and dyed, and salt was made in great marine pans.

Then, in the fifth century AD a German cloud appeared on the northern horizon.

THE GERMANIC PERIOD

For a considerable time, small groups of Teutonic peoples had been settling in the north of the Iberian Peninsula, when in the fifth century waves of their belligerent coun-

returned to Orthodoxy, but had established the precedent of uniting church and state. One group established its capital and a major bishopric in Braga, where the church held paramount ecclesiastical power for centuries in what was to become Portugal. They also began persecuting the Jews, with serious consequences for the whole of Iberia in time, Portugal as much as Spain. In the meantime a new force was gathering in the south, which early in the eighth century was poised to usher in five hundred years of a very different kind of order.

Celt-Iberian ruins OPPOSITE at the Citânia de Briteiros in the Minho. Évora's Temple of Diana ABOVE is the greatest single surviving monument of the Roman era.

THE MOORS

The Mohammedan hurricane had roared out of Arabia, clearing away everything in its path to north Africa. In 710 the Arabs (or Moors) and their Berber henchmen crossed the Mediterranean to Spain; they swept north to France, where they were stopped at the Battle of Pewters in 732. The Spanish had halted their advance at Covadonga in 718, but they established a caliphate at Córdoba to administer the Iberian Peninsula. Theirs was an era of tolerance and order, commerce and wealth. Scholarship in mathematics, medicine, engineering, navigation, architecture and philosophy flourished. Jews and Christians alike were allowed to practice their religions. Much has been written about the Christian resistance to Islam: the truth is that the inhabitants of Iberia were converted in swathes, and many churches rededicated as mosques. When the *reconquista* began many of the defenders were Iberian Mohammedans, fighting beside the Moors themselves. Beyond the sublime architecture which they left, the Moors brought new agricultural methods, such as the mechanized milling of corn and the construction of enormous water-wheels to lift water from the rivers into cultivated fields. They had an effect on the taste in music, and in architectural ornamentation, such as the use of decorative tiles.

Still, parts of the northern Iberian Peninsula had not been brought fully under Moorish control: forays were made into the territory under their sway by small Christian armies. Encouraged by the Pope and promises of help from northern Europe, they became increasingly aggressive; a long

war of attrition developed, in which Moorish strongholds fell to Christian forces, one after the other. The last to fall was Grenada in 1492.

However, history moves slowly, and there are wheels within wheels: far removed from the scenes of decisive battles, a gentleman from France was doing a little empire-building on his own account.

THE BIRTH OF PORTUGAL

The appeals of the Christian aristocracy to northern Europe for help in driving out the heathen Moor met with varying degrees of success. One of those who did assist was Earl Henri from Burgundy: he had taken control of the the town of Porto at the mouth of the Douro. On April 9th, 1097, he staked a claim to the land between the Douro and Minho rivers, so-called *Portucale.* Within a short time, Henri's son, Afonso Henriques made his capital the city of Guimaraes and proclaimed his earldom a kingdom. This was neither to the taste of the Mohammedans in the south, nor to that of the kings in the north who had conquered Castile. For the first time, but not the last, a Portuguese king had to fortify his country against Castilian attack. Still, Portugal continued its southbound conquests, taking Lisbon in 1147 after terrible fighting, and later the Algarve. Her historic misfortune was that Castile developed at the same time, was every bit as ambitious and had considerably more muscle.

Portugal's advance as a military power was a cultural and economic step backwards. Famine and disease accompanied the fighting, and religious repression began to manifest itself. The succession of her kings and the changes in power are are too complicated for a book of this kind, but what is worth mentioning is a problem that began about this time, enduring for hundreds of years: the king came into conflict with his nobles, who sought to limit his power. This had no altruistic motives. Indeed, at times the king attempted reforms which the nobility found threatening and prevented, to the country's detriment.

Portugal's mountain tops are crowned by sturdy castles and forts, many built in the fourteen century under King Diniz.

One could be forgiven for assuming that a country of Portugal's size had a fairly homogeneous social structure: in fact it was divided into three different societies. In the north was an agricultural economy worked by feudal lords: they provided their serfs with a little grain and a degree of protection from invading forces in return for labor. In the center, power resided in the municipal authorities, where wealth was generated by crafts, manufacture and trading. In the south were great estates, *latifundia*, ruled by knights of the religious orders and worked by Moorish slaves and Christian immigrants. There was a constant shortage of labor on the land, as people preferred to try and make a better living in the towns, despite opposition from the landowners; conversely, taxes were constantly being imposed in the towns for new fortifications.

As a result of these difficulties a revolution took place in 1383, bringing into prominence the House of Avis and ushering in a new era for Portugal. There was chaos: the peasants rose against the feudal lords, the townspeople rose against the king, and a number of contenders for power tried to make enough alliances to seize the throne. A palace revolt was led by Duke João of Avis, who was able to use his military contacts to get the support he needed. All of this was too much for Castile, which made a bid to wrest control, and by extension, Portugal. An outbreak of bubonic plague drove them away from Lisbon. Two years later in 1385, a group of aristocrats, churchmen and municipal representatives elected Duke João as king, with the title of João I. Castile made the mistake of invading again, and was soundly beaten at the Battle of Aljubarrota that August. In thanksgiving, the monastery of Batalha was built, and Portugal entered an age of unprecedented power.

THE HOUSE OF AVIS AND THE VOYAGES OF DISCOVERY

João's priority was now to weld new alliances to protect himself from Spain: a year after Aljubarrota, in 1386, he signed a perpetual alliance with England at Windsor, and for good measure got himself spliced to Philippa of Lancaster. Their children were immensely successful: Duarte became king and won the support of the nobility, Pedro became a patron of commercial development in the towns, and Henrique — remembered by posterity as Henry the Navigator — became commander of the Order of Christ. He established a tradition of maritime exploration and conquest which brought Portugal to the height of its greatness. João also had an illegitimate son, Afonso, who married into great wealth and founded the ducal House of Bragança. That family came into prominence 260 years later.

In 1415 Henry led an expedition to expel the Moors from Ceuta in North Africa, an event which marked a decisive shift in the whole mentality of Europe, turning its eyes to horizons of unimagined conquests beyond the known world.

This was the beginning of Portugal's imperial age, in which she took Madeira, the Azores and the Cape Verde Islands, charting the route around Africa in the voyages of Bartolomeu Diaz, finding the sea route to India in 1498 in the courageous voyage of Vasco da Gama and establishing colonies in Goa, Angola, Mozambique, Guinea, Macau, Timor and Brazil. She came to dominate the trade in gold from west Africa — transporting by sea what the Moors had transported by land — gaining great wealth for herself. And all this from a small country with a population of about one-and-a-half million! That little Portugal was unable to sustain such an empire is scarcely surprising, and even less so when she was persuaded by Spain to shoot herself in the foot.

SPANISH RULE

There were fundamental weaknesses in the social fabric of Portugal. For a start, opening up new colonies meant that significant numbers emigrated, reducing the population to about a million. Secondly, an increasing number of men had to carry out the conquests and defend the newly-won territories, diverting them from productive enterprise. (The situation was not improved by importing black slaves, who clearly had suspect loyalties and were hardly a stabilizing factor.) Thirdly, the great wealth flowing into the country did not percolate down to the common people: it stayed in the hands of the Roman Catholic Church, the aristocracy, the crown and a few merchants. The fourth reason was that the country's attention had been diverted from the development of local industry, and it was often cheaper to import than to buy locally. Finally, João III had the stupidity to introduce the Inquisition from Spain into Portugal in 1536, establishing a reign of terror. Many of

When the young King Sebastião went off to Africa in a campaign against the Moors and got himself and 8,000 men killed, Spain seized its chance and annexed Portugal in 1580 on the pretext that the king had left no heirs. Philip II of Spain was now also Philip I of Portugal, and promised to safeguard Portugal's language, currency, overseas empire and government. By and large he kept his word, but did not stop the Dutch and the British from nibbling away at the empire, while he *did* expect Portugal to help foot the bill for his ruinous wars. After another two

the professional and learned men were Jews, as were traders and bankers. (Following Spain's sudden conquest of the last Moorish kingdom on the Iberian Peninsula in 1492, Grenada, religious tolerance disappeared. In 1497 Portugal followed Spain's example and forbade public worship by both Jews and Mohammedans.) Large numbers were expelled, impoverishing not only cultural and scientific life but also the country's economic health. Reducing the population was bad enough, but the qualitative loss almost destroyed Portugal. Furthermore, the Inquisition created tension with England, Portugal's perpetual ally which was not on the best of terms with the Pope and Roman Catholic authorities.

conveniently-named Philips' had continued in the same vein, matters came to head in 1640 when there was a coup in Lisbon. An unwilling Duke of Bragança was proclaimed king by the nobility: João IV. His House ruled into the twentieth century, the last Portuguese dynasty.

THE FIRST BRAGANÇAS

The reluctant João struggled to maintain Portugal's independence, regain some of the lost overseas empire and make allies.

The sixteenth century Tower of Belém of Lisbon sits serenely on the Tagus like a tall ship at anchor.

This was a momentous time for all Europe: the great powers of England, France and the Netherlands were all in the throes of civil, religious and international wars. João finally had to sign a treaty with England, then under the sway of the Protestant Cromwell, anathema to the deeply conservative Portuguese. Fighting continued with Spain for nearly 30 years; finally her independence was recognized in 1668. Attempts were made again to stimulate the establishment of local industry, but once more these were set aside when gold and diamonds were discovered in Brazil in the 1690s. As before, this new-found wealth was misused in the building of extravagant churches and palaces, leaving Portugal's basic infrastructure weak and vulnerable, and her people poor. Although a number of important public works were constructed, these were of little benefit to the population.

A commercial landmark of the time was the signing in 1703 of the Methuen Treaty with England, in which the English — who had developed an unquenchable thirst for port wine — were granted preferential terms for the import of textiles into Portugal and her colonies (much to the disadvantage of the local weavers) in return for unrestricted access to England's wine market. The real effect was to give the British control of Portugal's port wine industry.

Fortunately for the country, which was about to experience the greatest natural catastrophe in its history, a ruthless, efficient and in many ways innovative official became chief minister: the results of the appointment of the Marquês de Pombal are still visible, two-and-a-half centuries later.

THE GREAT EARTHQUAKE

On All Saints' Day on the 1st of November, 1755, a violent earthquake struck Lisbon and other parts of Portugal. It happened while many were at Mass, and the lighted candles started fires which added to the horror. Some fled to the Tagus, into the arms of a tidal wave; ensuing epidemics completed the misery. The final death toll stood at around 40,000.

Pombal swiftly restored order, using the opportunity to introduce and enforce administrative and economic reforms in the name of the king. Plans were drawn up and carried out for the rebuilding of Lisbon and other towns in a practical grid pattern, industry was encouraged, the Jesuits thrown out, slavery abolished in metropolitan Portugal, the laws regarding wine production revised to reduce the advantage that the English had secured for themselves, and the excesses of the Inquisition curbed: institutionalized persecution of the Jews was terminated. Although he put an end to public executions by burning, he authorized the use of torture on his opponents, and ensured with savagery that his instructions were obeyed.

Having achieved so much he tried to usurp the throne in 1777: he failed and was banished. Later the queen restored certain religious elements of government abolished by Pombal, but his legacy was of lasting benefit.

THE PENINSULAR WARS

In 1807 Napoleon's army invaded Portugal. He had demanded in vain that she close her ports to British shipping. His force was under the command of General Junot, formerly the ambassador to Lisbon; a secret pact had been signed between France and Spain, in which Portugal would be divided into three parts; the north and south sections were to be awarded to Spain, while the center was to be made available to the Braganças if certain conditions were met. The Portuguese colonies in the Americas were also on the shopping list, with Spain intended as a major beneficiary.

In the meanwhile the royal family had been evacuated by the British to Brazil; although the Portuguese authorities made no trouble for the French invaders, their welcome began to wear thin. An expeditionary force under the future Duke of Wellington was dispatched from Ireland in 1808, and evicted Junot, then transported the invaders back to France with their booty. Further invasions increased the misery of the long-suffering Portuguese, who had also had enough of the British military dictatorship under Viscount Beresford, who ruled the country for 10 years. In 1820 open revolt broke out and smoldered for 31 years, going through the same destructive phases as the French revolution did. When the entire country was in a state of exhaustion, a constitutional monarchy was established. In the meanwhile Brazil had become a politically independent empire under a Bragança in 1822, which had the effect of driving Portugal away from its traditional system of government.

Portuguese Liberals were divided into two groups, one more radical than the other, and amidst acrimony and civil disturbances both of them steered Portugal through the ensuing decades, slowly bringing reforms to the economy, judiciary and administration.

THE END OF THE MONARCHY

The seeds had already been sown for a pluralist democracy in Portugal. When economic recession struck Europe in the 1870s, the old question of import-substitution and developing local industry arose. On the other hand, since the final loss of Brazil in 1898 — when it threw out its last Bragança monarch and became a republic — there was talk of reinforcing the African colonial empire, linking Mozambique and Angola and developing the territory between. This was rudely interrupted when the British demanded Portuguese withdrawal from the Zambezi heartland in 1890. Humiliated, Portugal had little choice but to agree. Republican sentiment began to simmer, and erupted in 1908 after economic deprivation had embittered the peasantry and the military: the king had been begged to rule by decree in those difficult times, but instead authorized his prime minister, João Franco to rule dictatorially, an unpopular decision. On the 1st of February of that year, King Carlos and his son were assassinated in the middle of Lisbon. His second son took the throne as Manuel II, but mounting pressure forced the unfortunate man to abdicate in 1910. So ended the power of the ancient House of Bragança; after 813 years of monarchy, Portugal had become a republic.

THE FIRST REPUBLIC AND SALAZAR

In 1911 a new constitution was adopted, and the Law of Separation declared Portugal a secular state.

Unfortunately things did not go as intended: there were 45 changes of government in the first 16 years of the republic's life. The arrival of the Great War did not help. Goaded by Britain, her perpetual ally, and fearful of the fate of her colonies in Africa, she declared war on Germany in 1917 with neither the manpower nor the stomach for the conflict.

In 1926 the army staged a coup, with General Carmona in charge; democracy had left Portugal, not to return for nearly 50 years.

In 1928, Antonio Salazar, an economist from the University of Coimbra, was appointed by Carmona as minister of finance. His condition for accepting was unrestricted control of the finances of all the ministries, and he was successful in many respects, using harsh austerity measures. In 1932 he became prime minister, and a year later established a dictatorship. His rule has been called fascist because he opposed pluralism and was prepared to use force: in fact, the comparison is facile. There was none of the rabble rousing, the grandiose parades, the quests for new empires, none of the racial dogma with demagogues screeching about their historic destiny. He even banned his own political party. It is true that he was able to impose his will on Portugal, riding the tidal wave which brought Mussolini and then Hitler and Franco to power, but there the similarity ends. He was a conservative man — much more so than his republican predecessors — and a deeply religious Catholic, although his faith did not stop him from using methods that Pombal would have admired. He was not a demagogue, but rather a secretive monocrat. His achievement was perhaps to give Portugal a measure of stability, and keep her out of the Second World War, avoiding the cataclysms which engulfed most of Europe from Spain to the Urals. He kept his country independent, but his people impoverished and backward. He has been described as a fascist without the attributes of fascism. Being a traditionalist, he did not tear down old buildings and go on a rampage of urban renewal, for which the modern traveler (grudgingly) owes him a debt of gratitude.

THE CARNATION REVOLUTION

In 1968 Salazar suffered a stroke which left him mortally ill; he was succeeded by Dr. Marcelo Caetano, who attempted to modernize and reform the government. It was too late. Hostility had grown, especially amongst the armed forces who had served in the colonies. They formed an organization called the MFA, the Armed Forces Movement. In the early hours of the April 25th, 1974, troops moved into Lisbon and took control in what is remembered as the carnation revolution, after the carnations which the soldiers had placed in the barrels of their rifles.

A provisional government representing all political factions was established under the respected military leadership of António de Spínola as president, and Mário Soares as foreign minister. Their first problem was to deal with the question of the African empire, a source of great dissent which lead to uprisings. In the first two years following the coup there were six governments as everyone jostled for political place. Impoverished Alentejan laborers seized farms owned by absentee landlords and set up co-operatives — with the usual consequences — while many industries, banks and insurance companies were nationalized.

Soares' plan for the careful dismantling of the colonies was ignored and the Portuguese simply turned their back on them, leaving chaos and bloodshed which persists to this day. In 1975 there was a flood of refugees into Portugal after the South African government had restricted the number of immigrants it was prepared to accept, and a population of 10 million was swelled by 700,000. A major insurrection was crushed by General Eanes in the same year: he then went on to win the presidential election, appointing Soares as prime minister.

In a swing to the right in 1987, the first majority government since 1974 came to power. At last the country seems to be on the road to modernity and progress, and Soares is now president.

Portugal has been a member of the European Union since 1986, a quirk of fate bringing her closer not only to the rest of Europe, but to the Spanish, whose history has yet again run parallel to her own. Industry has been re-privatized, private enterprise is flourishing as never before, and massive investments are being made, both from abroad and domestically. Although there is still much poverty and illiteracy, it must be remembered that Portugal has had only a little over 20 years of democracy and unfettered economic activity to catch up with Western European standards; given the industriousness of her people, there is every reason to be optimistic about the future.

GEOGRAPHY AND CLIMATE

Situated in the southwest corner of Europe, Portugal occupies a narrow strip on the Iberian Peninsula of 88,500 sq km (35,383 sq miles). From east to west it measures 220 km (137 miles) at its widest, and from north to south 560 km (348 miles). It is bounded by a land frontier with Spain of 1,215 km (755 miles), which has virtually no natural barriers, and the Atlantic Ocean. The four major rivers are the Douro and Minho in the north, the Guadiana in the southeast — which forms the border with Spain — and most important, the Tagus, which is the longest river in Iberia, Lisbon being located at its mouth.

North of the Tagus lies Portugal's more mountainous region, the highest range being the Serra de Estrêla in the northeast, rising to an altitude of 1,991 m (6,532 ft). South of the Tagus is the alluvial plain of the Alentejo and Ribatejo provinces.

The northern coast, sometimes called the Costa Verde, is a land of exposed sandy beaches, forests and green valleys. Its climate is temperate with warm, mainly dry summers and mild, wet winters while the sea tends to be cold and rough year round. This is also the country's most densely populated region. Inland, the harsh-featured Douro valley, the country's most famous wine-making area, has a more extreme climate with cold winters and searing temperatures in summer.

South of the Douro, the low-lying coastal belt is cooled by sea breezes and has heavy rain in winter. To the south lies Estremadura, the province stretching as far down as Setúbal, south of Lisbon. Its coastline is edged with sandy beaches and cliffs, and it is here that the Mediterranean Sea begins to affect the climate.

In the northeast corner beyond the Gerês and Marão ranges lies the isolated and

To the south lies Portugal's largest region, the Alentejo, which occupies nearly a third of the country's area. Stretching from Spain to the Atlantic, it is an area of rolling plains and reddish-brown soil. This is the breadbasket of Portugal, and the land where half the world's cork comes from. Summers are long and can be cruelly hot on these airless prairies, while the short winters can be extremely cold.

Separated from the Alentejo by the Serra de Monchique and the Serra do Caldeirão, the southernmost strip of Portugal has a

sparsely populated region of Trás-os-Montes, an area of high mountains, large plateaux and deep valleys. Less rain falls here but greater extremes of temperature occur than elsewhere in the north, as high as 40°C (104°F) in summer, and below freezing in winter.

South of the Douro, the northeasterly provinces of Beira Alta and Beira Baixa form Portugal's most mountainous area, an extension of the high plateau of central Spain.

The central zone consists of the coastal area around Lisbon and the inland province of Ribatejo on an alluvial plain, where temperatures are warmer than in the north, the rainfall lower and the summers longer.

subtropical climate. Winter temperatures in the Algarve rarely drop below 12°C (54°F) and in summer they average 24°C (75°F). The coast is lined with long, sandy, inviting beaches.

FAITH AND SUPERSTITION

RELIGION

Although the 1911 Law of Separation made Portugal a secular state, roughly 95 percent of the population are Roman Catholics, albeit

Windmill looms over whitewashed terrace at Peniche, Costa da Prata, to catch the Atlantic breezes.

with a strong local flavor. Pagan-based rituals are still practiced in parts of the country, and appeals from Rome to stop painful acts of personal sacrifice — such as walking on the knees and self-flagellation — have fallen on deaf ears.

In spite of the church's initial disapproval, the cult of Fátima grew and flourished. This relates to a vision of the Virgin said to have been seen by three children in 1917, when they were given three secrets. In October that year, although none but the children saw the Virgin, 70,000 people claim

to do things their own way. In the summer months, there is a plethora of religious processions, called *romariás*, especially in the northwest. Each village and town has its own celebrations: get hold of a pamphlet from the I.P.T. (Instituo de Promoção Turistica, (see page 76 for addresses) with details of what takes place and when. These festivals are an indelible part of Portuguese life.

A word on the subject of the Portuguese churches: these were built from the times of Roman and Visigoth occupation, and

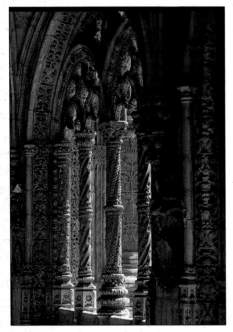

to have witnessed a miracle where the sun moved and the sick were cured of their illnesses. Salazar made good use of the opportunity to focus popular attention on a Portuguese miracle, and had an extravagant basilica built there.

Sometimes Christianity's darker roots show, particularly in the remoter northern regions, where superstition and belief in magic prevail. People still sometimes visit the local *bruxa* or witch, and strange rituals surround birth, death and fertility.

Now that contraception has become freely available, the birth rate suggests that many are making use of it; this goes to show that in spite of their adherence to a formal, strict religion, the Portuguese tend

display a remarkable diversity of styles, both architecturally and in their ornamentation. They range from the very simple and the starkly elegant to enormous structures, the extravagance of their sculpture and gold leaf inspiring awe in both the devout and mere visitors.

Heironymous Monastery cloisters, Lisbon ABOVE LEFT, Eglise de San Lauranção in the Algarve ABOVE RIGHT and Capella de Coimbras in Braga OPPOSITE display the rich diversity of styles and art in Portugal's magnificent heritage of religious monuments.

Lisbon
and
Environs

LISBON

Lisbon is a city with the stamp of past greatness. Overlooking the River Tagus, the gateway to the Atlantic, its weathered edifices are monuments to the days when Portugal was the vanguard of discovery of the world beyond the horizons of renaissance Europe. Although they recall an era of untold wealth, the older cathedrals and fortresses were witness to the worst natural cataclysm in her history, when in 1755 this proud and glittering city was reduced to rubble by a shattering earthquake. But Lisbon never lost the soul of Portugal: its faded beauty reflects not only nobility, but also the tribulations of a people who have known better times.

Background

Archaeological evidence suggests that the city's founding fathers were Phoenicians, who around 1200 BC colonized the hilltop where the Castelo São Jorge stands, naming their settlement Alis Ubbo, meaning Delightful Harbor. The Romans made the city an administrative center in 60 BC, and built new fortifications around the hilltop, traces of which are still in evidence.

Under Moorish rule the town flourished and became a center of learning. Several attempts to capture Lisbon from them ended in failure, but in 1147 Afonso Henriques, aided by an army of Crusaders, laid siege to it. After a grueling 17 weeks the Moors surrendered, and the Crusaders pillaged this cultured city like a pack of hyenas. Some of the English contingent, obviously liking what they saw, decided to stay on in the area and an English priest, Gilbert of Hastings, was made Bishop of Lisbon.

In 1256, after the Moors had been prised out of the Algarve, the capital was moved from Coimbra in the north, to the more centrally located Lisbon. The first university was founded shortly afterwards, nearly 700 years ago. The building of the city then began in earnest and Lisbon became an important trading port.

The fifteenth century brought the voyages of discovery, and by the sixteenth century, as the Spice Route to the Moluccas opened and Portugal began to exploit the wealth of her colonies, Lisbon became the hub of a great maritime empire and a major trading center, basking in undreamt-of wealth and glory. The population swelled to 165,000, making it the largest city on the Iberian peninsula; King Manuel I, who ruled from 1495 to 1521, launched a massive campaign of construction, enriching Lisbon with many beautiful and ornate buildings. Of those, fortunately the magnificent Convento dos Mosteiro dos Jerónimos in Belém and the Torre de Belém have survived.

Lisbon's and Portugal's fortunes waned thereafter, but the discovery of gold and diamonds in Brazil in 1705 fueled another wave of lavish building. Gold leaf glistened in the churches, a great aqueduct was built — with such engineering precision that it withstood the 1755 earthquake and stands to this day — and Lisbon emulated all the splendors of the French court. English merchants traded in the city and established a comfortable expatriate community, eventually setting up their own English church and cemetery in the Estrêla district.

Then, suddenly, disaster struck. While the devout were at Mass at 10 am on All Saint's Day, 1755, there began — in the words of an English nun's letter to her mother — a noise like the rattling of Coaches. It was the beginning of the great earthquake. Overturned church candles started fires that were fanned by the wind. People ran to the Tagus for safety, into the arms of death as tidal waves swept up the river.

The lower part of the town was destroyed, the docks were washed away and aftershocks continued for five days. After the inevitable epidemics had taken their toll, the number of dead was put as high as 40,000, nearly a quarter of its population. In the days that followed, King José I gave emergency powers to his prime minister, the Marquês de Pombal, who skillfully handled the situation, restoring law and order, closing the port, burying the dead, and punishing looters. His measures included dealing decisively with that thorn in Portugal's side for centuries, the Inquisition, which saw the earthquake as an opportunity to

The Alfama district's narrow shopping streets nestle far below the Castle of São Jorge.

start wholesale burnings at the stake. It was through Pombal's persuasion and planning that Lisbon remained the capital. A special tax was levied to finance the rebuilding of the city on a grid system of wide streets and large, airy squares, the sight that greets the visitor to central Lisbon to this day.

During World War II Lisbon again became a focus of international attention and regained a little of its lost glamor. Under Salazar, Portugal remained neutral and so thousands of Jewish refugees poured into Lisbon to await transportation to other safe

countries. It became a refuge for exiled European royalty and heads of state, while people of all nationalities mingled in the hotels and bars, and the city swarmed with spies.

The most recent drama in Lisbon's history came on April 25, 1974, when Salazar's successor, Caetano, was overthrown in the virtually bloodless military coup that has become known as the Carnation Revolution. The army entered amid scenes of jubilation, and truckloads of carnations, the symbol of the revolution, were brought into the city. The rapid decolonization that followed brought an influx of 700,000 refugees from Angola and Mozambique, many of whom chose to settle in Lisbon, making it delightfully cosmopolitan.

GENERAL INFORMATION

The best source of information in Lisbon, as elsewhere in Portugal, is the Tourist Information offices or *Turismos* operated by the I.P.T. (Instituo de Promoção Turistica). Most centrally placed is the one at Palácio Foz, Praça dos Restauradores, ((01) 346-3314 or 346-3624, just north of the Rossio. Another is at Avenida António Augusto Aguiar Nº86, ((01) 575091.There are four others at major transport points: Alcântara

Maritime Station, ((01) 600756; Rocha Maritime Station, ((01) 396-5018; Santa Apolónia Station, ((01) 886-7848; and Lisbon (Portela) Airport, ((01) 893689.

For information on the whole of Portugal go to the Direcção-Geral do Turismo at Avenida António Augusto de Aguiar Nº86, ((01) 575086, and I.P.T. at Rua Alexandre Herculano Nº51, ((01) 388-1174, 388-1175, 388-1176 or 388-1177.

For specific travel inquiries, the following telephone numbers may prove helpful:

Portela Airport ((01) 848-5974.

General rail information: ((01) 876027 or 877092.

Rodoviária Nacional (coach travel), ((01) 726-7123.

The main office of TAP Air Portugal is at Praça Marquês de Pombal N°3A, ((01) 544080. For details of ferry services contact Alcântara Maritime Passenger Station, ((01) 396-9111, in the main docks.

For motoring information, you can contact the Automóvel Clube de Portugal at Rua Rosa Araújo N°24, 1200 Lisbon, ((01) 736121.

WHAT TO SEE AND DO

Designated Europe's City of Culture for 1994, Lisbon is rich in attractions and with

sio square and down to the Praça do Comércio by the Tagus. The fact that Lisbon is built on a number of hills — seven of them, it is said — need not impair your visit: there are trams, buses, cheap taxis, funiculars, a metro system and even elevators to spare your feet if you don't feel up to longer walks. However, a comfortable pair of walking-shoes, preferably trainers, is essential. The amount of walking as you visit the sights is deceptive, especially in museums and galleries. What's more, the gorgeous mosaic pavements are hard on the feet as well.

the exception of the slightly out-of-center Belém district, the sights are within walking distance of one another. The best way of enjoying its atmosphere, shaded squares and magnificent views is on foot, making it possible to spend time at places of special interest without the tension of worrying about parking and transport, and to stop when the the spirit moves you at the old *pastelarias* and cafés.

In the center there are three main areas of interest: the western hilltop neighborhood of the Bairro Alto, the medieval Alfama district huddling below the castle on the opposite hillside, and the valley running between them from the Pombal statue at the top of Avenida da Liberdade, across the busy Ros-

The Baixa

The Baixa, or Lower City, was rebuilt after the 1755 earthquake; the Marquês de Pombal's majestic reconstruction of the commercial and business heart of the city was rational, and is sometimes referred to as Pombaline Lisbon, characterized by wide, straight streets lined with uniform neoclassical buildings. Its austerity imparts a touch of Pombal's own ruthlessness, but the overall effect is softened by the decorative black and white mosaic pavements.

The old gateway to the city (although for most visitors it will probably not be the point

The seven hills ABOVE of Lisbon rise up from the Tagus estuary while imperious arches LEFT are reminders of the nation's great seafaring age.

of entry) is the **Praça do Comércio**. Situated in the center of the port, one side of this square is open to the Tagus where marble steps lead down to a landing stage. The other three sides are lined with uniform buildings, all with arcaded lower storeys and many of which are now ministerial offices.

Comparisons with the squares of other European cities are pointless because they ignore the question of spirit of place, but with dimensions of 192 m (630 ft) long by 177 m (581 ft) wide its proportions are heroic. Sadly, it has been reduced to little more than a transport terminus, dominated by a huge car park; hopefully some day it will be earmarked for restoration and a clean-up. Where else could one sit and enjoy such splendid views of the Tagus?

It is interesting to note the various names by which the square is known. Although it's officially the Praça do Comércio, the citizens in true Portuguese fashion refuse to relinquish the past and refer to it as the Terreiro do Paço (the palace grounds) because a royal palace once stood there. The English, in contrast, named it Black Horse Square after the bronze equestrian statue of King José I at its center. As the statue has turned green, this tag is now puzzling for visitors. In the northwest corner where the main post office stands, King Carlos I and the Crown Prince were assassinated in 1908 in an open carriage, an event which triggered the end of the Portuguese monarchy.

The magnificent **Arco Monumental da Rua Augusta**, the triumphal arch at the northern end, presents one of the most striking views of Pombaline Lisbon. It is crowned with statuary and straight through it runs the Rua Augusta, one of three main parallel streets which together with the Rua do Ouro and the Rua de Prata form part of a geometric street grid leading to Rossio Square. These were assigned by Pombal to various businesses and named accordingly: Rua do Ouro (now called Aurea) means Street of Gold, Rua de Prata Street of Silver, to this day prime areas for jewelry shops and banks, while the neighboring Rua dos Fanqueiros, Drapers' Street, still has a few textile and clothing shops.

The **Praça do Dom Pedro IV**, better known as the **Rossio**, is the heart of the Baixa and the hub of Lisbon. The square was once the site of the Inquisition's *autos da fé* (acts of faith, the silky euphemism for burning at the stake,) but is now rather more cheery, with flower sellers and lottery-ticket vendors clustering around its fountains. It is lined with souvenir shops and some nonchalant old cafés including the ever-popular **Café Nicola** and the **Pastelaria Suiça**. There is a lot of traffic around the square, so it is a busy, noisy place. The north end is entirely occupied by the **Dona Maria II National Theater**, constructed in 1840 on the site of the Palace of the Inquisition and in front of which stands the statue of the sixteenth-century Portuguese playwright Gil Vicente. At the northwestern end of the square is the unmistakable **Rossio Station**, a nineteenth-century neo-Manueline structure with clumsy horseshoe-shaped entrances that gives it a slightly humorous appearance.

Just east of the Rossio is the quieter and very pleasant **Praça da Figueira** with its relaxed cafés. North and west of the Rossio at the **Praça dos Restauradores** an obelisk commemorates the overthrow of Spanish rule and the restoration of Portuguese independence in 1640. Tourists of all nationalities gravitate here because the *Turismo* is housed within the **Palácio Foz** on the west side of the square, facing the main **Post Office**.

The tree-lined **Avenida da Liberdade** runs north of the Praça do Restauradores, a wide, pleasant boulevard dotted with statues and fountains and lined with some of Lisbon's top hotels. It stretches for a stately 1,500 m (about a mile), sloping uphill and culminating at the **Praça Marquês de Pombal**, a circular intersection with a monument on which stands a statue of that gentleman. To its rear is the **Parque Eduardo VII**, a charming mixture of formal and informal gardens, well worth a visit for the sweeping view it commands over the city center to the Tagus. Within this park is the **Estufa Fria**, a greenhouse covered with green slats in which tropical rain forest vegetation thrives.

The Castelo São Jorge and the Alfama

Overlooking all is the imposing Castelo de São Jorge, its battlements crowning the steep

Flower sellers, fountains and the unpretentious old cafés OPPOSITE TOP give busy Rossio Square BOTTOM a unique charm.

hill east of the Baixa. If you don't feel up to the stiff walk, get a taxi or bus up to the castle, then explore the environs at an easier down-hill pace. This is the inner heart of Lisbon, the hilltop first colonized by the Phoeni-cians, later fortified by the succession of Ro-mans, Visigoths, Moors and Portuguese kings, and around which the city expanded.

The castle and ramparts have been heav-ily restored, and the medieval quarter of **Santa Cruz** huddles within its outer walls. The grounds have been landscaped and the castle ruins are surrounded and inter-spersed with lawns, fountains and pools, the domain of peacocks, swans and other fowl. Lisboetas and tourists alike come here to sit on the terraces and feast on magnificent views over the city and the River Tagus.

After the castle, wander through the Alfama: much of this quarter survived the earthquake and is a maze of narrow, winding lanes and alleys clinging to the hillside. Once an area of rich mansions, it is now a poor quarter largely occupied by fishermen and sailors wheresome homes have no in-door plumbing. Small squares and churches crowd the steep slopes, the wrought-iron balconies festooned with flowers, washing, and caged canaries. The area is a hive of activity in the mornings when the *varinhas* (fishwives) come up here to sell the freshly caught fish. Towards evening the street lan-terns are lit and *fado* music fills the *adegas*.

Stop for a while at the **Miradouro de Santa Luzia**, a small square close to the church of Santa Luzia where a terrace has been con-structed on some Moorish fortifications. Have a drink while you savor the views across the terracotta-tiled rooftops to the Tagus and port below. There's also a map on the street wall to help you find your way down through the maze of streets and passageways.

Around Alfama

Just west of the Alfama district, is the **Sé Patriarcal, (** (01) 866752, the imposing twelfth-century Romanesque cathedral that was Lis-bon's first church. It suffered damage during the earthquakes of 1344 and 1755, and has undergone extensive reconstruction. Being a patchwork of architectural styles, the interior is a little disappointing. The cloister contains pieces of Roman masonry unearthed during

the work, but for many the fourteenth-cen-tury tombs of Lopo Fernandes Pacheco and his wife are the highlight. His statue depicts an old man with his dog lying at his feet, and his wife's is also surrounded by hounds; the touching domesticity seems to bridge the gap in time. A chapel contains a baroque nativity scene by one of Portugal's most famous sculptors, Machado de Castro. The cloisters are open from 9 am to noon and from 2 pm to 5 pm but are closed on holidays.

East of the Castelo de São Jorge lies **São Vicente de Fora**, a sixteenth-century domed renaissance church and former monastery commissioned by Portugal's Spanish king Philip II. The cloisters are tiled with a vast number of *azulejos* depicting scenes from La Fontaine's *Fables*, and in a chapel are the

tombs of many of the Braganças and for the time being at least, King Carol II of Rumania, who lived in exile at nearby Estoril. Open from 10 am to 12:30 pm and 3 pm to 6 pm; closed on Mondays.

Further east of the Alfama in the Xabregas district and closer to the Tagus is the **Igreja da Madre de Deus** (Church of the Mother of God) with its **Museu Nacional do Azulejo** (National Azulejo Museum), ((01) 814-7747, both well worth a visit. *Azulejos* are the distinctive glazed tiles which were a feature of Islamic architectural embellishment, and which the the Portuguese encountered during their conquest of Ceuta in Morocco; they adapted the designs and manufactured them to their own taste. Early styles often included blue and yellow

glazes, later superseded by the blue and white of of imported Delft-ware. They form murals or sometimes purely decorative bands and panels; the museum's importance lies in its display of the stylistic evolution of these tiles from the fourteenth century to the present day. Of special interest are those portraying Lisbon in her pre-earthquake splendor. Open from 10 am to 5 pm, closed on Mondays and holidays. Admission is free on Sundays until 2 pm.

Bairro Alto
West of the Baixa and looking across to the Alfama is the Bairro Alto (Upper City) district.

Views over Lisbon and the Tagus estuary are reason enough to check out São Jorge castle, itself an attraction with landscaped terraces and fountains.

To get there you can walk uphill through the Chiado shopping area, or take the funicular tram either from Calçada da Gloria by the Praça dos Restauradores up to Rua São Pedro d'Alcântara, or from the Calçada do Combro to the Rua do Boavista. A quicker option is to ride up to the Largo do Carmo in the **Elevador de Santa Justa** that stands just off the Rua do Ouro, a fancy and very comfortable iron elevator, or lift built by a student of Gustave Eiffel.

The Bairro Alto with its Bohemian reputation and cafés attracts trendies and tourists alike, and remains Lisbon's most

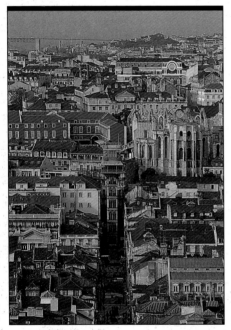

appealing district. In the early sixteenth century aristocratic families settled up here, but although many buildings survived the earthquake the district's fortunes declined, becoming the hang-out of writers and artists. In spite of the hilly terrain the streets are straight and narrow, and lined with wine shops, cafés, bars, *fado* clubs, restaurants, art galleries, and bookshops. It is the center of Lisbon nightlife and stays awake until the early hours of the morning.

On a steep hill at the top exit of the Elevador de Santa Justa is the rather dour shell

Ride the fancy iron lift ABOVE up to Largo do Carmo to see the world at your feet, or simply stroll Lisbon's streets to admire the beautiful *azulejo* tile paintings OPPOSITE.

of the fourteenth-century **Convento do Carmo**, founded by a military leader in honor of a vow he made at the Battle of Aljubarrota. During the earthquake the roof caved in on the congregation, leaving its forlorn arches to stand as their memorial: it is best seen from the inside.

From here it is a short walk to the Rua São Pedro d'Alcântara and the **Igreja São Roque**, late sixteenth-century church founded by the once-powerful Jesuits and designed by Felipe Terzi (architect of the Igreja de São Vicente). It survived the earthquake in spite of damage to the facade; behind the clumsily restored exterior lies surprising opulence including painted Italianate ceilings, fine *azulejos*, and a series of side chapels. But what draws visitors here is the **Chapel of São João Baptista** (fourth to the left of the altar), legendary for its phenomenal cost. In 1742 King João V commissioned it to be built by Luigi Vanvitelli in Rome, and in Rome it was built. Upon completion it was consecrated by the Pope, dismantled and transported to Lisbon. An extravagant creation with columns of lapis lazuli, angels of white Carrara marble and ivory, walls and floors covered in mosaic, its ceilings and capitals of gold and silver, the chapel's equally extravagant treasures are displayed in the Museu de São Roque, ((01) 346-0361, adjoining the church. Opening hours are from 10 am to 5 pm October to April and from 10 am to 6 pm June to September; it is closed on Mondays.

After visiting São Roque you can stroll around the **antique shops** of Rua São Pedro d'Alcântara, or partake of some refined refreshment in the **Solar do Vinho do Porto** (Port Wine Institute) at 45 Rua São Pedro de Alcântara, ((01) 342-3307, open between 10 am and midnight Monday to Saturday. Here you can relax in easy chairs in the magnificence of an eighteenth-century mansion and order a glass of port from the enormous list. Close by is the heart of the Bairro Alto, a maze of narrow, cobbled streets that predate the earthquake.

Between the Rossio and the Praça Luís de Camões is the **Chiado**, Lisbon's smartest shopping area. This lies on the Rua do Carmo from the Rossio, centering on the Rua Garrett and the Largo do Chiado and encompassing boutiques, bookstores, *pastelarias*,

and Lisbon's few department stores. In 1988 a fire that started in the Rua do Carmo devastated the area, destroying a large number of beautiful old shops including Grandela, one of Europe's oldest department stores. Restoration work is currently in progress. Be sure to visit **A Brasileira, (** (01) 346-9541, Rua Garrett N°120, an art nouveau café that has become a Lisbon institution. It was once the meeting place of the literati; today you can rub shoulders with the great twentieth-century poet Fernando Pessoa whose statue sits on a chair among the tables on the sidewalk terrace.

Belém

The riverside district of Belém (meaning Bethlehem) is about six kilometers (four miles) from the center of Lisbon. To get there take a tram or bus from the Praça do Comércio or an inexpensive taxi-ride. There are several museums here and two major sights not to be missed: the Torre de Belém and the Mosteiro dos Jerónimos, both exceptional examples of the uniquely Portuguese Manueline style.

The majestic **Mosteiro dos Jerónimos** (Hieronymite Monastery), was built in jubilant thanksgiving for Vasco da Gama's discovery of the Spice Route to India. It was worked on by a succession of architects, initially the Frenchman Boytac who began the work in 1502, followed by the Spanish João de Castilho. The result is one of Portugal's greatest and most original architectural achievements: a subtle fusion of Gothic and renaissance styles stamped with Manueline ornamentation, rich

The Jerónimos monastery's Manueline architecture ABOVE AND OPPOSITE bursts with the exuberance of Portugal's great Age of Discovery.

in seafaring motifs and other images evocative of the Voyages of Discovery.

In the southern facade stands a grand doorway surrounded by a mass of elaborately carved stonework featuring the figure of Henry the Navigator; its church of **Santa Maria** has an interior of somber magnificence. Slender, delicately-sculpted columns support a fan-vaulted ceiling that rises to a height of 75 m (246 ft) over the three aisles. The lower chancel contains the tomb of the national hero Vasco da Gama and a monument to the poet of the Portuguese epic *Os Lusíadas*, Luís de Camões. Camões' body is not interred here: in good artistic tradition he died in poverty and was probably buried in an unmarked pauper's grave. The cloisters are magnificent, each column differently carved with coils of rope, sea monsters, coral, and the like. Opening hours are from 10 am to 1 pm and from 2:30 pm to 5 pm (until 6:30 pm in the summer months). For details telephone **(** (01) 362-0034.

There are other museums in and around the monastery, but my advice is to proceed first to the Monument to the Discoveries and the Torre; if you have time, energy, and inclination afterwards, visit them when you return this way to pick up transport home.

Across the road from the monastery and overlooking the Tagus is the **Padrão dos Descobrimentos** (Monument to the Discoveries). Shaped like a ship's prow, the figures of those who played a major role in the Voyages of Discovery are sculpted upon it. Prince Henry the Navigator heads the procession, and alongside him stand Vasco a Gamaes brandishing his book. The ground before it is inlaid with a huge mosaic compass and map of the world in colored marble with the dates of the Discoveries. Inside the monument is a museum and a lift to the the top for some views of the Tagus and Belém. The lift and museum, **(** (01) 616228/9, are open from 9 am to 6 pm (until 7 pm in the summer) but closed on Monday mornings.

From here, if you walk westwards to the **Torre de Belém**, you'll stumble across the oddly situated **Museu de Arte Popular** (Museum of Folk Art), a good place to study traditional handicrafts if you're considering some quality souvenirs of Portugal. Beyond it the magnificent Torre appears before you

like a mirage. The Torre is five stories high with loggias at the third level; in front of it projects an artillery platform, producing a slightly nautical effect. It was built in 1515 in Gothic style with delicate Moorish embellishments; at that time it stood in the river but because of land reclamation it's now on the bank. Many voyages began from here and for the sailors on their long, perilous voyages it became a symbol of the beloved homeland that they longed for. The tower, (01/362-0034, is open from 10 am to 5 pm (to 6:30 in the summer), and closed on Mondays. Admission is free on Sundays until 2 pm.

The **Museu da Marinha** (Naval Museum) is housed in the west wing of the monastery (an incongruous nineteenth-cen-

tury addition) displaying every imaginable kind of vessel, from warships to fishing boats as well as beautiful scale models of ships, old sea charts (some of them reproductions), and the royal barges. You can wonder at the extravagance of the royal yacht and see the seaplane that made the first crossing of the South Atlantic. Opening hours are from 10 am to 5 pm, closed Mondays, ((01) 362-0010.

An annex to the monastery houses the **Museu Nacional de Arqueologia e Etnologia** (Archaeological and Ethnological Museum) with its collection of artifacts dating from prehistoric to Roman times. Open from 10 am to 12:30 pm, 2 pm to 5 pm, closed on Mondays, ((01) 362-0000 or 362-0022.

Close by stands the **Museu dos Coches** (Coach Museum), appropriately housed in

TransTejo (**(** (01) 75058) can take you on a two-hour scenic trip or a romantic evening cruise. Boats leave from the Praça do Comércio at 3 pm and 9 pm.

The **Ponte 25 de Abril** suspension bridge spans the Tagus and at 2,278 m (one-and-a-half miles) it is longer than San Francisco's Golden Gate Bridge, with the longest central span of any bridge in Europe. It offers some spectacular views of Lisbon, especially if you're not driving, and brings you within a couple of miles of the monument of **Cristo-Rei**, which you will have noticed by now, a scaled-down version of the statue of Christ in Rio de Janeiro; if you just can't get enough of those views, a lift will take you to the top.

Elsewhere in Lisbon

Art lovers can't afford to miss out on the **Calouste Gulbenkian Museu**, Avenida de Berna N°45, **(** (01) 793-5131, which is in the Saldanha district and within walking distance of the Pombal monument. Calouste Gulbenkian was an eccentric Armenian oil tycoon who lived in Portugal from 1942 until his death in 1955, and bequeathed his wealth and superb art collection to the Portuguese nation. The Gulbenkian Foundation has been a major supporter of the arts and has concert and exhibition halls within the Foundation building, a symphony orchestra, ballet and choral companies, and libraries.

Housed in a cool, modern building set in parkland, the museum's original art collection consisted of around 3,000 works, many of which were bought in the 1920s from the Hermitage in St. Petersburg when the former U.S.S.R. was more in need of foreign currency than usual. Others have been added since Gulbenkian's death; there are collections of ancient art dating from 2700 BC, oriental art, Islamic works and European painting from the medieval period to the nineteenth century, covering a range from Rembrandt to Renoir. One room is devoted to Lalique (the French Art Nouveau jeweller), and if the idea of coins makes you yawn, prepare for instant conversion at the sight of the Hellenic collection. Gulbenkian's urge to possess seems to have been inspired by a

what was once the Royal Riding School. The collection is usually billed as the world's largest and best: certainly there are some wonderful examples, especially the glittering baroque ones. Hours are 10 am to 1 pm, 2:30 pm to 6:30 pm (5:30 pm in the winter), closed on Mondays, **(** (01) 363-8022. Admission is free on Sunday.

The Tagus

For a different perspective of the city take a ferry trip across the Tagus. It runs from Cais do Sodré or the Praça do Comércio to **Cacilhas** on the south bank, where a a view of Lisbon and lunch can be combined in one of the many fish restaurants. The journey takes approximately 10 minutes each way. If you prefer a longer and more leisurely journey,

The Tagus quay side is punctuated with monuments to the explorers who made Portugal a world power in the fifteen and sixteenth centuries.

love of beauty, not greed. He collected by elimination rather than accumulation, when quality mattered, not quantity. From July to September the Museum is open from 10 am to 5 pm, on Wednesdays and Saturdays from 2 pm to 7:30 pm; October to June it's open from 10 am to 5 pm but closed on Mondays; admission is free on Sundays.

In the grounds of the Foundation is the **Centro de Arte Moderna** (Center of Modern Art), ((01) 734309, with its modern Portuguese works by Edouard Viana, Paula Rego, Amadeo de Souza Cardoso, Maria Helena Vieira da Silva, Almada Negreiros and others. The opening hours are as for the museum: admission is also free on Sundays. The foundation, incidentally, has a very good but busy self-service restaurant.

A little further north, the **Museu Nacional do Traje** (National Costume Museum) is housed in a seventeenth-century palace in Largo Julio de Castilho, ((01) 758-2739, in the Lumiar district. There are excellent displays of eighteenth-century gowns, wedding dresses, accessories, traditional costumes and very old fabrics. Opening hours are from 10 am to 1 pm, from 2 pm to 5 pm, and it is closed on Mondays.

Moving south to the Lapa district, a seventeenth-century palace has been converted and extended to house the **Museu Nacional de Arte Antiga** (Museum of Ancient Art), Rua das Janelas Verdes N°95, ((01) 672725. The third floor is devoted to Portuguese art of the fifteenth and sixteenth centuries, dominated by the polyptych by Nuno Gonçalves dating from around 1470. It depicts the Adoration of St. Vincent, patron saint of Lisbon; famous people of the time also appear in the painting, including the artist himself. On the first floor of the museum are works by foreign painters including Holbein, Dürer, Piero della Francesca, and Poussin. There are also collections of ceramics, carpets, porcelain, and gold and silverware. Open from 10 am to 1 pm and from 2:30 pm to 5 pm, but closed on Mondays. Admission is free on Sunday mornings.

If you have time, take a stroll around the Estrêla district just northwest of the Bairro Alto, clearly once a focal point of British life here, with the British Hospital, the English

Church of St. George, and worryingly close to the hospital the **English Cemetery**, where the novelist Henry Fielding is buried. Set in the lovely **Estrêla Gardens** is the domed eighteenth-century **Basilica da Estrêla**. The rather frosty marbled interior contains a life-sized crib carved by the sculptor Machado de Castro. The basilica is closed between 1 pm and 3:30 pm.

GETTING AROUND

Lisbon has a subway system, the Metropolitano, which connects the Baixa and the newer areas of Lisbon. Though not extensive it is straightforward, cheap, and efficient, and a flat fare of 135 escudos (about $1) is charged. A fun way of getting around is the old tram system dating from the late nineteenth century which negotiates some very steep hills. Routes of both the bus system and the trams are easy to use as the routes are outlined at bus stops.

For metro, bus, and trams you can purchase a tourist pass or a book of tickets, both of which constitute good savings on fares, from the Cais do Sodré station, the Restauradores ticket office, the Elevador de Santa Justa or main terminals, and while you're there pick up a free route map showing tram and bus routes. If you want a tourist pass, you'll need to show your passport. In addition to the usual modes of public transport, there's a special sightseeing tram that tours the major monuments. It leaves the Praça do Comércio three times daily and tickets for it cannot be booked in advance. Taxis are plentiful except during the lunch hour, and are easily recognizable by their green roofs. Fares are relatively inexpensive and a taxi can be cheaper than taking a bus if there are a few of you sharing. Fares are metered except outside the city limits, in which case check the fare before leaving to be sure you don't get overcharged. Whatever form of transport you use, the same rule applies: avoid rush hours if you can.

SPORTS

Soccer enthusiasts may be interested in seeing a Lisbon match. Benfica and Sporting are the two main Lisbon teams and matches are

A stone's throw from the Presidential Palace, the Belém tower now houses a museum of weaponry.

guaranteed to draw big crowds; as many fans have season tickets there can be a problem getting hold of tickets. Try the ticket kiosk in the Praça dos Restauradores, failing which the stadia ticket offices. **Horse racing** is another popular spectator sport here, and if interested you should go along to the Campo Grande Hippodrome, close to the city university.

Tennis enthusiasts will find courts in Monsanto Park and near the Campo Grande. For details of how to book get in touch with the Club Internacional de Ténis,

One of the two main shopping areas in central Lisbon is the **Chiado** area west of the Rossio and centering around the Rua do Carmo and the Rua Garrett. Despite the devastating fire of 1988 it still has some of Lisbon's most fashionable shops, a few department stores. Rua Garrett has excellent bookshops some of which stock foreign language books. The other main shopping district is in the **Baixa** along the Rua Augusta (now a pedestrian mall), and the neighboring streets forming the geometric grid north of the Praça do Comércio. These roads, particu-

Rua Professor Sousa Camara Nº193, ((01) 682084. There are several **swimming** pools in Lisbon. There is the Piscina do Ariero in the Avenida de Roma, the Piscina do Parque de Campismo de Monsanto in the huge Parque Florestal Monsanto west of the town center, but the most centrally located is the Piscina do Lisboa-Sheraton Hotel.

SHOPPING

Lisbon shops are stocked with an extensive range of local craftwork. As elsewhere in Portugal, leather goods, embroidery, and porcelain are all particularly good buys. Some lovely gold jewelry is available and the filigree work, a traditional craft, is popular.

larly the Rua Aurea and the Rua da Prata, are known for their jewelry shops, but for something really special go along to Rua Nova da Almada Nº9, where the **Casa Batalha**, one of the oldest jewelers in town sells some fabulous costume jewelry.

The **Bairro Alto** is a good area for antique shopping, particularly the Rua do Alecrim, the Rua da Misericórdia, Rua São Pedro d'Alcantâra, and the Rua Dom Pedro V. Over in the **Alfama** district there's a **flea market** held on Tuesdays and Saturdays behind the Church of São Vicente in the Campo Santa Clara.

Azulejos can make the ideal souvenir as well as a beautiful adornment for your home: two factories in Lisbon make these tiles to old designs. One, the **Fabrica Sant'Anna**, has its shop in the Rua do Alecrim Nº95, ((01) 322537, and the other, **Fabrica Viúvia Lamego**, is at Largo do Intendete Nº25. For some genuine antique *azulejos* there's a shop in Rua Dom Pedro V that has a large selection at vastly varying prices.

Most shops open from 9 am to 1 pm and from 3 pm to 7 pm on weekdays, from 9 am to 1 pm on Saturdays, and are closed all day Sunday. There are exceptions and if you want late-night shopping there's **a mall** at the Rossio railway station open until mid-

The **Teatro Nacional de Dona Maria II** at Praça Dom Pedro IV (the Rossio), ((01) 322210, has a season of Portuguese and foreign plays that usually runs between autumn and spring, but performances are in Portuguese. The opera and ballet season tends to be between December and June at the **Teatro Nacional de São Carlos**, Largo São Carlos, ((01) 346-5914, and at the **Teatro Municipal de São Luís**, Rua António Maria Cardoso Nº40, ((01) 327172. These grand old theaters attract top international companies. The **Fundação Calouste Gulbenkian**, Avenida

night seven days a week. Outside the center there's the huge **Amoreiras Center** at Avenida Duarte Pacheco, ((01) 692558, an ungainly post-Modernist lump of a building. This commercial center with over 300 shops stays open until midnight every night, with restaurants and cinemas, the largest of its kind on the Iberian Peninsula.

ENTERTAINMENT

The Portuguese daily *Diário de Notícias* carries a useful entertainments listing, as does the weekly *Sete* that comes out on Wednesday afternoons. The *Turismos* are always a good source of information and publish an entertainments guide called *What's On in Lisbon*.

de Berna Nº45, ((01) 735131, has its own ballet company and symphony orchestra, and also hosts performances by other companies and performers. An elaborate **cultural center** was opened recently in Belém with two auditoriums, one seating 1,800 and the other 400.

Lisbon has a large number of cinemas where foreign films are shown with their original soundtrack and Portuguese subtitles, which is good news for visitors. Tickets are cheap, seats are assigned, and there are intervals allowing time for a drink at the bar. Eating and drinking are not allowed in the cinema, a welcome change.

OPPOSITE Lisbon's quality shopping ranges from designer labels to jewelry while noisy barter takes place among street traders in the Alfama district ABOVE.

Lisbon, unlike most other places in Portugal, has a nightlife and the action goes on until 2 or 3 am, but it's mostly found in the **Bairro Alto**, the hilltop district that rises to the west of the Rossio. No visit to Lisbon is complete without a visit to a *fado* club. These clubs or *adegas* usually have a cover charge which can be spent on food or drink. Up until about 10:30 pm they usually function as restaurants where you can enjoy your meal as the singers perform, often interspersing the *fado* with folk music, but after about 10:30 tables are cleared, the place becomes a drinking club, and the singing begins in earnest. Although these *adegas* are scattered around the older neighborhoods such as the Alfama and Lapa districts, the majority are to be found in the Bairro Alto. **Machado** at Rua do Norte Nº91, ℂ (01) 346-0095, is popular with both tourists and *Lisboêtas*; at **Lisboa a Noite**, Rua das Gáveas Nº69, ℂ (01) 346-8557, the owner is herself a respected *fadista* who gives performances at the club; and **A Severa** at Rua das Gáveas Nº49-57 is a well-known and popular spot. One of the foremost (some say it's the best) is **Senhor Vinho** in the Lapa district at Rua do Maio a Lapa Nº18, ℂ (01) 677-4546, while over in the Alfama close to the docks there's **Parreirinha de Alfama**, Beco do Espírito Santo Nº1, ℂ (01) 886-8209, and the more upmarket **Coata D'Armas**, Beco de São Miguel Nº7, ℂ (01) 886-8682.

Spend an evening in Lisbon at one of the many bars or cafés. You'll find them scattered throughout the city, but some deserve special mention. At the lovely **Café A Brasileira**, Rua Garrett Nº120, you can enjoy the ambience of the Bairro Alto. **Bachus** at Largo da Trindade Nº9 is a very smart but friendly spot that serves food at the bar, and at the **Pavilhão Chinés**, Rua Dom Pedro V Nº89, you can enjoy a drink surrounded by chinoiserie. Also along Rua Dom Pedro V close to the Principe Real, is **João Sebastião**, an intimate place with a Bohemian feel about it where singers entertain on certain nights.

Down in the Rossio Square there's **Café Nicola**, another Lisbon institution, and between the Rossio and the Restauradores the **Casa Alentejana** at Praça da Goa Nº2, is a beautiful old building with good cheap food and a bar. If you want cool and sophisticated

try the **Sheraton Hotel's Panorama Bar** along Rua Latino Coelho, perched near the top with some superb views over Lisbon.

For music and dancing, again the Bairro Alto has several places to offer. Music from Cape Verde plays live at **Lontra** at Rua São Bento Nº157, and also at **Clave di Nos**, Rua do Norte Nº100, where it's mixed in with Latin American sounds. The lively **Gafiera** on Calçada de Tijolo has live Brazilian music, and down near Cais do Sodré, **The Jamaica**, Rua Nova do Carvalho Nº6, plays recorded rock and reggae music. Moving upmarket but staying dockside is **Banana Power** at Rua de Cascais Nº52 in the Alcântara district, an exclusive spot with a restaurant; near the Sheraton hotel there's **Whispers**, Avenida Fontes Pereira de Melo Nº35. A favorite with the young set is **Rock Rendez Vous** close to the Gulbenkian Museum on Rua da Beneficência, where live Portuguese bands play, but the trendiest place to be seen at the moment seems to be **Fragil** at Rua da Atalaia Nº128.

WHERE TO STAY

Luxury
For old-time splendor you can't do better than the **Hotel Avenida Palace**, Rua 1º de Dezembro Nº123, 1200 Lisboa, ℂ (01) 346-0151, fax: (01) 342-2884, a building very centrally placed by the Rossio Square. During World War II the Avenida was a hotbed of espionage; there used to be a secret exit to the Rossio Station, but in case you're thinking of doing a bunk it's been bricked up. Long known and loved for its faded grandeur, it has been elegantly refurbished and upgraded to a five-star hotel. While the bad news is that the price has rocketed, the good news is that the refurbishment has retained much of the old character, sympathetically blending modern comfort with classical style.

The **Hotel Ritz Inter-Continental**, Rua Rodrigo da Fonseca Nº88, 1093 Lisboa, ℂ (01) 692020, fax: (01) 691783, is a large, modern five-star hotel built in the 1960s. The heavily-marbled interior is tastefully decorated with tapestries, sculptures, and other works of art. Some of the airy guest rooms have terraces overlooking the park, but the suites provide accommodation which is exceptional.

Next door is **Le Meridien Lisboa**, Rua Castilho Nº149, 1000 Lisboa, ((01) 690900 or 690400, fax: (01) 693231. Facing the Edward VII Park with excellent views of the river and city, this modern building contains restaurants, health club, business center and shops, meeting the high standards one would expect.

Located on Lisbon's main street, the **Hotel Tivoli Lisboa**, Avenida da Liberdade Nº185, 1200 Lisboa, ((01) 530181, fax: (01) 579461, has an impressive range of facilities, including a health club, tennis court and a swimming pool set in a garden.

sympathetic to the age of the building. Antique furnishings, marble tiles, and polished wooden floors set a traditional, peaceful, and friendly scene. Prices vary between mid-range and luxury. The nearby **York House Residencia**, Rua das Janelas Verdes Nº47, is under the same management. This eighteenth-century mansion was once the home of the novelist Eça de Queiroz, and has 17 rooms. Prices are slightly lower than at York House.

Hotel Veneza, Avenida da Liberdade Nº189, 1200 Lisboa, ((01) 352-2618, fax: (01) 352-6678, is an old building with grand

The **Tivoli Jardim**, Rua Júlio César Machado, 1200 Lisboa, ((01) 539971, fax: (01) 355-6566, stands close to its big sister, the Tivoli Lisboa on the Avenida da Liberdade. Less pricey than the Tivoli Lisboa, it is well located, offers comfort, good facilities and the rooms at the back overlook the garden.

Mid-Range

Close to the Museu de Arte Antigua, a flight of steps leads up to a seventeenth-century convent now called **York House** (Rua das Janelas Verdes Nº32, 1200 Lisboa, ((01) 396-2435, fax: (01) 397-2793). This provides some of the most charming accommodation in Lisbon. Overlooking a delightful courtyard, it has 37 rooms, all exceptionally well decorated in a manner

public areas and a bar. All 38 rooms have soundproofing, air-conditioning, satellite television and minibar. Prices vary from mid-range to luxury. **Hotel Eduardo VII**, Avenida Fontes Pereira de Melo Nº5, 1000 Lisboa, ((01) 530141, fax: (01) 533879, is a modern establishment just north of the Pombal statue. Rooms are comfortable, well-equipped and those at the front have excellent views of the city, but being on a busy main road it's not exactly peaceful. Perched on a hilltop in the Graça district (neighboring the Alfama) **Albergaria Senhora do Monte**, Calçada do Monte Nº39, 1100 Lisboa, ((01) 886-6002,

Lisbon's nightlife stays alive until the early hours with *fado* singing mainly in the Bairro Alto district, and nightclubs around the Alfama.

fax: (01) 877783, commands magnificent views of Lisbon and the Castelo, and offers agreeable rooms with bathroom, television, telephone, and air-conditioning.

The **Quinta Nova da Conceição**, Rua dos Soeiros Nº5, 1500 Lisboa, ((01) 778-0091, at São Domingos de Benfica, presents an interesting option — it's a guesthouse operating under the TURIHAB scheme (see under ACCOMMODATION in the TRAVELERS' TIPS section). This eighteenth-century house set in a large garden offers just two rooms: one with double bed, and another with two beds and sitting room. This kind of accommodation has to be booked well in advance and for a specified minimum period of stay.

Inexpensive

In the Bairro Alto, right next to the famous Café A Brasileira, the **Hotel Borges**, Rua Garrett Nº108-110, 1200 Lisboa, ((01) 346-7159, has an old-fashioned feel about it despite modernization. There are around 100 rooms, some with bathroom, and prices vary between inexpensive and mid-range. Also very central is the **Hotel Internacional**, Rua da Betesga Nº3, 1100 Lisboa, ((01) 346-6401, fax: (01) 347-8635, just off the Rossio where the rooms all have bathrooms, telephones, and television. It's busy, popular for its central location, and good value.

At the top exit of the Gloria Elevador in the Bairro Alto there's the **Pensão Londres**, Rua Dom Pedro V Nº53, 1200 Lisboa, ((01) 346-2203, a large, high-ceilinged townhouse with airy rooms, good views, and friendly staff. The **Pensão Casa de São Mamede**, Rua da Escola Politécnica Nº159, 1200 Lisboa, ((01) 396-3166, is a large nineteenth-century house, now operating as a family-run hotel that retains some old-time appeal. Rooms have baths, phones, and television.

Close to the Castelo São Jorge, the aptly named **Pensão Ninho das Águias** (Eagle's Nest), Costa do Castelo Nº74, 1100 Lisboa, ((01) 886-7008, is a strange little place with some wonderful views over Lisbon and plenty of character. Rooms are simple but clean, and some have baths. More centrally located is the **Residéncia Florescente**, Rua das Portas de Santo Antão Nº99, 1100 Lisboa, ((01) 342-6609, which is close to the Restauradores Square.

WHERE TO EAT

If you intend dining at one of the restaurants in the expensive category bookings are usually required, while for those listed in the moderate section bookings are still advisable. All the restaurants listed in the expensive category serve a variety of local and international dishes.

Expensive

The Bairro Alto presents an excellent range of restaurants, among them **Tavares**, Rua da Misericórdia Nº37, ((01) 321112 or 342-1112, one of Lisbon's best known dining spots since the late eighteenth century and said to be Lisbon's oldest restaurant. Take an apéritif in the salon while you peruse the menu, then sit back and enjoy the chandeliered and stuccoed dining room. Equally prestigious is **Restaurant Avis** at Rua Serpa Pinto Nº12B, ((01) 328391 or 342-8391, established by the chef of the grand old Avis Hotel that is no more. Wood paneling, marble columns, and crystal give it the air of a gentleman's club, and the top-class cuisine together with excellent service make this a special dining experience. Closed on Sundays.

Also in the Bairro Alto is **Tágide**, Largo da Academia Nacional de Belas Artes Nº18-20, ((01) 342-0720 or 346-0570, an old townhouse with an elegant upstairs dining room with views over the Tagus and across to the Castelo. The menu is extensive and everything presented with care. It is closed on Saturdays and Sundays. Tucked behind the Rossio's National Theater is another of Lisbon's top restaurants, **Gambrinus**, at Rua das Portas de Santo Antão Nº25, ((01) 342-1466. The menu is varied, but specializes in seafood. Not far away is **António Clara**, Avenida da República Nº38, ((01) 796-6380. Located in an Art Deco house that was once the home of a famous local architect, it is decorated with antique furniture, gilt mirrors and frescoed ceilings. Closed on Sundays.

Moderate

Within the walls of the Castelo de São Jorge, **Michel**, Largo de Santa Cruz do Castelo Nº5, ((01) 886-4338, serves excellent French food in

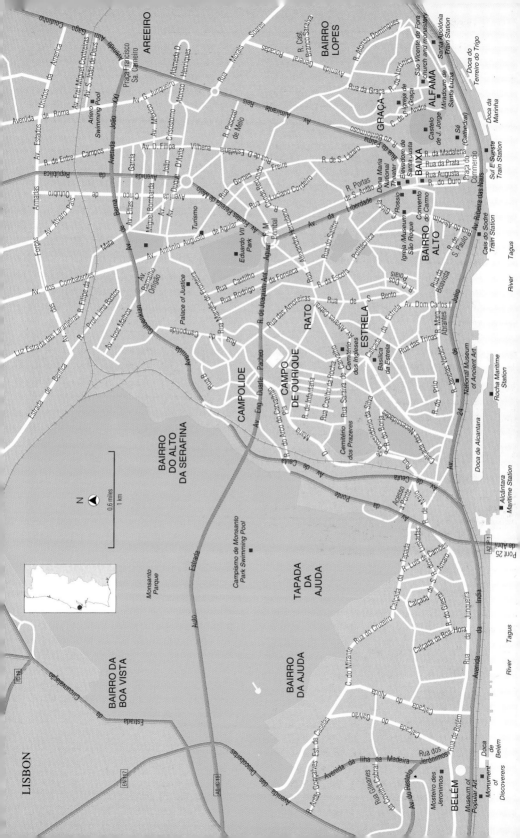

a bistro atmosphere. The restaurant occupies three old buildings, one of which was formerly a smithy, as the decor suggests. Closed on Sundays and Saturday lunchtime. In the neighboring Graça district, the **Restaurante O Faz Figura**, Rua do Paraíso Nº15B, ((01) 868981, is a traditional, friendly place serving local and international fare, with a dining room overlooking the river. Closed on Sundays.

On the hillside facing the Bairro Alto, **Bachus**, Largo da Trindade Nº9, ((01) 342-1260, serves continental cuisine in a congen-

your visit to Lisbon you should try, at least once, to go to the cavernous **Cervejaria da Trindade**, Rua Nova de Trindade Nº20C, ((01) 342-3506. It's an institution that's been going since the nineteenth century, and as the name suggests a lot of beer gets swilled here, often followed by vast quantities of seafood; as this is extremely busy you'd be well advised to visit outside peak lunch and dinner hours. It's open every day from 9 am to 2 am.

Well worth a visit is the **Casa do Alentejo**, Rua das Portas de Santo Antão Nº58,

ial ambience and stays open from noon until 2 am. Inside a converted bakery, **Pap'Açorda**, Rua da Atalaia Nº57, ((01) 346-4811, is popular, with a well-patronized bar at the front of the restaurant. **Sua Excelência**, Rua do Conde Nº40-42, ((01) 308-3614, offers good service and the menu includes some unusual creations. Closed during September.

Inexpensive

In the Bairro Alto, **Bota Alta**, Travessa da Queimada Nº35-37, ((01) 342-7959, is a bistro serving regional cuisine. It's open from Monday to Saturday, and you may have to queue for a table. So does **O Funil**, Avenida Elias Garcia Nº82A, ((01) 796-6007, and being popular, bookings are a good idea. During

((01) 328011. You walk up a closed-in staircase on to a tiled courtyard with Moorish overtones; the interior is similarly decorated and Alentejan specialties are served. For some colonial flavor try the **Velha-Goa**, Rua Tomás de Anunciação Nº41B, ((01) 600446, where Goanese cuisine is offered from noon until midnight. Close by, behind the theater at the north end of the Rossio, the Travessa de Santo Antão has a good selection of restaurants. One of the most popular is **Bonjardim**, ((01) 342-7424, which serves local fare in slightly rustic surroundings. The roast chicken is said to be the best in town, and the smells are irresistible. There are two dining rooms and a bar for aperitifs. Open every day from noon to 11 pm.

HOW TO GET THERE

For details of air and rail services to Lisbon see GETTING AROUND and GETTING THERE sections of TRAVELERS' TIPS. Linha Verde buses leave the airport for the city center at 15-minute intervals and the Nº44 and 45 local buses also link the airport with the center. By taxi the airport is a 20-minute drive from the center and the fare costs between 1,500 and 2,000 escudos, ($10 and $14).

Several bus companies operate express services linking Lisbon with major towns and cities throughout the country. The national bus company, Rodoviária Nacional, has its main station in the Avenida Casal Ribeiro near the Saldanha metro station.

Lisbon is connected by motorway to Porto, 314 km (195 miles) to the north, and to Faro, 300 km (186 miles) to the south. Beware of dangerous driving along these routes: the Lisbon to Faro stretch of motorway has a particularly high accident rate.

AROUND LISBON

QUELUZ

Just 15 km (nine and a half miles) northwest of Lisbon, the town of Queluz is graced by the **Palácio de Queluz** (Queluz Palace), ((01) 435-0039, a pink rococo affair built in the spirit of Versailles. On the orders of the Infante Dom Pedro, younger son of João V, work began on the palace in 1747 and was completed in 1760. It became the home of Dom Pedro's wife and niece, Queen Maria I whose reign was cut short by insanity. During the brief period of French occupation General Junot set up headquarters here. And in the reign of King João VI, his Spanish wife, the bizarre Carlota Joaquina, led a life of extraordinary dissipation here while conspiring with her son and anybody else who was interested, to overthrow her husband. The palace was badly damaged by fire in 1934, but has since been carefully restored.

As royal palaces go Queluz is quite intimate in scale, but has a surprisingly dilapidated exterior. I say surprising because it is

still used to accommodate visiting royalty and heads of state. I find its proportions a little clumsy, but many are enraptured by the place. The highly elaborate rooms have daintily painted walls and ceilings, gilt, chandeliers, chinoiserie and eighteenth-century furnishings, although many original pieces were removed, either by the royal family as they fled to Brazil or by the French who occupied it soon afterwards. The **Throne Room** is a glitter of mirrored walls and chandeliers occasionally used for banquets. A good way of savoring the atmosphere may be to go along to one of the summer concerts held in the ornate **Music Room**.

The carefully tended formal gardens are an elegant composition of topiary, clipped box hedges, trees, and flowerbeds interspersed with fountains, pools, and statuary. Cages which once held wild animals for royal amusement now stand empty, but the **Dutch Canal** lined with azulejos remains, specially constructed so that the royal party could take boating trips through the grounds. What could be more agreeable?

If you wish to extend your visit, there is a gourmet restaurant inside what used to be the palace kitchen. Aptly named **Cozinha Velha** (old kitchen), ((01) 435-0740, it serves both local and international fare and is open for lunch, dinner and tea every day. The palace is open from 10 am to 1 pm and from 2 pm to 5 pm except on Tuesdays; entrance is free on Sunday mornings.

How to Get There

From Lisbon take a train from the Rossio station or inquire at the Turismo about coach trips. If you're driving from Lisbon, you need to take the divided highway west of the Praça Marquês de Pombal through Monsanto Park, then after five kilometers (three miles) turn right onto Estrada Nacional 117. Four kilometers (two-and-a-half miles) along the road turn left on to the Estrada Nacional 249 for Queluz and Sintra, and after approximately two-and-a-half kilometers (one-and-a-half miles), a turning to the right will bring you to the palace.

Men sit chatting, usually about soccer, outside the Alfama district's Nossa Senhora da Graça church.

SINTRA AND ENVIRONS

The beauty of Sintra has moved a succession of poets and writers to sing praises of its every facet. Nestled in the **Serra de Sintra**, it stands on a remote ridge rising north of the Tagus estuary, washed with Atlantic rain and covered in lush and varied vegetation. The hills are often shrouded in damp mists that seem to drift into the town, keeping it cool and verdant even at the height of summer, but occasionally hiding it in fog.

For centuries Sintra has been a favored summer retreat, acquiring palaces and splendid manor houses. Perhaps it is the coolness and the verdure which drew the British here, a people especially entranced by its beauties. Even Lord Byron, who for some reason loathed the Portuguese, thought it possibly the most beautiful village in the world. He wrote: It contains beauties of every description, natural and artificial. Palaces and gardens rising in the midst of rocks, cataracts and precipices; convents on stupendous heights — a distant view of the sea and the Tagus. Go there, but be warned: you may never want to leave.

Background

Prehistoric peoples and the Lusitani tribe lived in the area long before the Romans arrived and fell in love with it. The Romans called it the *Serra Mons Lunae* — Hills of the Moon, where they worshipped Artemis (Diana), the goddess of the moon. The Moors in turn expanded the town and either built the castle or rebuilt it on Roman foundations: it still bears the unmistakable imprint of their occupation. In the fifteenth century King João I brought Philippa of Lancaster and the court to the Palácio da Vila, which remained the favored summer residence of the royal families until the nineteenth century when Queen Maria II's consort, Dom Ferdinand, built the Pena Palace nearby.

General Information

There is a *Turismo* in the center of Sintra, close to the Palácio Nacional in the Praça da República, ((01) 923-1157 or 923-3919, fax: (01) 923-5176. There are others in nearby Colares at Avenida Linhares de Lima, ((01) 929-2638, and at Cabo da Roca, ((01) 929-0981.

What to See and Do

Sintra is really three villages, all on the north side of the Serra: the **Vila Velha** (Old Town), the modern **Estefânia**, and **São Pedro**, which is furthest up the escarpment. At the center of the Vila Velha is the **Palácio Real** ((01/923-4118), a bulky, irregular building from which two strange oast-house-like chimneys protrude. Don't be put off by the slightly gloomy exterior — this is well worth a visit. Built on the site of a Moorish palace, it has been added to throughout the centuries. The first major building work was carried out at the behest of King João I in the late fourteenth century and was strongly influenced by Moorish taste. The interior is decorated with some exceptional polychrome *azulejos*, particularly in the **Arab Room**, and there are

several Moorish-style courtyards. Of particular note is the **Armory**, which has a domed ceiling painted with the coats of arms of sixteenth-century noble families, the **Mermaids' Room**, with its delightful pictures of sirens and ships, and the particularly grand **Swan Room** which has a paneled ceiling painted with white swans, each with a golden crown around its neck.

Most memorable of all has to be the **Magpie Room**, where the pictures have a tale to tell. João I and his English wife Philippa had set new standards of morality for the court: João himself broke with the kingly tradition of begetting bastards after his marriage. However, he was caught kissing a lady-in-waiting, and that inevitably set the court gossiping. In retaliation he had the ceiling of

this room painted with magpies, one, it is said, for every lady-in-waiting, each with a rose and the motto *por bem* (meaning well meant) clasped in its beak. Whether or not the king was guilty of less noble intention, the ceiling has remained a rather touching testimony both to his affection for Philippa and to his indignation. The palace operates guided tours and is open from 10 am to 12:30 pm and from 2 to 5 pm, but is closed on Wednesdays. Admission is free on Sundays.

This pretty village has a number of antique and handicraft shops, restaurants and cafés. The nearby **São Pedro de Sintra** holds

The National Palace at Sintra was a favorite retreat for Portuguese royalty from the fourteen century, with successive monarchs adding their own architectural flourishes.

a **Country Fair** on the second and fourth Sundays of each month, selling craftwork, antiques, pottery, and local produce. Similar but on a larger scale is the annual **Feira Grande de São Pedro** held at the end of June.

From the town center you can taxi, drive, take a *calèche* (at a price), or, if you're in the mood for a stiff but scenic walk, hoof it up to the **Castelo dos Mouros** (Moors' Castle). If you're driving, take the Estrada da Pena which twists and rises southward from town, passing the **Estalagem dos Cavaleiros** where Byron wrote part of *Childe Harold's Pilgimage*, and turn left at the crossroads, which will bring you to a car park. From here you can walk up to the ruins of this Moorish fortress. Built in the eighth or ninth century, its crenellated walls and towers have been partially restored. You can climb a staircase to the top of the main tower for some sweeping views over Sintra and its *quintas*, or country houses, to the coast beyond. Admission is free and the opening hours are from 9 am to 5 pm (6 pm in the summer).

Back at the car park, an iron gateway leads to the lovely **Pena Park**. You can drive through it, though a walk is more rewarding; above stands the much photographed **Palácio da Pena** (Pena Palace), an architectural nightmare with superb panoramic views of the countryside and coastline. It was the brainchild of King Ferdinand of Saxe Coburg Gotha, Queen Maria II's German consort, who engaged one of his countrymen, Baron von Eschwege, to begin work on it in 1840. A sixteenth-century Hieronymite monastery once occupied the site but was destroyed by the 1755 earthquake, although some ruined cloisters and a chapel still stand in the palace grounds. The chapel contains an alabaster and marble altar by Nicholas Chanterène, whose work you may already have admired at Lisbon's Hieronymite Monastery.

Inside the palace things have been left as they were when the last Portuguese royal family fled the country. Little everyday items are scattered through the rooms, giving us an intimate picture of the royal lifestyle. We are now allowed to see King Ferdinand's private chamber, decorated with paintings of naked ladies, all of whom are said to have been acquaintances of his. The palace is open from 10 am to 1 pm and from 2 to 5 pm, but closes on Mondays. Telephone (01) 923-0227 for information.

Just outside Sintra, along the road that leads to Colares, is the **Palácio de Seteais**, now a luxury hotel. The name means Palace of Seven Sighs referring either to the beauty of the surroundings, or possibly to the despair of the Portuguese when French and English generals signed the Convention of Sintra here in 1809, granting the French a safe passage out of Portugal with their loot. The palace was originally built in 1787 for a Dutch merchant: its interior with frescoed walls and ceilings is delightful. If you can't afford to reside in this expensive establishment, try to stay for tea, drinks, or perhaps a meal.

About four kilometers (two-and-a-half miles) along the road from Sintra to Colares is the **Quinta da Monserrate**, a fanciful pseudo-Moorish villa built by Englishman Sir Francis Cook in the mid-nineteenth century. It stands on the site of a house once occupied by another English eccentric, the millionaire writer William Beckford who imported a flock of sheep from England to remind him of his home in Fonthill. You can visit the **botanical garden** (✆ (01) 923-0137) and the greenhouse here that was filled in the 1850s with exotic plants from all around the world, a massive undertaking for its time. Open from 9 am to 5:30 pm April to November and until 4:45 pm the rest of the year.

Continuing along the road we come to **Colares**, nine kilometers (five-and-a-half miles) from Sintra. This charming old hillside village with its winding lanes has Moorish arches, a square and vineyards of particular interest to wine enthusiasts; in the latter half of the nineteenth century while the root-eating phylloxera beetle destroyed most European vines, necessitating replanting with vines grafted on to tougher American root-stock, in Colares the phylloxera was unable to penetrate the sand. The result is that the vines here are still wholly European. The output is small and Colares wines are difficult to find, but visitors are welcome to call in at the **Wine Lodge** on weekdays. From Colares it is only another six kilometers (four miles) to the southwesternmost point of Europe, the wild and windswept headland called **Cabo da Roca**.

Where to Stay

Top of the list has to be the **Hotel Palácio de Seteais**, Avenida Barbosa do Bocage Nº8, Seteais, 2710 Sintra, ((01) 923-3200, fax: (01) 923-4277, an eighteenth-century palace which has been converted into a five-star hotel under the management of the Tivoli Hotels Company. Surrounded by lawns, it has an exquisite interior, tennis courts, and a swimming pool. Reservations are needed and the prices are high in the luxury bracket.

There are three particularly lovely houses in the area that offer guest-house accommodation under the TURIHAB scheme. Close to the Quinta da Monserrate Palace there's the **Quinta de São Thiago**, Estrada de Monserrate, 2710 Sintra, ((01) 923-2923, a former sixteenth-century convent which has 10 rooms, one suite, a music room, and a library. The **Quinta da Capela**, Estrada de Monserrate, 2710 Sintra, ((01) 929-3405, is a farmhouse-like collection of buildings offering 10 airy rooms with views over the countryside, some self-catering accommodation, and a gymnasium. In the old town itself, there's the **Vila das Rosas**, Rua António Cunha Nº4, 2710 Sintra, ((01) 923-4216, fax: (01) 923-4216, a nineteenth-century villa surrounded by a garden with a tennis court, and offering four rooms. Prices are moderate.

At the cheaper end of the range is the **Hotel Central**, Largo Rainha Dona Amélia, 2710 Sintra, ((01) 923-0963, in the main square across from the Palácio Nacional. It's a rambling old tiled building that forms a large part of the square; the rooms, not all with bathroom, have simple, old-fashioned furniture. Also inexpensively priced is the **Pensão da Raposa**, Rua Dr. Alfredo Costa Nº3, ((01) 923-0465, fax: (01) 923-5757, a homely old place with nine rooms. Cheapest of all is the **Pensão Nova Sintra**, Largo Afonso de Albuquerque Nº25, ((01) 923-0220, a building dating from the early 1900s in the Vila Estefânia.

In Colares there's the **Pensão do Conde**, Quinta do Conde, 2710 Sintra, ((01) 929-1652, an early eighteenth-century farmhouse that has been extended. Set on the slopes north of the village and surrounded by orchards, this has views of the sea and mountains. Run by an English couple, it consists of a cottage and 10 guestrooms. The prices here are inexpensive to moderate.

Where to Eat

Even if the food weren't good it would still be worth eating at the **Hotel Palácio dos Seteais** for its sumptuous surroundings, described above. Fortunately the food is excellent, and both local and international dishes are served in its elegant dining room. It's expensive. In the old town probably the best place to dine is the excellent **Tacho Real**, Rua da Ferraria Nº4, ((01) 923-5277, an elegant restaurant with vaulted ceilings, tiled floors and an extensive wine list. Both regional and international dishes are served

here and the prices are moderate. For inexpensive dining there are a few restaurant-bars scattered around; in Sintra itself the **Adega das Caves**, Rua da Pendoa Nº2A, Largo da Vila Velha de Sintra Nº10, ((01) 923-0848, is cozy and unpretentious, as is the **Tulhas-Bar** at Rua Gil Vicente Nº4. Right on the main square you'll see the busy **Café Paris** with its canopied pavement terrace, a good spot to sit and watch the world go by.

São Pedro has quite a few restaurants and cafés, one of the most unusual being the **Galeria Real**, Rua Tude de Sousa, ((01) 923-1661. A mixture of restaurant and antique

Pena Palace rises as in a fairy story, out of Sintra's dense, green forests.

gallery, its eighteenth-century setting offers some good regional cuisine. Its prices are moderate to expensive. Also in São Pedro is the moderately-priced **Restaurante Solar S. Pedro**, Largo da Feira Nº12, ((01) 923-1860, which specializes in French food but also offers a selection of local and Italian dishes.

How to Get There

Sintra is 32 km (20 miles) northwest of Lisbon, approximately 45 minutes by train from Rossio Station. For details of bus services to Sintra check with the R.N. bus company, Avenida Fontes Pereira de Melo Nº33, Lisbon, ((01) 563451, or with the *Turismo*. The R.N. Gray Line service conducts sightseeing tours which take in Sintra, and from Sintra itself a Gray Line tour departs from the *Turismo* for a tour of the Mosteiro Capuchos, the Pena Palace, Colares, Cabo da Roca, and the coastline.

If you're driving from Lisbon, take the route described in the section on Queluz, but continue along the N249 until the Estrada Nacional 9 turn-off into Sintra.

ESTORIL

Estoril is Portugal's answer to Cannes, a seaside resort with palm-lined streets bounded by flower-beds, where sandy beaches and spa waters have attracted wealthy Europeans and Portuguese since the turn of the century. During the World War II it gained a certain cachet from exiled European royalty, heads of state, and aristocrats who resided there. Although most of the royals have left and the older villas and hotels have been overshadowed by large new complexes, Estoril remains one of the most fashionable resorts in Europe.

General Information

You'll find the *Turismo* at the edge of the public park, at Arcadas do Parque, ((01) 468-0113.

What to See and Do

The real attractions here are the recreational facilities. The **Casino** is the hub of the town, a smart white building surrounding by carefully tended gardens. It has gambling machines, bingo, a cinema, restaurant, theater, night club and of course the gaming room.

The cabarets are glitzy extravaganzas, all of which attracts many big name entertainers.

The **Clube de Golf do Estoril**, Avenida da República, ((01) 468-0176, has what is said to be one of the most beautiful golf courses in Europe. Its nine- and 18-hole courses are sometimes used for international championships. Golfers can also go to the nine-hole Estoril-Sol Golf Course at Linhó, ((01) 923-2461, off the road to Sintra. **Tennis** enthusiasts go to the **Clube de Ténis do Estoril**, Avenida Amaral, Estoril, ((01) 468-1675 or one of the other numerous courts in town. For **water sports** there's the **International Windsurfing School**, ((01) 268-1665, but beware of swimming: this part of the coast has suffered badly from pollution, so read the warning notices or check before rushing in for a dip.

Estoril is the venue for the **Portuguese Formula One Grand Prix** motor race at the **Autodromo** and draws big crowds, as does the annual **Port Wine Rally** which also begins and ends at the Autodromo.

Where to Stay

You would expect Estoril to have plenty of hotels, and most are large, modern establishments with three- or four-star ratings. Surprisingly, though, the only five-star hotel is the show-stealing **Hotel Palácio**, Parque do Estoril, 2765 Estoril, ((01) 468-0400, fax: (01) 468-4867. Built in the 1930s in the grand European manner, it has accommodated many a royal visitor, with its classic chandelier-and-drapes style and swimming pool set in carefully manicured gardens. The prices here vary considerably, all within the luxury category.

Golfing is the theme at the luxury **Estalagem Lennox**, Rua Eng. Alvaro Pedro de Sousa Nº5, 2765 Estoril, ((01) 468-0424, fax: (01) 467-0859, which is set on a hillside close to Estoril beach, the best accommodation being inside the main building: other rooms are located in newer structures within the grounds. The hotel can arrange golfing holiday packages and lays on free transport to the Quinta da Marinha where there are riding stables and a golf course, thus adding a country club service to its friendly ambience.

Hotel de Inglaterra, Rua do Porto Nº1, 2765 Estoril, ((01) 468-4461, fax: (01) 468-2108, is partly mansion, partly new buildings, a popular choice for families because it is situated only a few minutes' walk from the beach. Prices are around the higher end of mid-range. The mid-range **Lido**, Rua Alentejo N°12, 2765 Estoril, ((01) 468-4123, fax: (01) 468-4098, is good value. The hillside location of this modern hotel is a quiet residential area, a little way from the Casino, with simple rooms equipped with telephone; a large swimming pool lies within the grounds.

At the inexpensive end of the range there is the modern **Hotel Alvorada**, Rua de

The moderately priced **English Bar** in Monte Estoril on the Estrada Marginal, ((01) 468-1254, overlooks the sea, and despite its name, serves good Portuguese and international dishes, seafood being a specialty. **Pak Yun**, close to the Casino at Centro Comércial, Estorial Parque N°5, ((01) 467-0692, serves some of the best Chinese food in the area, and for Japanese cuisine, try **Furusto**, Praia do Tamariz, ((01) 468-4430. Both are moderately priced. For inexpensive eating, there are plenty of pleasant cafés and snack bars scattered around the town.

Lisboa N°3, 2765 Estoril, ((01) 468-0070, fax: (01) 468-7250, opposite the Casino, and the older **Pensão Continental**, Rua Joaquim Santos N°2, 2765 Estoril, ((01) 468-0050 or 468-4026.

Where to Eat

Probably the best restaurant in Estoril, and certainly the most expensive, is the **Four Seasons Grill** in the Hotel Palácio, Parque do Estoril N°4, ((01) 468-0400. It serves international cuisine, and the menu changes periodically. If you want to throw yourself into the spirit of Estoril, go to the **Grand Salon Restaurant** in the Casino, which serves first-rate food. Expensive.

How to Get There

Estoril is only 24 km (15 miles) away from Lisbon: fast electric trains leave at frequent intervals from Lisbon's Cais do Sodré Station, stopping at Oeiras, Estoril, sometimes Monte Estoril, and Cascais.

If you're traveling from Lisbon by car, take the Avenida 24 de Julio along the bank of the Tagus west of the Praça do Comércio, which becomes the Avenida da India around Belém, then turn into the Marginal where the bridge crosses the Tagus. Beware, though: this dangerous stretch of road has a notoriously high accident rate even by

Ritzy Estoril was a hotbed of espionage during the Second World War. Later, the resort was a repository for deposed crowned heads.

Portuguese standards. If the prospect of driving along it scares you — and so it should — leave Lisbon on the divided highway from the Praça Marquês de Pombal (see Queluz section), and stay on the A5, turning off to the south close to Estoril. If you're driving from Sintra, Estoril is only 13 km (eight miles) away along the N6. From either Lisbon or Sintra, a taxi to Estoril is well within economical range.

CASCAIS

Further along the coast about six-and-a-half kilometers (four miles) west of Estoril and 29 km (18 miles) from Lisbon, Cascais is both a fishing village and a major holiday resort: such is the charm of Cascais that its popularity has begun to rival that of Estoril.

In 1879 King Luís I and his royal entourage descended on the village and spent summer in its seventeenth-century citadel, still in use as a residence for the Head of State. In the 1930s Cascais was discovered by artists and writers who delighted in its ambience.

General Information
The *Turismo* is at Rua Visconde da Luz, ((01) 486-8204.

What to See and Do
One of the few buildings here that did survive the great earthquake is the **Church of Nossa Senhora da Assunção** at the western edge of town. It particularly merits a visit for its paintings by Josefa de Óbidos, a seventeenth-century Portuguese artist. Along the road to Guincho, the **Castro Guimarães Museum**, ((01) 284-0861, is housed in a nineteenth-century building set in parkland, in which are displayed various antiquities well worth seeing.

But the real attraction here is the fishing port itself, where you can watch them bringing in the catch, taking it to the **Fish Market** near the Praia da Ribeira and selling it by Dutch Auction. In this the auctioneer starts off at an excessive price, dropping it until he gets acceptance: the first one secures the fish on offer.

The pretty fishing port of Cascais has become a popular tourist resort and commuter town for wealthy Lisbon folk.

The beaches in Cascais can be unfit for **swimming** because of periodic pollution: swim there only if it has been declared safe to do so. However, many of the hotels have their own pools and there are plenty of other interesting distractions. You could either go along to the **riding** club at Centro Hipico de Cascais, Quinta da Guia, ((01) 284-3563, or to the one at Quinta da Marinha, ((01) 289881, along the road to Guincho. Quinta da Marinha also has an 18-hole **golf** course and **tennis** courts.

One of the best unpolluted **beaches** on the coast is at **Guincho**, eight kilometers (five miles) west of Cascais, sandy, beautiful and with rough sea, but popular with **windsurfers**. There is a windsurfing school here and several hotels, but without the big crowds of Estoril and Cascais.

Where to Stay
There's plenty of accommodation in Cascais, but as in Estoril, bargains are few and far between. Because of its popularity, reservations are a good idea, if not essential.

The choicest spot in town is the well-known and perfectly located **Hotel Albatroz**, Rua Frederico Arouca N°100, 2750 Cascais, ((01) 483-2821, fax: (01) 484-4827. This hotel is a magnificent nineteenth-century house built for the Portuguese royal family; since operating as a hotel it has been favored by royalty and celebrities. Inevitably a modern wing has been added containing a series of balconied rooms, a swimming pool and sun terrace, the whole complex being situated on a rocky promontory overlooking the sea. The restaurant is the best in town and enjoys panoramic views. Definitely in the luxury class.

Estalagem Senhora da Guia, Estrada do Guincho, 2750 Cascais, ((01) 486-9239, fax: (01) 486-9227, is located two kilometers (one mile) outside Cascais and four kilometers (two-and-a-half miles) from Estoril, close to the Quinta da Marinha with its tennis courts, riding center, and golf course. Built in traditional style this beautifully furnished house has a large saltwater pool and terrace. Prices vary between mid-range and luxury. The **Estalagem Senhora das Preces**, Rua Visconde da Gandarinha N°43, ((01) 483-0376, fax: (01) 483-1942, is close to the beach and

golf courses of Cascais and combines the atmosphere of an old manor house with modern comforts. Mid-range.

For something out of the ordinary, the centrally-placed **Casa da Pérgola**, Avenida Valbom Nº13, ℂ (01) 484-0040, is a family house with a stuccoed facade, carefully decorated rooms, and gardens. Operating under the TURIHAB scheme, its 10 rooms are to let at inexpensive to mid-range prices. The **Pensão Dom Carlos**, Rua Latino Coelho Nº8, ℂ (01) 486-8463, is a restored sixteenth-century mansion with eight rooms, simply furnished and inexpensive, while the similarly priced **Albergaria Valbom**, Avenida Valbom Nº14, ℂ (01) 486-5801/2/3/4/5, is a rather faceless modern building, but offers comfortable rooms with private bath, balcony, and telephone.

For those who prefer a more isolated setting or are mad about windsurfing, the **Hotel do Guincho**, Praia do Guincho, 2750 Cascais, ℂ (01) 487-0491, fax: (01) 487-0431, is in a seventeenth-century fort on a cliff near Cabo da Roca. The rooms are individually decorated and overlook the sea. Prices vary from mid-range to luxury.

Where to Eat

Cascais has an excellent choice of good restaurants. Considering the town's popularity as a holiday resort and the reasonable prices, you are well-advised to make reservations. The best restaurant of all, and arguably of the whole Costa do Sol, is the elegant **Restaurant Albatroz**, Rua Frederico Arouca Nº100, ℂ (01) 483-2821. Although expensive you must book. Close to the fish market the **O Pescador**, Rua das Flores Nº9, ℂ (01) 483-2054, is considered the best fish restaurant in town. It has a relaxed atmosphere and is expensive; reservations are essential.

Overlooking the harbor, **Gil Vicente**, Rua dos Naveganes 22-30, ℂ (01) 483-2032, is a bistro in what used to be a fisherman's cottage. Both ambience and food are excellent, and prices moderate, as are those of **Baluarte**, Avenida Dom Carlos I, ℂ (01) 486-5471, a smart, trendy establishment which serves international dishes as well as some very good seafood.

For inexpensive local cuisine and particularly good seafood, try **Restaurante O**

Batel, Travessa das Flores 4, ℂ (01) 483-0215. If you like being where the action is, **Aláude**, Largo Luís de Camões Nº8, ℂ (01) 483-0287, opens on to a very busy square and offers inexpensive international cuisine in a lively atmosphere.

How to Get There

From Lisbon's Cais do Sodré station the train takes approximately half-an-hour to reach Cascais.

Cascais is just three kilometers (two miles) along the coastal road from Estoril, (see Estoril section for directions) and from Sintra is a straightforward drive along the N9.

THE SETÚBAL PENINSULA

For a peaceful alternative to the busy resorts of the Estoril coast, try the Setúbal peninsula to the south of the Tagus. The opening of the Ponte 25 Abril has brought this region within easy reach of the city, and its clear waters with long sandy beaches have made it a popular getaway for *Lisboetas* who refer to it as the *Outra Banda*: the other shore. Increased interest in the area has brought a certain amount of change, not all of it for the best, so catch it while you can.

General Information

The *Turismo* at Costa da Caparica is at Avenida da República Nº18 ℂ (01) 290-0071; at Sesimbra, it's at Largo da Marinha Nº26-27, ℂ (01) 223-5743. At Setúbal the main office is at Travessa Frei Gaspar Nº10, ℂ (065) 524284 with branches at the Praça de Quebedo, ℂ (065) 529507 and Cámera Municipal, Praça do Brocage, ℂ (065)522105.

What to See and Do

Along the west coast of the peninsula lies the **Costa da Caparica**, an eight-kilometer (five-mile) stretch of sandy beaches where the sea is safer and cleaner than along the Estoril coast. Although it's far from quiet, the beaches are considerably less crowded than those of Estoril and the hotels and restaurants more moderately priced.

On the south side of the peninsula the **Serra da Arrábida**, a small limestone ridge,

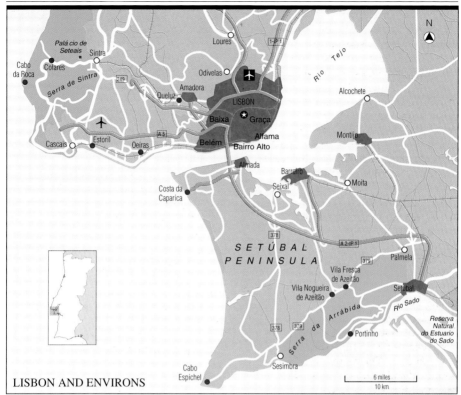

LISBON AND ENVIRONS

covers the 35 km (22 miles) between Cape Espichel and Palmela, rising in a series of smooth hills to a height of 550 m (1,600 ft) then sloping down into the Atlantic, where some of the loveliest beaches and coves are to be found. Now a designated nature park, the Serra is partially covered in dense, typically Mediterranean vegetation and is at its best in springtime when a stunning variety of wildflowers burst into bloom.

Too easily accessible for its own good, the old fishing village of **Sesimbra** lies on the southern slope of the Serra da Arrábida, just 25 km (15 miles) from Setúbal. It remains a busy fishing port packed with colorful trawlers, but unchecked development around the old town has turned Sesimbra into a crowded resort, threatening its warrens of steps and whitewashed cottages.

Heading northeastwards along the N379, a turn-off to the right onto the N379-1 will take you through the Serra da Arrábida. After about four kilometers (two-and-a-half miles) a fork in the road offers you the choice between going deeper into the Serra or going along a coastal road. To get to the

small village of **Portinho da Arrábida** and to one of the most beautiful beaches you could hope for, bear right here and watch out for the narrow turn-off down to Portinho. Unfortunately the beach is also popular, and if you're going during the peak summer months don't drive down this turn-off unless you're comfortable with having to reverse up a steep, narrow road. Sometimes there isn't enough space to park, in which case you'll have quite a hike from the top road.

Backed by green hills, the crescent-shaped bay with its white sand and clear blue waters is an idyllic place to relax and swim. Amongst the many caves along this stretch of coastline is the **Lapa da Santa Margarida**, one that the enraptured Hans Christian Andersen described as a veritable church. Other lovely beaches such as **Praia dos Coelhos** lie further along the coast. Access is not easy, but if you're prepared for a bit of a climb you will be rewarded with some real peace and quiet.

Back up on the N379 along the northern edge of the Serra, vineyards, olive groves and orchards thrive, and you should stop off at **Nogueira de Azeitão**, a pleasant town to wander around. Take a look at the **Tavora Palace**, a sixteenth-century renaissance building that once belonged to the Dukes of Aveiro, and at the tiled interior of the nearby church of **São Lourenço**. The town has a more hedonistic appeal, too: near the palace, you'll find the old nineteenth-century **José Maria da Fonseca Winery**, and, more importantly, the **New Fonseca Winery**, ((01) 208-0227, on the edge of town where you can tour and sample some of Portugal's best

red wines and the sweet muscatel for which Setúbal is famous.

Close to the village of **Vila Fresca de Azeitão**, off the N10, look out for the bus station opposite which the **Quinta de Bacalhôa**, as featured on one of the famous Fonseca wine labels, lies hidden behind a wall. This beautiful renaissance-style villa was built in the late fifteenth century and rescued from dilapidation by an American lady who bought it in the 1930s. The house itself is not open to the public as the family still owns and occupies it, though you may be shown around the lovely garden if you call between 1 and 5 pm on any day but Sunday, allowing you glimpses of the house itself.

The town of **Palmela** sits, pretty and whitewashed, in the foothills of the Serra, about 39 km (24 miles) from Lisbon and five kilometers (one-and-a-half miles) north of Setúbal, overlooked by the imposing **Castelo de Palmela**, parts of which have been modified over the years. Some of the Moorish fortifications can still be seen, and the fifteenth-century monastery has been con-

verted into a pousada. Even if you're not staying or dining here, come up for the superb views over the Serra da Arrábida and the neighboring province of Alentejo.

Setúbal stands on the bank of the river Sado, 48 km (30 miles) from Lisbon, a large city by Portuguese standards with a population of around 100,000. It is a fishing port and industrial city — sardine canning and car production — but from the tourist's point of view there are just two reasons to come here: one is the the **Igreja de Jesus** (Church of Jesus) at the Praça Miguel Bombarda, built in the Manueline stylistic period by Diogo Boytac, with a vaulted ceiling supported by six columns sculpted like twisted nautical rope. Adjoining it is a **Museum** with a collection of renaissance Portuguese paintings.

The other reason to visit is just outside Setúbal, the **Castelo de São Filipe**, a sixteenth-century castle-turned-*pousada* on a hill overlooking the port.

Where to Stay
In Sesimbra the **Hotel Espadarte**, Avenida 25 de Abril Nº10-11, 2970 Sesimbra, ((01) 223-3189, fax: (01) 221-4699, right on the esplanade, offers simple rooms at mid-range prices. In the Vila Fresca de Azeitão, the **Quinta do César**, 2925 Vila Fresca de Azeitão, ((065) 208-0387 operates under the Turismo de Habitação scheme, and has four rooms, one of which is in an annex; inexpensive.

On a hilltop just outside Setúbal is the **Pousada de São Filipe**, 2900 Setúbal, ((065) 523844 or 532538, fax: (065) 523844, preserves the original character without compromising comfort. Some rooms are split-level with the bedroom on the lower floor and a sitting room above. Luxury. Nearby, the **Quinta do Patrício**, Ecosta de São Filipe, 2900 Setúbal, ((065) 522088 or 524373, an eighteenth-century house with views over Setúbal and the River Sado also participates in the TURIHAB scheme; three mid-range rooms, two in the house and one in an adjacent windmill.

In Palmela the only place to stay is the **Pousada do Castelo de Palmela**, 2950 Palmela, ((01) 235-1226, fax: (01) 235-1395, built as a monastery in 1482 inside the castle walls. Skillful conversion and clever use of glass have combined to retain the feeling of cloisters while creating a comfortable environment. What used to be the monks' cells now make comfortable, large guest rooms with magnificent views. Luxury.

Where to Eat
Near the beach in Sesimbra the **Restaurante Ribamar**, Avenida dos Náufragos, ((01) 223-4853, specializes in seafood and is moderately priced. In Portinho da Arrábida there are a couple of eateries on the beach, and at Azeitão the **Quinta das Torres**, Estrada Nacional 5, ((065) 208-0001, offers simple

across the river (the cost is included in the rail ticket) and from there a regular train service operates to Palmela and Setúbal. To reach the Caparica Coast, you can pick up a bus from the ferry-landing in Cacilhas on the south bank of the Tagus in Lisbon; during summer there's a narrow-gauge train to take you along the various beaches. Quicker, but not so much fun, is the bus from Lisbon's Praça de Espanha to Setúbal and Sesimbra, and there's also a service to Costa da Caparica. Local buses run between Sesimbra and Setúbal.

local cuisine in the large old dining room. In Palmela you can dine or lunch at the **Pousada do Castelo de Palmela**, ((01) 235-1226, in what was once a monks' refectory. Moderate.

In Setúbal, the **Pousada de São Filipe**, ((065) 532538, is a little out of town but worth the trip to eat in sixteenth-century surroundings. Plenty of cheap, small restaurants in town cater mainly for locals. While there, be sure to taste some of the muscatel brandy or fortified muscatel wines made in the Setúbal region.

How to Get There
A ferry from the Praça do Comércio in Lisbon will take you to the Barreiro station

Driving to Setúbal from Lisbon is straightforward: after you cross the bridge, keep going on the A2-IP1. To reach the Costa da Caparica turn off at the first junction after the bridge, which will join with a coastal road. To go direct from Lisbon to Sesimbra, you need to come off the A2-IP1 at the second junction after the bridge, turning on to the N378 that runs southwards.

Big, gutsy Portuguese red wines OPPOSITE make up in character, what they lack in finesse. Cabo Espichel ABOVE is one of the most dramatic headlands on the Arrábida peninsula.

Estre-
madura
and the
Ribatejo

ESTREMADURA is the coastal province northwest of Lisbon, edged with dramatic cliffs and sandy beaches and containing some outstanding monumental architecture. Much of Estremadura is within easy reach of Lisbon and can alternatively be covered in day trips. It also includes the Setúbal Peninsula, covered in LISBON AND ENVIRONS, page 106.

The neighboring inland province of the Ribatejo, meaning "banks of the Tagus," lies in the valley of that river, for the most part on fertile alluvial plains planted with rice and cereals. This is Portugal's prairie, synonymous with horse and bull breeding, and *campinos* (herdsmen) in their green stocking-caps, black knee breeches and red waistcoats. Its attractions lie in the lovely town of Tomar, home of the Convent of Christ, and several small riverside villages of undisturbed beauty.

ESTREMADURA

MAFRA

Forty kilometers (25 miles) northwest of Lisbon, 18 km (12 miles) north of Sintra, Mafra is a small town overshadowed by the hulking **Mafra Monastery and Palace, (** (061) 52332.

Like so many Portuguese monuments, Mafra was built in fulfillment of a vow. King João V pledged that he would build a monastery if the union with his Austrian wife was blessed with a child, and in 1717, six years and three children later, work began. The building was completed in 1735.

The cost was almost more than the country could bear. The brief had been to build something to rival Philip of Spain's Escorial near Madrid, including a church, monastery and palace, to be paid for out of the newly discovered wealth of gold and diamonds in Brazil. Mafra almost ruined Portugal by draining not only its coffers but also the country's work force: as many as 50,000 men were employed to work on it at one point, many of whom were never paid.

Mafra's vital statistics (the most remarkable thing about it) include 4,500 doors and windows, a three-storey, 220-m (722-ft) long facade, and a total area of four hectares (ten acres). The Italianate **basilica** sits at the cen-

ter of the facade, its porch filled with large Carrara marble statues; it is flanked by two long wings, each topped by a squat, rather squashed dome. Two belfries containing carillons rise over the basilica and between them carry over 100 bells which can be heard for miles around. These were made in Belgium, and the story goes that when King João was told the immense cost of one set, he promptly replied I'll take two! That just about sums up Mafra.

After the building of the monastery, a school of sculpture was set up there between 1753 and 1770 to make the most use of the expertise of those summoned to work on the palace. Today the building is largely used by the army, only 10 percent of it being open to the public, although a tour still takes about one-and-a-half hours. The highlight is the **Baroque Library**, a barrel-vaulted room 65 m (213 ft) long packed with over 35,000 volumes. Other areas open to the public include the pharmacy with a rather grisly array of medical instruments, the infirmary, the monks' cells, and the kitchens. Occupied by royalty into the twentieth century, the chambers are filled with antique furnishings and tapestries.

To see inside Mafra you will have to join one of the guided tours which operate from 10 am to 1 pm and from 2 to 5 pm Wednesday to Monday. Closed on Tuesdays, admission is free on Sunday mornings.

Near Mafra, the village of **Turcifal** makes a pleasant stop for coffee. Its streets are lined mainly with eighteenth-century buildings, and it has a church built from Mafra's left-over stone.

General Information

There is a *Turismo* in Mafra at Avenida 25 de Abril, ((061) 812023.

How to Get There

A bus service runs every hour between Lisbon and Mafra. For details of services check at the *Turismo* or the R.N. bus depot. The R.N. Gray Line operates sightseeing tours that take in Mafra, Sintra and Estoril. For details contact them in Lisbon at ((01) 577523/538846.

If you are driving from Lisbon, take the Avenida da República from the city center,

Ocean and continent clash at Cabo Carvoeiro OPPOSITE on Estremadura's rugged Atlantic coast.

continue north out of the city and join onto the A8-IC1. About 33 km (20 miles) out of Lisbon, turn left onto the N116 to Mafra. From Sintra, Mafra is a 18-km (12-miles) drive along the N9.

IN AND AROUND ERICEIRA

The Estremadura coast is dotted with ancient and often picturesque fishing villages, with modern hotel complexes shooting up and making tourism an increasingly important alternative to income derived from traditional sea fishing. Fifty kilometers (32 miles) northwest of Lisbon along the N116 lies the small fishing port of Ericeira from which the last king and his family sailed off into exile in 1910. Perched on cliffs overlooking the Atlantic, it has four gently curving beaches, each separated from the other by rocky headlands. Its squares and narrow cobbled streets snake uphill from the harbor, lined with seafood restaurants and lively with visitors. Stroll over to the dazzling white **Hermitage of São Sebastião**, a seventeenth-century domed circular building of North African design with an *azulejos*-lined interior, which overlooks São Sebastião beach; also on the cliff above the harbor is the **Chapel of Santo António**, which has tiles portraying the departure of the royal family.

One of the main amusements remains the **fishing beach**, where you can watch the gaily-painted boats return and unload their catch. The overcrowding may spoil the town for you, but comfort yourself with lunch at one of the seafood restaurants: Ericeira is famed for the variety of it, particularly its lobster.

General Information
The *Turismo* is at Rua Eduardo Burnay Nº33A, ((061) 63122.

Where to Stay
The **Estalagem Morais**, Rua Dr. Miguel Bombarda Nº3, 2655 Ericeira, ((061) 864200/08, fax: (061) 864308, is a cheerful establishment with 40 rooms, swimming pool and a decent restaurant. Prices are around the

low end of mid-range. The **Hotel Vilazul**, Calçada da Baleia Nº10, ((061) 864303, fax: (061) 62927, offers good views, comfortable and inexpensive accommodation, bars and a restaurant.

Where to Eat
Ericeira's **O Poco**, Calçada da Baleia Nº10, ((061) 63669, serves good seafood dishes and is quite inexpensive.

How to Get There
Express buses run from Lisbon to Ericeira via Mafra. By road, Ericeira lies 12 km (seven-and-a-half miles) west of Mafra along the N116, 50 km (32 miles) northeast of Lisbon (see also Nazaré, below).

PENICHE AND THE BERLENGA ISLANDS

Moving north of Ericeira, and 96 km (60 miles) north of Lisbon, is Peniche, once an island but now connected to the mainland by a thin isthmus flanked by sandy beaches. This lackluster fishing and canning center has a population of around 15,000: take a boat trip out to **Berlenga Grande**, the only one of the misty Berlenga Islands which can be visited, and now a bird sanctuary. Surrounded by cliffs it is only about one square mile in size, but it is possible to camp there or lodge in the island's seventeenth century **fortress**, now a hostel, that sits on an islet connected to the island by a stone staircase. It stands on black rocks pounded by the sea, and lies in the shadow of a sprawling sixteenth-century **Fortress**, once the Fortaleza Prison controlled by Salazar's secret police and used to incarcerate his opponents, but now an innocuous museum of local history.

The sandy beaches along the isthmus from Peniche have good water for surfing but not for swimming. Further north along the coast where the Óbidos lagoon meets the sea, **Praia da Foz do Arelho** is a quiet, sandy beach that can also offer the tranquil, though at times polluted, waters of the lagoon. Fourteen kilometers (nine miles) further north, the village of **São Martinho do Porto** has a virtually landlocked bay, calm waters and an inviting sandy beach. It is best enjoyed off-season, however.

The people of Nazaré, trace cultural traits and the design of their fishing boats, back to Phoenician traders.

General Information

In Peniche there is a *Turismo* at Rua Alexandre Herculano, ((062) 789571, which also has information on the Berlenga Islands. At São Martinho do Porto, the *Turismo* is on Avenida 25 de Abril, ((062) 989110 or 989440, .

Where to Stay

In Peniche there are no hotels of interest but on Berlenga Grande the seventeenth-century fort has been converted into a hostel, **Casa Abrigo São João Baptista,** ((062) 72271, where you need to take your own food and bedding, and in the summer there's also the **Pensão Mar e Sol**, ((062) 72031, which offers a handful of rooms and a reasonable restaurant. Both are inexpensive.

In São Martinho do Porto, the **Hotel do Parque**, Avenida Marechal Carmona N°3, 2465 São Martinho do Porto, ((062) 989506, is set in private grounds with a tennis court. The rooms are clean and homely, all with bathrooms, but there is no restaurant on the premises. It is open only from March to October. Prices mid-range to inexpensive.

Where to Eat

In Peniche the **Restaurante Nau Dos Corvos**, Cabo Carvoeiro, ((062) 722410, with glass walls overlooking the rocks of Cabo do Carvoeiro, naturally offers seafood on its moderately priced menu.

How to Get There

São Martinho is served by rail. It lies on the line from Lisbon to Leiria on which the train also stops at Óbidos, Caldas da Rainha, and Valado. A bus connects Caldas da Rainha and São Martinho do Porto with Peniche, another connects Nazaré with Leiria. There's a service between Nazaré and Valado, just four kilometers (two-and-a-half miles) away. Express buses run from Lisbon to Peniche.

Until the N8 from Lisbon reaches the Nazaré area the road doesn't run close to the coast, so for Peniche, São Martinho, and Praia da Foz do Arelho you will have to turn off and strike out westwards. At Caldas da Rainha you have the option of hiving off the N8 onto the quieter N360, a coastal road which will take you westwards to Foz do Arelho, then north to Nazaré via São Martinho do Porto.

NAZARÉ

Thirteen kilometers (nine miles) further along the coast is the pretty but overcrowded fishing village of Nazaré. Here the locals sometimes wear their distinctive traditional dress: fishermen's capes, plaid shirts and stocking caps, while the women wear seven petticoats beneath wide skirts. More color is added by the brightly decorated narrow boats, particularly the *meia-lua* (half-moon) type, on whose graceful crescent-shaped prows are painted eyes, stars, or other symbols.

The town is on two levels. The lower is a jumble of narrow lanes and cottages, and 109 m (360 ft) above it is the **Sítio**, the site of the original town before the sea receded. A

funicular takes you up to where you can see the **Ermida da Memória** (Memory Chapel), a tiny white chapel with blue borders built to commemorate the miracle that saved the life of Fuas Roupinho, the companion in arms of Afonso Henriques, in 1182. While in pursuit of a white deer (said to be the devil in disguise), the mist caused Fuas to lose his way. Our Lady appeared and halted his horse just in time to prevent it and Fuas from falling over a cliff, where a hoofprint is still embedded in the edge. If you do decide to stay in Nazaré, this is where you have a view of the harbor spread out below; down on the beach you'll find yourself hassled constantly by souvenir sellers or by locals trying to persuade you to take a room.

General Information

Most accesible is the branch office of the *Turismo* at Rua Mouzinho de Albuquerque N°72, Avenida da República, ((062) 561120. The main office is in Avenida Guinariãs, ((062) 561194.

Where to Stay

Nazaré has several modern hotels, but to my mind the most pleasant accommodation is the inexpensive **Pensão Restaurante Ribamar**, Rua Gomes Freire N°9, 2450 Nazaré, ((062) 551158, an old inn on the waterfront. Some of their rooms have balconies

The fisher folk of Nazaré dry splayed sardines and jackfish over wooden racks on the beach.

overlooking the fishing beach, and all have traditional furnishings.

Where to Eat
The **Pensão Restaurante Ribamar** (see above) serves traditional dishes under oak beams; the **Restaurante Mar Bravo**, Praça Sousa Oliveira, ((062) 551180, is located on a square overlooking the sea. Both are inexpensively priced.

How to Get There
From Lisbon, take the N8 north through Torres Vedras, Caldas da Rainha and the outskirts of Nazaré.

ÓBIDOS

The medieval town of Óbidos, 95 km (59 miles) north of Lisbon and 16 km from the coast east of Peniche, sits on a hill surrounded by a fertile and cultivated plain, crowned by a castle — now an excellent *pousada* — and surrounded by yellow crenellated castle walls. Within is a jumble of alleyways and small squares leading off a main street, where whitewashed houses have brightly-colored terra-cotta roofs: vivid flowers seem to sprout from every corner and balcony. It can be seen on a day trip from Lisbon, but if you are on the way north this is a good spot to spend the night.

Background
In its early days Óbidos stood by the sea with boats moored alongside the lower wall, but centuries of land reclamation have left the town miles from the coast. The saintly Queen Isabella was so charmed by it that in 1282 her husband King Dinis made her a gift of Óbidos, after which it became a tradition for the town to be presented to the queens of Portugal, earning the title *Casa das Rainhas* (House of the Queens). It was to Óbidos that the wife of João II, Queen Leonor, came to mourn the death of her only son, Prince Afonso, who met his end in a riding accident. His body was borne back in a fisherman's net, which Queen Leonor took as her emblem: you can see it carved on the town's pillory.

Another famous resident was Josefa de Óbidos (1634–1684), one of the few known artists of the feminine gender in the seventeenth century. Her religious paintings and more popular studies of still life are scattered around the country, and several of them can be seen here.

General Information
The *Turismo* is on the main street, Rua Direita, ((062) 959231.

What to See and Do
If you're driving here, leave your car in the parking lot because the narrow streets of the town are difficult to negotiate. One of the first obstacles is the **Porta de Vila**, a double gateway through which you have to zig-zag; inside is a renaissance balcony brightened with eighteenth-century *azulejos*, contrasting with the ancient yellowing stone walls. The gateway opens on to the narrow main street, lined with old houses and shops where you can sometimes see weavers making the town's famous cotton carpets.

Moving along the Rua Direita, just past the *Turismo*, in the square to the right stands the handsome **Igreja de Santa Maria** (St. Mary's Church), where blue and white seventeenth-century tiles painted with African-inspired designs cover the walls all the way to the ceiling. Paintings by Josefa de Óbidos of the life of St. Catherine adorn a side chapel. Open from 9:30 am to 12:30 pm and from 2:30 pm to 7 pm, ((062) 959231.

Also in the square is the **Museu Municipal** (Municipal Museum), ((062) 959263, established with the help of the Gulbenkian Foundation, which has some works from the fifteenth century onwards, including paintings by Josefa de Óbidos. Opening hours are from 9 am to 1 pm and from 2 to 6 pm.

The pillory bearing the coat of arms of Queen Leonor stands in this square. The pillory or *pelourinho* was a place of punishment in Portugal, and a symbol of authority. Often elaborately carved, you will find one in the main square of virtually every town.

Close by the museum stands the **Igreja da Misericórdia** built by Queen Leonor in 1498, and the fourteenth-century **Chapel of São Martinho**. One of the other churches in town, the **Church of São Pedro**, contains the tomb of Josefa de Óbidos. At the end of the Rua Direita is the **Castelo**, part of the twelfth-century fortifications turned into a royal palace in the sixteenth century and into an excellent *pousada* in the twentieth.

Where to Stay

The place where everyone wants to stay in Óbidos is the **Pousada do Castelo**, 2510 Óbidos, ℂ (062) 959105, fax: (062) 959148, built into a restored section of the Manueline-ornamented sixteenth-century castle. It retains the atmosphere of a castle with antique furniture and medieval weaponry on the walls. Only six rooms and three suites are

and a bar, where there's *fado* singing on Fridays and Saturdays. Both are inexpensive.

Where to Eat

The **Pousada do Castelo**, ℂ (062) 959105, has an excellent restaurant furnished in provincial style which serves local and continental food at moderate prices. The restaurant at the **Estalagem do Convento**, ℂ (062) 959214/7, offers moderately priced continental cuisine in an old-fashioned dining room or *al fresco* in warmer weather. **Restaurante Alcaide**, Rua Direita, ℂ (062) 959220, serves regional

available, all with views over the surrounding countryside. Prices are expensive, but drop into mid-range off season. The second choice for accommodation is probably the **Estalagem do Convento**, Rua Dr. João d'Ornelas, ℂ (062) 959214/7, fax: (062) 959159, a converted eighteenth-century convent just below the walls. The furnishings are old but comfortable and all rooms have bathrooms and minibars. Mid-range prices apply.

Two places in town operate under the TURIHAB scheme: the **Casa do Relógio**, Rua da Graca, ℂ (062) 959194, comprising a medieval building and eighteenth-century mansion with six rooms, and the **Casa do Poco**, Travessa da Rua Nova, ℂ (062) 959358, a building of Moorish origin with six rooms

dishes and is open for tea or drinks in the afternoons. If you are early you may get a balcony table. Prices range between inexpensive and moderate.

How to Get There

Trains run frequently from Lisbon's Rossio station to Óbidos with a journey time of about two hours. By bus you will need to take the service to Caldas da Rainha and change there for Óbidos.

The motor-route out of Lisbon is the same as for Mafra, but instead of turning on to the N116 continue along the N8 to Óbidos.

For generations, Romantic Óbidos, tightly clustered within its formidable town wall, has inspired poets and lovers.

BATALHA

Three important centers of religious life mark the drive to Tomar and merit a visit.

The **Monastery of Santa Maria da Vitória**, better known as Batalha Abbey, (technically just inside Beira Litoral province rather than Estremadura) towers over a collection of small houses and shops at the side of the busy N1 motorway. Nevertheless, Batalha, a magnificent Gothic extravaganza with Manueline flourishes, is curiously divorced

delicate Gothic tracery is embellished with Manueline plants and flowers of the newly discovered lands, as well as more common seafaring motifs.

An opening off the cloister leads to the **Chapter House** where a soldier guards the **Tomb of the Unknown Soldiers**, two Portuguese casualties of the First World War. The single-span vault was a very daring construction in its time, rising as it does to a height of 20 m (60 ft) without intermediary supports. Condemned criminals were recruited to build it, and the blind Afonso

from its surroundings. It was built by King João I in thanksgiving for the Portuguese victory over strong Spanish forces at the Battle of Aljubarrota in 1385, a honey-colored mass of limestone spires, flying buttresses, balustrades, and pinnacles, edged with filigree-like stonework as delicate as starched lace. The soaring interior is no less impressive.

Batalha was built between 1388 and 1533, years which saw the evolution of the Manueline style. At the southern end is the **Capela do Fundador** (Founder's Chapel), an octagonal domed lantern within a square structure, with a star-vaulted ceiling. It contains the tombs of João I and Philippa of Lancaster together with those of their sons. In the **Claustro Real** (Royal Cloister) the

Domingues, the first architect to work on Batalha, found it necessary to spend a night under the Chapter House roof to convince people that it was safe.

Outside the abbey there is access to the **Capelas Imperfetas** (Unfinished Chapels) through a vast Gothic doorway covered with extravagant sixteenth-century carving. Band upon band of delicate lace work carry the words of Dom Duarte's motto, *tam yasary* ("I shall be loyal"), repeated in the tracery. This octagonal structure with seven chapels was commissioned by Dom Duarte as a mausoleum in 1435, only three years before his death; its pillars and arches end in mid-air all at the same height, as though someone had sliced through the roof leaving the chapels forever open to the elements. The Abbey is open from 9 am to noon and from 2 to 5 pm (until 6 pm in the summer months) but is closed on Mondays.

General Information
In Batalha the *Turismo* is close by the Abbey at Largo Paulo VI, ((044) 96180.

Where to Stay and Where to Eat
The **Pousada do Mestre Afonso Domingues**, Largo Mestre Afonso Domingues, 2440 Batalha, ((044) 96260/1, fax: (044) 96260,

is right next to the monastery, a modern but traditionally styled establishment with 20 rooms and one suite. Some have splendid views of the monastery. Mid-range prices apply here: modern *pousadas* often cost less than those housed within historic buildings.

The **Residencial Batalha**, Largo da Igreja, ((044) 767500, fax: (044) 767467, is a spanking new hotel linked to a shopping center, its 22 rooms including bathroom, telephone, satellite television, and sound insulation. Prices are mid-range. Under the TURIHAB scheme there is the **Quinta do Fidalgo**, ((044) 96114, a seventeenth-century house facing the abbey and surrounded by gardens and trees. There are four rooms and the

prices vary between inexpensive and mid-range.

There are several restaurants and cafés, probably the best of which is the **Pousada do Mestre Afonso Domingues** in Largo Mestre Afonso Domingues, ((044) 96260/1, which has a good restaurant with inexpensive to moderate prices.

How to Get There
The nearest rail link to Batalha is at Leiria (11 km or seven miles to the north. Trains arrive from Lisbon's Rossio station and from

Coimbra. There is a bus service to Batalha from Leiria.

To drive from Lisbon, take the airport road and continue north along the A1-IP1 motorway. The Fátima–Batalha turn-off is some 125 km (78 miles) from Lisbon.

ALCOBAÇA

Twenty kilometers (12 miles) south of Batalha, the **Mosteiro de Santa Maria** (Santa

---

The awesome Batalha Abey OPPOSITE was built in thanksgiving for victory over the Spanish. The faithful find Fátima ABOVE LEFT a rich source of spiritual energy. Lovers Pedro and Inês at Alcobaça ABOVE RIGHT will rise up to face each other on judgement day.

Maria Monastery) at Alcobaça is the largest church in Portugal. Before the battle of Santarém Portugal's first King, Afonso I, vowed to build a monastery there if he won. He duly captured Santarém from the Moors in 1147 and handed over the domain of Alcobaça to the Cistercians.

Work began on the monastery in 1178; it is believed once to have housed 999 monks. The facade is a mixture of baroque and Gothic, altered by seventeenth- and eighteenth-century work which left only the doorway and rose window of the original facade. It was ransacked during the Peninsular Wars and the monks finally left under the 1834 ban on religious orders.

The interior of the church is impressive but simple: three aisles stretch out amid a forest of graceful columns, and the original serenity achieved through the use of space has been returned by stripping out the later additions. The tombs of King Pedro and his beloved mistress stand in the north and south transept, a testimony to one of Portugal's great love stories and the rage and vengeance of the grief-stricken king.

Afonso IV's son Pedro was betrothed to Constanza, a princess of Navarre, but instead fell in love with her lady-in-waiting, a Castilian noblewoman named Inês de Castro. Inês was exiled from the court by Afonso, but returned upon the death of Constanza to settle in Coimbra where she raised her royal children; she claimed that she had been secretly married to Pedro. Fearful of the harm that this union and Inês' ambitious family could cause, Afonso had her murdered. Two years later in 1357 Pedro came to power and exacted terrible revenge: he traced two of the assassins and had their hearts torn out. The story goes that he had Inês body disinterred, set upon the throne, robed and crowned, and had the entire court kiss her decayed hand in homage. Pedro became obsessed with the dispensation of justice and was often harsh, acquiring the sobriquet "The Cruel."

Their two white tombs were placed foot to foot so that on the Day of Judgment their first sight would be of one another: Inês' effigy, now without its nose which disap-

peared during the Peninsular Wars, lies supported by six angels. The panel at the head of her tomb depicts the Crucifixion, and the one at her feet shows Judgment Day and the damned being cast into the jaws of hell. The tomb is supported by animals with human faces, which some believe represent her assassins. Dom Pedro's tomb is similarly guarded by angels, a faithful hound at his feet and the wheel of fortune at his head.

A Manueline doorway leads from the chancel to the sacristy, beyond which is a circular chapel lined with golden baroque carvings and busts of saints. A doorway from the nave leads into the **Cloister of Silence** dating from the fourteenth century with a Manueline upper storey, where there is access to the vast dormitory.

General Information
The *Turismo* is at Praça 25 de Abril, ((062) 42377.

Where to Stay and Where to Eat
The **Hotel Santa Maria**, Rua Dr. Francisco Zagalo, 2460 Alcobaça, ((062) 597395, fax: (062) 596715, is a modern hotel in its own gardens, standing in front of the monastery. All rooms have bathrooms, phones, and are inexpensive. The **Pensão Mosteiro**, Avenida João de Deus Nº1, ((062) 42183, is an inexpensive, homely place, a little the worse for wear but very friendly.

The **Restaurante Trinidade**, Praça Dom Afonso Henriques Nº22, ((062) 42397, serves meals and snacks. **Restaurante Frei Bernardo**, Rua Dom Pedro V Nº17-19, ((062) 42227, is a late nineteenth-century building with a large dining room serving traditional, inexpensive fare, occasionally to the accompaniment of live music.

How to get There
The nearest railway station is Valado de Fráles, only five kilometers (three miles) away from which buses connect with Alcobaça. There is also a bus service from Leiria to Alcobaça and express busses run from Lisbon.

To drive from Lisbon, exit on the airport road and continue north along the A1-IP1 motorway, leaving it at the Fátima–Batalha

OPPOSITE: Wisened old lady of Ribatejo.

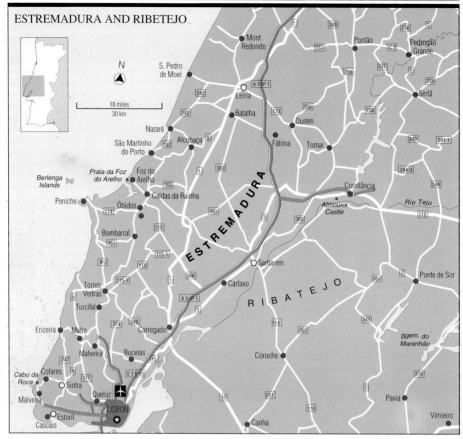

ESTREMADURA AND RIBETEJO

N

S. Pedro de Moel

18 miles
30 km

Mont Redondo
Pontão
Pedrogão Grande
Leiria
Batalha
Ourém
Fátima
Tomar
Sertã
Nazaré
São Martinho do Porto
Alcobaça
Berlenga Islands
Praia da Foz do Arelho
Foz do Arelho
Caldas da Rainha
Constância
Peniche
Óbidos
Almourol Castle
Rio Tejo
Bombarral
ESTREMADURA
Torres Vedras
Santarém
Ponte de Sor
Turcifal
Cartaxo
RIBATEJO
Ericeira
Mafra
Carregado
Bgem. do Maranhão
Malveira
Bucelas
Coruche
Cabo da Roca
Colares
Sintra
Queluz
Pavia
Malveira
LISBON
Estoril
Cascais
Canha
Vimieiro

turn-off some 125 km (78 miles) from Lisbon. To reach Alcobaça from Batalha take the N8 south for 20 km (12 miles).

FÁTIMA

Nineteen kilometers (12 miles) east of Batalha is Fátima, revered as a place pilgrimage second only to Lourdes in France. On May 13, 1917 the Virgin appeared to three children, and again on the thirteenth of every month until October that year. It was during her final appearance (she was only visible to the children), that thousands witnessed a miracle, when the sun rotated in the sky and its rays cured many of the sick. Under Salazar a vast basilica — a rather cold structure of no great architectural merit — and square were constructed there. This is not a place for casual sight-seers but rather for the deeply religious, a place of prayer. In fact, notices at Fátima give the same advice.

General Information

The *Turismo* is at Avenida Dom José Alves da Silva, ((049) 531139.

Where to Stay and Where to Eat

There are over 30 hotels and *pensãos* in Fátima priced from moderate to inexpensive. At the higher end, the **Cinquentenario**, ((049) 533465, fax: (049) 532992 is modern and clean and near the shrine.

The **Estalagem Dom Gonçalo**, ((049) 533062, fax: (049) 532088, Rua Jacinto Marto Nº 100, 2495 Fátima, low-rise and set in its own grounds yet near to the shrine. Inexpensive to stay, and a good place to eat is **Pensão Restaurante Estrêla de Fátima**, ((049) 531150, fax: (049) 532160, Rua Cónega Formigão Periera, 2495 Fátima.

How to Get There

The nearest rail link to Fátima is at Leiria 20 km away, where trains arrive from Lisbon's Rossio station and from Coimbra. From

Leiria there is a bus service to Fátima. There is also an express bus service from Lisbon.

If you're driving from Lisbon, take the airport road and continue north along the A1-IP1 motorway, leaving it at the Fátima–Batalha turn-off some 125 km (78 miles) from Lisbon; then follow the signs.

RIBATEJO

TOMAR

Tomar is 72 km (48 miles) west of Fátima,via Vila Nova de Ourém, on N113, 140 km (87 miles) from Lisbon and 197 km (122 miles) from Porto, on the banks of the River Nabão at the foot of a hill. Dominated by the famous Convent of Christ — the Ribatejo's main tourist attraction—it merits a visit in its own right.

Background
Tomar was founded by the Knights Templar in 1160 and remained their stronghold until King Dinis disbanded the order in 1314 to reconstitute it as the Order of Christ, under the Grand Mastership of the younger sons of the Kings of Portugal. One was Prince Henry the Navigator, who used the Order's wealth to finance some of the Voyages of Discovery: his sails bore its cross. Some of the money earned from these voyages was spent on turning the monastery into a symbol of the Discoveries, and of the Order's power and prosperity.

General Information
The main *Turismo* is on Rua Serpa Pinto Nº 1, ((049) 313013 with a branch on Avenida Dr. Candida Madureira, ((049) 312487

What to See and Do
The main attraction is the monastery, the **Convento de Cristo**, which was begun in the twelfth century and finished in the seventeenth. It is entered through the 16-sided Charola, based on Jerusalem's Holy Sepulcher; to the west an archway links it to an elaborate sixteenth-century Manueline **Chapterhouse** by Diogo de Arruda. From the Santa Barbara Cloister you can see *it*: the famous **Manueline window**, a seething

mass of ropes, knots, cables, coral and sea-weed, all curled around two masts at either side of the window and topped by the cross of the Order of Christ. You may need some time to recover.

A passageway leads you from the chapterhouse to the top storey of the sixteenth-century **Main Cloisters** by Diogo de Torralva, essentially an Italian renaissance structure in which its beauty lies in its simplicity. The cloisters stand in complete contrast to the choking ornamentation of the chapterhouse above. They provide an

overview of the whole building from the spiral staircase in the eastern corner. Open from 9:30 am to 12:30 pm and 2 to 5 pm (until 6 pm in the summer months). Entry is free Sunday mornings.

Halfway down the hill is the **Capela de Nossa Senhora da Conceição** (Chapel of Our Lady of the Immaculate Conception), a renaissance building, pure in form and proportion. Opening times are as for the monastery. The old part of town has cobbled streets lined with seventeenth- and eighteenth-century houses, and is strewn with parks and gardens. In one of the backstreets is a fifteenth-century **synagogue** which over the years has served a variety of secular purposes. It is now a **Luso-Hebraic Museum** and its hall is sometimes used for concerts.

Where to Stay
The **Estalagem de Santa Iria**, Parque do Mouchão, 2300 Tomar, ((049) 321238, is in

Every May 13th, anniversary of the Virgin's first apparition at Fátima, upwards of 100,000 pilgrims gather at her shrine.

the park by the river, moderately priced, with a bar and restaurant. The **Pensão Nuno Alvares**, Avenida Dom Nuno Alvares Pereira Nº3, ((049) 312873, offers agreeable guest rooms and a good restaurant. There are a couple of modern hotels in town, the largest being the **Hotel dos Templários**, Largo Cândido dos Reis Nº1, ((049) 321730, fax: (049) 322191, with a wide range of facilities including pool and tennis court. Mid-range.

Where to Eat

The **Pensão Nuno Alvares** (see above) has an excellent restaurant, while the **Bela Vista**, Fonte do Choupo Nº4, ((049) 312870, as its name suggests, has good views of the town as well as inexpensive food. **Chico Elias**, Algarvias, ((049) 311067, is slightly outside the town but well-patronized, serving moderately priced regional dishes, and in the old quarter near the river **Chez Nous**, Rua Dr. Joaquim Jacinto Nº31, ((049) 312294, has a mixture of French and local cuisines at similarly moderate prices.

How to Get There

Trains from Lisbon's Santa Apolónia station and from Porto run to Entroncamento, where there is a frequent service to Tomar. An express bus service runs from Lisbon via Santarém to Tomar.

From Lisbon (140 km or 87 miles away) the fastest route to Tomar is along the main Coimbra–Lisbon motorway, the A1, turning on to the N3 running east to Entroncamento after 103 km (64 miles,) where you head north on the N110 to Tomar.

SANTARÉM

The capital of the Ribatejo is the hilltop city of Santarém, 65 km (40 miles) south of Tomar, an agricultural center with plenty of cafés, restaurants, and excellent views over the surrounding pasturelands. The real highlight of any visit here is the nearby **Church of São João de Alparão**, located towards the end of the Avenida 5 de Outubro and now a museum displaying a ragbag of unrelated pieces. There is a Gothic tomb bearing a long inscription, erected by the widow of Duarte de Meneses who died at the hands of the Moors while defending

his King. The fight was evidently a long and hard one, for in a glass case in the museum is all that remained of Dom Duarte when it was over: one rotten tooth. More complete members of the Meneses family are interred in the fifteenth-century **Church of Nossa Senhora da Graça**. For spectacular views over the surrounding plains and a restaurant with some of the best food in town, go to **Portas do Sol**, a small public garden at the end of the Avenida 5 de Outubro.

General Information

For information on the Ribatejo as a whole contact the Regiáo de Turismo de Ribatejo in Santarém, ((043) 26318 or 2637. Santarém also has a local *Turismo* at Rua Capelo Ivens Nº63, ((043) 23140.

How to Get There

There is a frequent train service linking Lisbon with Entroncamento via Santarém, and trains from Porto and Coimbra run to Entroncamento. Frequent R.N. express buses operate between Lisbon and Santarém.

Santarém is 78 km (48 miles) from Lisbon just off the LisbonPorto A1 motorway on the N114. To drive to Santarém from Tomar (a distance of approximately 60 km or 37 miles) take the N243 joining the N118 after 30 km (19 miles), then turn on to the N114 at Almeirin. It can be seen on a day trip from Lisbon if you are basing yourself there.

ELSEWHERE IN RIBATEJO

Ourém

The fortified hilltop village of **Ourém** lies 20 km (12 miles) northwest of Tomar on the N113, its summit studded with olive trees and crowned with the ruins of a fifteenth-century castle. In its grounds lies a renaissance palace, the **Paço dos Condes** (Palace of the Counts), built by Dom Afonso, the bastard son of João I. The towers have parapets supported by pointed arches. To visit the palace you enter through one of the two huge gateways, but will probably have to leave your car outside at Vila Nova de Ourém (the busy modern part of town), as driving through them would be a tight squeeze. Climb up the square tower for panoramic views of the countryside.

Below the castle, part of the old town is protected by its walls. Go into the **Colegiada** (Collegiate Church) where you can see the highly ornate limestone tomb of Count Dom Afonso.

For those who want to stay over, Ourém has a few *pensãos* and also the **Quinta da Alcaidaria-Mor**, 2490 Vila Nova de Ourém, ((049) 42231, a splendid old house which offers accommodation under the TURIHAB scheme.

Almourol Castle

Just a few kilometers away from Constância, 22 km (14 miles) south of Tomar, Almourol Castle stands on a small craggy island in the Tagus, built in 1171 on the site of a Roman fortress (parts of the lower walls are Roman). You can be ferried across by a boatman who will wait to row you back; this picture-book structure has never suffered attack, but stories of princesses and giants cling to it. On St. John's Eve it is said to be haunted by the ghosts of a Moorish boy, a Christian girl and an angry, heartbroken

Constância

Situated southeast of Tomar, the sparkling white town of Constância sits in a natural amphitheater at the confluence of the Tagus and Zêzere rivers, a cluster of stepped streets all bedecked with brightly colored flowers. Camões was exiled here between 1548 and 1550 because of his affair with a young lady-in-waiting, Catarina d'Ataide, the Natercia of his love poems. You can still see the shell of the Casa dos Arcos where he used to live.

A delightful place to base yourself is the **Casa O Palácio**, 2250 Constância, ((049) 932249, a lovely nineteenth-century mansion sitting on the riverbank which offers TURIHAB accommodation.

father, protagonists in a romantic and tragic legend. The outer wall is flanked by 10 round towers, the whole dominated by the square keep which you can climb for good views of the river.

There is a train service from Entroncamento to Almourol, from which it takes approximately 20 minutes on foot to the castle.

Troubadores in traditional costume make merry at Abrantes, on the alluvial plains of the Tagus estuary.

Coimbra
and the
Beiras

THE BEIRAS

The three provinces of Beira Baixa, Beira Alta and Beira Litoral (Lower, Upper and Coastal Beira) together form a large block of land stretching from the coast to the Spanish frontier, bordered in the north by the Alto Douro and in the south by the provinces of Ribatejo and Estremadura. This area encompasses the Dão wine growing area, the Mondego and Zêzere valleys, and coastal plains laced with lagoons and edged with long, sandy beaches.

Beira Alta and Beira Baixa make up Portugal's most mountainous region, its principal range being the Serra da Estrêla. Because cultivation is difficult and the way of life hard, its population is sparse. Many settlements are encircled by stout fortifications, for this was the pathway into Portugal for invaders.

In contrast, the Beira Litoral is a low-lying area, well irrigated and fertile. Pine woods line the sandy coastal strip broken by the Aveiro lagoon, but this area lacks the natural grandeur of the mountain Beiras. Nonetheless, there are two important sights: the romantic, historic city of Coimbra, and the uniquely beautiful Buçaco Forest with its magnificent Palace Hotel.

In and Around Castelo Branco

The prosperous capital of the Beira Baixa lies 249 km (155 miles) northeast of Lisbon at the center of the exposed Idanha plain in the south of the province. Castelo Branco makes a convenient base for seeing nearby Monsanto, Idanha-a-Velha and surrounding villages which lack accommodation for visitors, but has little else to offer. The history of Castelo Branco goes back to Roman times, but because of its proximity to the Spanish frontier most traces of its past have been eradicated by centuries of looting and sacking. This largely modern town has an old quarter of modest proportions in the shadow of the ruined castle.

General Information

The *Turismo* is in the center of town at Alameda da Liberdade, ((072) 21002, and can supply information on Castelo Branco and

the surrounding area. Outside Castelo Branco, you may find another office open in Penamacor at the Rua 25 de Abril, ((077) 34316.

What to See and Do

Take a walk around the older part of the town, and go up to the ruins of the **Templar castle** where there's a **miradouro** (viewing point) set amid pleasant gardens. Be sure to visit the eighteenth-century **Jardim do Antiga Paço Episcopal** (Gardens of the old Episcopal Palace). Small and rather quaint, its paths, stairways and pools are lined with statues of saints, apostles, Portuguese kings and the unwelcome Spanish rulers (much smaller than the others), personifications of zodiac signs, the seasons, and the Virtues. Empty plinths recall those statues looted by the French invaders.

The Episcopal Palace itself dates from the sixteenth century and now contains the **Museu de Francisco Tavares Proenca Júnior**, ((072) 24277, which has a collection of prehistoric and Roman relics, Flemish tapestries, sixteenth-century and modern Portuguese art, antique furniture, and some old examples of the embroidered bedcovers or *colchas* for which Castelo Branco is famous. These are embroidered with brightly colored silks in old designs which sometimes incorporate motifs symbolizing love and marriage. The museum incorporates a school where the art is taught and practiced.

Other places to peruse in the area include **São Vicente da Beira** which lies 30 km (19 miles) north of Castelo Branco, and a little to the northeast, **Castelo Novo**, with its granite buildings and cobbled streets. If you would like to spend a night in the area other than in Castelo Branco, try **Alpedrinha**, one of the larger villages about four kilometers (two-and-a-half miles) north of Castelo Novo, where some grand old houses hide in the maze of streets twisting away from the main road. Thirty kilometers (19 miles) east of Alpedrinha and 43 km (27 miles) northeast of Castelo Branco along the N223, **Penamacor** sits up on a hill and harbors a medieval village within its ancient castle. Continuing northward, twelfth-century walls enclose the old quarter of

---

Castelo Branco OPPOSITE is a good base for exploring the mountains and isolated villages of the Beiras.

quarter of **Sortelha**, which overlooks the fertile valley of the River Côa.

Where to Stay

In Castelo Branco accommodation is limited: the choice is between the **Pensão Arriana**, Avenida 1° de Maio N°18, 6000 Castelo Branco, ((072) 21634/7, fax: (072) 31884, where rooms are simply furnished but all have private baths, telephones, and televisions; or the **Pensão Caravela**, Rua do Saibreiro N°24, ((072) 23939/40, basic but clean, some rooms having bathrooms. Both are inexpensive.

How to Get There

The railway line running through Castelo Branco links Lisbon with Guarda, calling at Castelo Branco and Alpedrinha. Some trains continue to Vilar Formoso on the border where there are connections to Salamanca in Spain. If you are traveling from Coimbra you need to take the train to Guarda and change there for Castelo Branco; from Porto you change at Pampilhosa for Guarda. Express buses run to Castelo Branco from Coimbra, from Lisbon, and from Porto.

In Alpedrinha, there is the **Estalagem São Jorge**, Largo da Misericórdia N°5, 6095 Alpedrinha, ((075) 57154 or 57354, which has a good restaurant and 10 rooms, all with telephone and bath. You have another choice: the lovely **Casa de Barreiro**, Largo das Escolas, ((075) 57120, a large rambling house offering accommodation under the TURIBAB scheme. Both are inexpensive.

Where to Eat

Castelo Branco has several restaurants, and most of them serve traditional fare at inexpensive prices. Specialties of the region are *cabrito* (kid), as well as the locally produced goat's cheese.

Castelo Branco lies 58 km (36 miles) west of the border town of Segura, and 249 km (155 miles) northeast of Lisbon. If you're driving, take the A1 from Lisbon for 103 km (64 miles) then turn eastwards on to the N3 until the junction with the N18-IP2, where you continue northwards. Castelo Branco lies 103 km (64 miles) south of Guarda along the N18-IP2.

If you are planning excursions out to the villages, there are trains to Alpedrinha from Castelo Branco.

MONSANTO AND IDANHA-A-VELHA

Forty-eight kilometers (30 miles) northeast of Castelo Branco are the eerie and isolated remains of Idanha-a-Velha, once a Celtic settlement, which in 16 BC became the site of the Roman city of Egitania, rebuilt by the Visigoths in the sixth century and said to be the birthplace of King Wamba. Abandoned in the early fifteenth century because of a 100-year-long plague of ants, it remains more or less untouched and unexcavated. An ancient **basili**ca, in part Visigoth, contains a collection of fragments of statues found on the site and stones bearing Roman inscriptions. A small chapel contains finds of Roman coins and pottery.

do Castelo. Its origins lie in a long siege which took place centuries ago, in Moorish or possibly Roman times. The hungry but defiant inhabitants threw the last of their food over the castle walls—a fatted calf with its stomach filled with wheat—presumably to convince the enemy that they had abundant supplies or as a sign of determination. Either way, the ploy worked and the siege was lifted. Commemorating this act of fortitude during the Festa, the women throw a calf made of roses and jugs of flowers from the walls.

The most well-known and photogenic of the Beira Baixa's fortified villages has to be **Monsanto**, 50 km (31 miles) northeast of Castelo Branco and just 15 km (eight miles) northeast of Idanha-a-Velha. Clinging to a steep rocky hill, it has withstood many a battle and exudes an air of primitive magic. The granite houses, many of which are very basic, are built between or into the rocks. Looking down on the village from the ancient stone fortifications, it is difficult to tell where the hill ends and the walls begin. Climb to the castle for some wonderful views across the surrounding plain.

In May, Monsanto is the scene of a strange ritual that forms part of the **Festa**

How to Get There

Two buses a day leave Castelo Branco for Monsanto and one leaves for Idanha-a-Velha. A problem arises because the daily Idanho-a-Velha bus returns immediately to Castelo Branco; this all highlights the fact that by far the best way to explore this region is by car.

IN AND AROUND GUARDA

The town of Guarda lies 352 km (219 miles) northeast of Lisbon at the northeastern edge of the Serra da Estrêla and at an altitude of

"Cold, rich, strong and ugly" Guarda OPPOSITE and ABOVE is at the heart of a high, rocky region where age-old farming methods are still practiced.

1,000 m (3,281 ft), it is Portugal's highest town, its one and only distinction. Trains run here from Spain, crossing the border at Vilar Formoso only 47 km (29 miles) away, from Lisbon, and from Coimbra. It offers a fair range of accommodation, making a good base for touring the villages to the north as well as the lovely Serra da Estrêla. The Portuguese say damningly of Guarda that it is *fria, farta, forte, e feia*: cold, rich, strong, and ugly.

General Information

The *Turismo* is near the cathedral in the Edificio da Câmara at Praça Luís de Camões, ((071) 22251. Outside Guarda, and useful if you are touring the villages, there is a *Turismo* in the border town of Vilar Formoso, close to Almeida, ((071) 52202, and another at Trancoso open only during the summer.

What to See and Do

The main sight is the **Sé**, or Cathedral, a somber building at the center of the town founded in the fourteenth century; it took until the sixteenth to complete. The granite exterior, with its twin octagonal towers, pinnacles and particularly threatening gargoyles gives it a fortress-like air, and although it was worked on by the sons of Mateus Fernandes (the architect of Batalha) and later by Boytac (who worked on Jerónimos), in no way does it rival either of these buildings. Inside, twisted Manueline columns mix with Gothic and renaissance features. The gilded altarpiece in the chancel is an elaborately carved bas-relief attributed to the sixteenth century French sculptor Jean de Rouen.

Excursions

North and northeast of Guarda the landscape is a mixture of wild countryside and fertile valleys scattered with small towns and villages, many of them set high on hillsides or outcrops of rock and fortified against Spanish invasion by the prudent King Dinis. Among these are **Castelo Bom**, **Castelo Mendo**, **Castelo Rodrigo**, **Castelo Melhor**, and **Marialva**, all within easy driving distance of Guarda.

The N16-N221 runs northeast of Guarda to the fortified town of **Pinhel**, 33 km (29 miles) north of the city and close to the Spanish border. The vineyards and wine co-operative are a reminder of one of the town's main products: Pinhel wine, similar in some ways to the smooth Dão red. The old town itself is well preserved, including several noble houses decorated with coats-of-arms.

From here it is a scenic drive across a lonely plateau to **Almeida** 29 km (18 miles) southeast of Pinhel and 40 km (25 miles) northeast of Guarda. Located 10 km (six miles) from the Spanish frontier, this quiet little town was once an important military stronghold, rendered particularly striking by its perfectly preserved 16-point fortifications in double star form, built in the eighteenth century and said to have been completed by Vauban himself. Understandably the town has attracted tourists in recent years, and a *pousada* has been built into the town walls.

Forty-seven kilometers (29 miles) northwest of Guarda the medieval town of **Trancoso** is still partly enclosed by stout walls and dominated by a squat **castle tower** at the northeast corner. Beflowered balconies overlook the arcaded lower stories of the buildings, and coats-of-arms adorn some of the nobler dwellings. Trancoso seems greatly to have appealed to King Dinis, for he married the 12-year-old Isabel of Aragón here in 1282 and gave her the town as a wedding present.

If you have any film left in your camera or fuel in your tank, consider going on to **Penedono**, 29 km (18 miles) north of Trancoso. Sitting on a craggy hilltop, the granite village lies below a triangular sixteenth-century castle whose angular crenelations on the turrets impart a fierce appearance: it is believed by some to have been the home of the legendary Alvaro Gonçalves Coutinho, otherwise known as *o Magrico*, whose chivalrous deeds were recalled by Camões in *Os Lusíadas*.

Where to Stay

Hotel Turismo da Guarda, Avenida Coronel Orlindo de Carvalho, 6300 Guarda, ((071) 212205/6, fax: (071) 212204, is Guarda's top hotel. It's a large, centrally-located, traditional building with good facilities and a large restaurant. Prices are mostly mid-

Sleepy, tumbledown little Almeida OPPOSITE belies an action-packed past as a fortified frontier town.

range. Moving downmarket, the **Pensão Gonçalves**, Rua Augusto Gil N°17, ((071) 212501, is friendly, clean, and a boon for the budget-conscious. Under the TURIHAB scheme there is the **Solar de Alarção**, Rua Dom Miguel de Alarção, N°25-27, ((071) 21275 or 24392, a splendid seventeenth-century manor house in the old part of town. Prices are inexpensive to mid-range.

Around the villages, the choicest place to stay — indeed one of the very few — is in Almeida at the aforementioned **Pousada da Senhora das Neves**, 6350 Almeida, ((071) 54283/90, fax: (071) 54320. This relatively new building conforms to the high standards of the *pousada* system. Prices go from inexpensive to mid range depending on the season.

Where to Eat

Guarda has quite a few places to choose from. The two best are the **Belo Horizonte**, Largo São Vicente N°1, ((071) 211454, and **O Telheiro** on the edge of the city at Estrada Nacional 16, ((071) 212493, a large restaurant with magnificent views. Inexpensive.

How to Get There

Two main railway lines link Guarda with Lisbon: one via Coimbra, while the other runs through the Beira Baixa stopping at Castelo Branco, Alpedrinha, Fundão and Covilhã, where you may have to change. People traveling from Porto need to change at Pampilhosa for Guarda. Guarda's railway station is about three kilometers (two miles) out of town but a frequent bus service links it to the center.

Express buses run to Guarda from both Lisbon and Porto, and an international bus service linking Lisbon with Paris calls at Coimbra and Guarda. Local buses connect Guarda with Viseu and Covilhã. Places mentioned under Excursions are best explored by car, as buses from Guarda and between the towns are infrequent and trains non-existent.

Guarda is 352 km (219 miles) northeast of Lisbon, and if you're driving, follow the route described for Castelo Branco, continuing north on the N18. From Coimbra it is about 159 km (99 miles) along the N2-IP3 to Viseu, where you head east along the N16-IP5 to Guarda.

SERRA DA ESTRÊLA

The poetically named Serra da Estrêla (Mountains of the Star) is Portugal's highest mountain range, with its highest point, the Torre, touching 2,000 m (6,562 ft). The lower wooded slopes are cut by deep, mostly cultivated valleys, while the granite crags above sometimes take on eerily human forms. In winter snow settles on the peaks, giving rise to Portugal's newest sport, skiing. Don't get too excited as there isn't always enough snow, but summer in the Serra offers plenty of other sporting possibilities such as climbing, walking, and trout fishing.

The town of **Covilhã** in the southeastern foothills close to the Zêzere Valley on the road to Lisbon is regarded as the major gateway to the Serra, and a good base for excursions. A wool center with several mills and a population of around 22,000, this charming old town lies upon the steep mountainside and commands some excellent views. A short drive or bus journey along the N339 takes you to the winter sports resort of **Penhas da Saúde**, 11 km (seven miles) to the northwest, which also makes a good starting point for hiking or climbing. Penhas da Saude is near the lofty **Torre** with unbeatable views of the region, although the welter of souvenir stalls at the summit slightly mars the romance of the scene.

Between Penhas da Saúde and the Torre, a turning off the N339 takes you along the Zêzere Valley to the small spa town of **Caldas de Manteigas**, and then on to the larger town of **Manteigas**, one of the prettiest in the Serra. If you come here be sure to make the short excursion to **Poço do Inferno** (Hell's Well), a wooded gorge with a waterfall that freezes over in winter. North of Manteigas along the road to Gouveia there is a welcoming *pousada*.

Gouveia and **Seia**, both on the western side of the mountain range, are points of access to the **Parque Natural Serra da Estrêla**, being served by public transport. Another gateway to the park is **Celorico da Beira** at the northern tip, with an impressive castle. The medieval town of **Linhares** sits upon a rocky outcrop overlooking the Upper Mondego Valley 16 km (10 miles) southwest of Celorico. Take a walk along the town walls for some excellent views, and then wander among the old granite houses, some of which date from the fifteenth century. The two churches — the **Misericórdia church** and the **Parish church** — have fine examples of Portuguese primitive paintings, some of which are believed to be the work of Grão Vasco.

The **Serra de Açor** is a southwestern extension of the Serra da Estrêla. One of its most picturesque villages is **Piódão**, where houses built of shale stand on a terraced hillside, looking for all the world as if they had sprouted out of it.

Northeast of Piódão is the village of **Avô**, worth visiting for its setting along the steep bank of the River Alva, spanned by a graceful arched bridge and backed by wooded hills.

General Information

In Covilhã the *Turismo* is at the Praça do Municipo, ((075) 22170 or 22151. Gouveia has one at Avenida 1° de Maio, ((038) 42185, and there is another at Seia in the Largo do Mercado, ((038) 22272.

Where to Stay

Covilhã has several *pensãos* to choose from. Among the better ones are the **Residencial Santa Eufêmia**, Sítio da Palmatória, 6200 Covilhã, ((075) 26081, a newish and inexpensive place out of the center of town, and the **Pensão Restaurante A Regional**, Rua das Flores N°4, (075) 322596, excellent value with decent rooms (some of which have private bath) and a good restaurant. There is also the **Hotel Turismo**, a modern establishment with 60 rooms, ((075) 323843, fax: (075) 313013.

In Caldas de Manteigas the inexpensive **Hotel de Manteigas**, 6260 Caldas de Manteigas, ((075) 98514/27, is a spa hotel with fitness facilities and tennis courts. In Manteigas itself there are a few *pensãos* and also the **Casa de São Roque**, Rua de Santo António N°63, 6260 Manteigas, ((075) 98125, a Turismo de Habitação place in the center of town. About 13 km (eight miles) north of Manteigas the **Pousada de São Lourenço**, 6260 Manteigas, ((075) 981321, fax: (075) 981664, is a modern building admirably situated for mountain views, with the

warm, lodge-like feel you need at the end of a good hike. Prices here vary between inexpensive and mid-range depending on the season.

How to Get There

Internal flights serve Covilhã from Porto and Lisbon. Trains running between Guarda and Lisbon stop at Covilhã, and a bus service connects Coimbra, Viseu, Guarda, and Castelo Branco to Covilhã. Buses also run between Celorico da Beira, Gouveia, and Linhares, and between Seia and Corvilha via a southern route. At weekends there is a bus service between Covilhã and Penhas a Saúde

For drivers, the best access points to the park are through Gouveia, Seia, Covilhã, and Valhelas (southwest of Guarda) which link easily to the most scenic roads through the Serra da Estrêla.

IN AND AROUND VISEU

Viseu, set in pine forested hills alongside the River Pavia, is the capital of Beira Alta, deserving of the title *Antigua et Nobilissima Cidade* (Ancient and Most Noble city). It lies about 292 km (181 miles) north of Lisbon. The medieval core is centered around a square at the city's highest point, within the scant remains of the old walls. In the sixteenth century it was the center of a school of painters led by Gaspar Vaz and Vasco Fernandes (remembered as Grão Vasco: the Great Vasco), who was influenced by the Flemish school. Viseu continued to grow into an agricultural center, its wealth evidenced by its fine Renaissance and baroque buildings.

This center of viticulture is famous for the smooth and aromatic red Dão wines. It's a good base for exploring the cluster of ancient, scenic villages within a manageable radius of the city, if you have your own transport. While you can stay in or around Viseu, it is an easy car trip from Coimbra if you are based there.

General Information

The *Turismo* is in the modern part of Viseu on the Avenida Gulbenkian, ((032) 279994, not far south of the Praça da República.

What to See and Do

The old town can be entered in grand style through a fifteenth-century gateway, the **Porto do Soar**, and is laid out around the dignified **Praça da Sé** (Cathedral Square). Here you will see the somber twin towers of the **Sé**, built between the thirteenth and eighteenth centuries; although predominantly Romanesque, it embodies the usual range of styles. Upon entering, the golden colors come as a pleasant surprise. The most notable feature is the Manueline ribbing of the vaulted ceiling, carved in the form of knotted ropes and supported by Gothic pillars. A gilt baroque altarpiece replaces the earlier paintings of Grão Vasco, now located in the neighboring museum.

The ground level of the renaissance cloisters are tiled with eighteenth-century *azulejos* and on the upper floor the old chapterhouse now houses the cathedral's **treasury**, which has a couple of thirteenth-century Limoges enamel caskets, a twelfth-century Bible, and some other interesting odds and ends. The **sacristy's** ceiling is painted with satyrs, strange animals, birds, and flowers, and in the *coro alto* they are carved into the choir stalls, further celebration of the Voyages of Discovery.

Next door to the Sé is the **Grão Vasco Museum**, ((032) 26249, housed within the former episcopal palace and filled with paintings by Grão Vasco and others of the Viseu school. One room is set aside for his 14-panel work depicting scenes from the life of Christ, which once graced the high altar of the cathedral. Spanish works, nineteenth- and twentieth-century Portuguese paintings, and a collection of sculpture from the thirteenth to the eighteenth centuries form the museum's collection. Open from 10 am to 1 pm and from 2 to 5 pm, closed on Mondays. Admission is free on Saturdays and Sundays.

While the Sé's exterior belies its more interesting interior, the reverse is true of the eighteenth-century **Misericórdia Church** just across the square. Typically Portuguese baroque with whitewash and granite, elegantly twirled and scrolled, its form is pleasingly symmetrical with a tower at each end. Should it be closed, comfort yourself with the knowledge that you have seen the best part.

Otherwise, the main attractions are the narrow streets and alleyways of the old quarter around the Cathedral square, with their mixture of sixteenth- and eighteenth-century houses ranging from the grand to the very humble. Those running south are lined with restaurants and shops selling local produce and crafts.

The modern part of town centers around the **Praça da República**, commonly called the Rossio, is southwest of the Sé, where a **market** is held every tuesday at the junction of the Rua Formoso and Rua de Luís Ferreira. In September each year the city bristles with life as the **Feira de São Mateus** comes to town.

Excursions

The town of **São Pedro do Sul** lies 22 km (14 miles) northwest of Viseu along the N16, in a verdant riverside setting amid orchards and vineyards. Just four kilometers (two-and-a-half miles) southwest, **Termas de São Pedro do Sul** is believed by some to be the oldest spa in Portugal; the ruined Roman

baths near the new spa are evidence of its continuity. The setting close to the River Vouga among pine trees and with a fair choice of *pensãos* and hotels, is itself a tonic.

The charming town of **Vouzela**, three kilometers (two miles) south of Termas and west of Viseu, sits on a hillside overlooking the lush Vouga Valley. There man-made beauties equal natural ones: several remarkable buildings remain, manor houses amongst them. The **Misericórdia Church** faced with *azulejos* stands out, as does the curved facade of the **Chapel of São Frei Gil**. Beautiful in its simplicity, the thirteenth-century **Igreja Matriz** (Parish Church) fuses the Gothic with the Romanesque. It is set in peaceful gardens, its doorway and rose window screened by the bell tower that rises before it. Note the gutter supports carved with human faces. And don't leave without trying the town's specialty, *pasteis de Vouzela*, sweet egg pastries.

Caramulo lies 43 km (27 miles) southwest of Viseu, some 800 m (2,625 ft) up in wooded Serra do Caramulo where the clear air is reputedly good for respiratory problems.

This is the unlikely location for an exceptional museum, the **Fundação Abel de Lacerda**, ((032) 861270, with an equally unlikely combination of exhibits. The bequest of Portuguese philanthropist Abel de Lacerda, the museum houses paintings by the so-called Portuguese Primitives including work by Grão Vasco, and an exceptional collection of nineteenth- and twentieth-century work by, among others, Picasso, Dali, Dufy, Léger and Chagall. There are exhibits of furniture, sculpture, archaeological finds, porcelain, and Tournai tapestries bearing fanciful interpretations of the arrival of the Portuguese in India. The eclecticism doesn't end there: on the lower levels is a collection of vintage motorcycles and cars.

A 40-minute walk up the road from the village brings you to the top of **Carmulinho**, the highest point in the Serra, with some dazzling vistas. If you want to stay on, there is a good *pensão* in the village and the **Pousada de São Jerónimo** on a nearby ridge.

The busy agricultural town of **Mangualde** lies 15 km (nine miles) east of Viseu. Its old quarter is a warren of narrow, twisting medieval streets. At its heart is the seventeenth-century **Palácio des Condes de Anadia** (Palace of the Counts of Anadia), pink, baroque and open to the public from roughly 10 am to noon and from 2 to 6 pm.

Santar, 15 km (nine miles) south of Viseu and once known as the Court of the Beiras, is a rewarding side trip. Many of its manor houses have retained their elegance.

Where to Stay

The top-rated hotel in Viseu is the centrally placed **Grão Vasco**, Rua Gaspar Barreiros, 3500 Viseu, ((032) 423511, fax: (032) 27047, with lots of comforts including a swimming pool. Mid-range prices. For something different, and to my mind preferable, head for the inexpensive **Pensão Rossio Parque**, Rua Soar de Cima Nº55, ((032) 422085, an old-fashioned establishment.

In Termas de São Pedro do Sul there are several inexpensive to mid-range prices hotels and *pensãos*. One of them is the **Pousada de São Jerónimo**, 3475 Caramulo, ((032) 861291, taking full advantage of the splendid views and clear air, with appearance slightly reminiscent of a Swiss chalet.

Where to Eat

There's no shortage of good eating in Viseu, where one or two establishments offer *fado* entertainment, and locally produced Dão wines are much in evidence. **O Cortico**, Rua August Hilário N°47, ((032) 423853, is generally regarded as the best place in town. It certainly is well patronized, so book first. **Trave Negra**, Rua do Loureiros N°40, ((032) 26138, is a close contender, being popular for its very good traditional food served by candlelight. Prices for both vary from inexpensive to moderate.

How to Get There

Strangely, trains no longer run to Viseu; much to the distress of railroad enthusiasts the world over, the scenic narrow-gauge line was axed a few years ago. You can travel from Lisbon or Guarda by rail only as far as Nelas where there is a bus connection for the remainder of the journey. If you are arriving from Porto or Coimbra, you will need to change at Aveiro for Sernada or at Pampilhosa for Nelas and complete the journey by bus. Bus services also run to Viseu from Lisbon, from Coimbra, and from Porto.

Viseu lies 85 km (53 miles) northeast of Coimbra, from which you drive north on the N1, turning on to the N2-IP3 to Viseu after about four kilometers (two-and-a-half miles). From Lisbon it is 292 km (181 miles) north along the A1-IP1 to the point just north of Coimbra where you turn on to the N2-IP3.

COIMBRA

The ancient capital of Beira Litoral and one-time capital of Portugal is 196 km (122 miles) from Lisbon, 117 km (73 miles) from Porto, on a steep hillside overlooking the Mondego River. This is the seat of Portugal's first university (and one of the world's oldest) and its main center of renaissance art. Portugal's most prestigious university remains the source of much of Coimbra's charm. Camões studied here and the city has its own strain of *fado* music, more intellectual and romantic than Lisbon's.

All this aside, Coimbra is a commercial center with thriving textile and handicraft industries; over the years some unsympa-

thetic and often downright ugly building has gone on here, cheek to cheek with structures of great antiquity. Don't be put off by this aspect of Coimbra or its traffic: after parking, make your way through the old section, and you will see beauty and charm everywhere.

BACKGROUND

To the Romans who had established a city at nearby Conimbriga, it was *Aeminium*, until it acquired a new name, Coimbra — a corrupted version of Conimbriga — as the Roman settlement declined. Between the ninth and eleventh centuries, Moors and Christians fought over it until 1064 when it finally came under Christian control. In 1143 on the accession of Portugal's first king Afonso Henriques, the capital of Portugal was moved here from Guimarães until around 1250.

The famous university was founded in 1290 in the new capital, Lisbon but later moved to Coimbra, then back again to Lisbon before settling finally in Coimbra in 1537. Jesuits and teachers from other great universities arrived in droves; in the sixteenth century the Coimbra school of sculpture developed here under Italian-inspired French sculptors Nicolas Chanterène and Jean de Rouen, who joined forces with the Portuguese João and Diogo de Castilho.

GENERAL IFORMATION

The main tourist office for the central region is Regiao de Turismo do Centro, Largo da Portages, 3000 Coimbra, ((039) 33028, fax: (039) 25576.

WHAT TO SEE AND DO

The **Velha Universidade** (Old University) crowns the hilltop on which the old city is built. To get there you must weave through a maze of steep and narrow streets. If this is too much of a hardship there are plenty of taxis around, but be sure to walk back through this most lovely part of Coimbra. Entering through the seventeenth-century **Porta Férrea** you find yourself in the courtyard known as the **Patio das Escolas** around which the principal old buildings are arranged. A large eighteenth-century clock known as *cabra* — the goat — stands in the courtyard as does King João III, who was responsible for returning the university to Coimbra in the sixteenth century and making a gift of this palace to it.

To the right, a fancy staircase leads up to the **Sala dos Capelos**, a hall with a seventeenth-century painted and gilded ceiling, hung with portraits of Portuguese kings who lend suitable gravity to the graduation ceremonies and other academic rituals here. The catwalk balcony has wonderful views over the city.

To the left of the courtyard a doorway heavily emblazoned with the coat-of-arms of King João V leads into Coimbra's magnificent **library**, a glittering piece of early eighteenth-century baroque that outshines that of Mafra, built by King João in 1724. Its three rooms lead one into another, at the end of which hangs a portrait of its benefactor, King João, theatrically framed by carved wooden curtains held open by cherubs.

Nearby, in what was once the archbishop's palace, is the **Museu Nacional Machado de Castro**, ((039) 23727. It is worth a visit just to look around the sixteenth-century building and see the decoration in some of the upper rooms. The palace was built over subterranean vaulted passages constructed

by the Romans, which now form the basement. The sculpture, spanning the fifteenth to the eighteenth centuries, is exhibited on the ground floor and some of the first floor.

The first floor also contains liturgical gold and silverware, jewelry, ceramics, oriental carpets, porcelain, and Portuguese and Flemish art spanning the same period. The museum is open Tuesdays to Sundays, 9:30 am to 12:30 pm and 2 to 5 pm. Admission is free on Sundays.

The nearby **Sé Nova** (New Cathedral) can be skipped in favor of the more interest-

ing Romanesque **Sé Velha** (Old Cathedral), a fortress-like place dating from the twelfth century. The renaissance portal added in the sixteenth century is believed to be the work of Jean de Rouen, but is in bad condition. The cavernous interior has been returned to its original simplicity and the eye is therefore all the more drawn to the gilded wooden altarpiece carved by Flemish artists in the early sixteenth century.

The streets surrounding the cathedral have bars frequented by students where you may be able to hear some *fado* music. Look out for the **Paço de Sub-Ripas**, on Rua

Coimbra University ABOVE is one of Europe's oldest seats of learning. Its library LEFT houses more than a million tomes.

Sub-Ripas, a sixteenth-century residence built in Manueline style and incorporating part of the old city walls. The doors and windows are Manueline and the walls covered with bas-reliefs by Jean de Rouen. As this is a private residence you must be content with looking at it from the outside.

Continue down through the city to the **Mosteiro de Santa Cruz**, a sixteenth-century Augustinian Monastery where there are numerous examples of the Coimbra school of sculpture on display. The renaissance entrance is the work of Chanterène

and Diogo de Castilho, now sadly damaged by pollution and weathering. Afonso Henriques and Sancho I, the first two kings of Portugal, lie here in richly carved tombs on either side of the high altar, and some wonderful gilded wood carving in the stalls of the *coro alto* incorporates images of Vasco da Gama's voyages. Open from 9 am to noon and from 2 to 6 pm; ((039) 22941.

Over the bridge and just off the bridge road is one of Coimbra's strangest sights, the **Convento de Santa Clara-a-Velha**. This fourteenth-century Gothic church was abandoned in the late seventeenth century because of flooding from the Mondego. It is now a ruin partially submerged in the silt and waters of the river its beautiful interior has an almost Romanesque simplicity.

The church was founded by Queen Isabel, at whose hands gold turned to roses. That may not sound the right way round for a miracle, but according to legend her husband did not entirely approve of her great generosity with gold. When he accosted her during one of her charitable sorties, she said,

not quite truthfully, that her apron was full of flowers. The king insisted on seeing what it was that she carried, and miraculously her apron was indeed full of roses.

On a nearby hill the **Santa Clara-a-Nova** (New Convent of St. Clare) looks down on the river with some excellent views of Coimbra. Built in the seventeenth century as a replacement for the old convent, New is something of a misnomer. These days it is partly used as a barracks and houses a military museum, and despite some glittering baroque carving it has acquired a slightly martial air. It lacks the simple beauty of its precursor, but go there to see the original fourteenth-century stone tomb of Queen Isabel, Coimbra's patron saint, removed from the old convent and stationed behind a grille. Her statue shows her in the plain garments of a Poor Clare nun with her dogs beside her. She now lies in the elaborate silver tomb on the high altar, and it is said that when her body was transferred it was redolent of the perfume of flowers, showing no sign of decay although she had died some 300 years previously, a sure sign of sainthood. Opening hours are from 9 am to 12:30 pm and from 2 to 5 pm. The convent is closed on Sundays and Mondays.

There are many more churches and chapels to see, if you desire. To get the feel of Coimbra you could easily wander the streets for a couple of days, listening to *fado* music, relaxing in cafés, *pastelarias*, or bars, and watching life go by.

WHERE TO STAY

Surprisingly, there is not much choice, but here is a selection of what's on offer.

Mid-range

Coimbra's grandest hotel is the three star **Hotel Astória**, Avenida Emidio Navarro Nº21, 3000 Coimbra, ((039) 22055 or 22229, fax: (039) 22057, a 1930s building overlooking the Mondego River and Santa Clara, edged with balconies and topped with a blue cupola, the inside a well-preserved 'thirties time warp. The restaurant offers the rare opportunity of tasting the famous Buçaco wines made on the premises of the Astoria's big sister, the Buçaco Palace Hotel in the

Forest of Buçaco (see page 000. There's nothing else in Coimbra to touch it.

Coimbra's only four-star hotel is the very modern **Hotel Tivoli Coimbra**, Rua João Machado N°4, ((039) 26934, fax: (039) 26827, with 90 rooms, 10 suites, and an arresting range of facilities, given the general standard of accommodation here. It has a health club, swimming pool, and sauna.

Inexpensive

Residencial Larbelo, Largo da Portagem N°33, ((039) 29092, is on a main square down

serves good local and continental food to the accompaniment of *fado* music. **Piscinas**, Piscinas Municipais, ((039) 717013, is a large restaurant with great views, located in a sports center. The food is again a mixture of local and continental and is considered some of the best in town. **Dom Pedro**, Avenida Emidio Navarro N°58, ((039) 29108, offers an upmarket setting and a similar menu. In contrast, **O Alfredo**, on the other side of the Santa Clara bridge, is much more low-key. It serves traditional fare, with seafood being a specialty.

by the river: the rooms are simply furnished, all with private bath. The **Pensão Internacional**, Avenida Emidio Navarro N°4, ((039) 25503, is close to the railway station with a down-at-heel grandeur. Rooms are clean but basic and do not have private bathrooms. The **Pensão Alentejana**, Rua Dr. António Henrique Seco, ((039) 25924 or 25903, is a villa with great character offering rooms with private baths and telephones.

WHERE TO EAT

Moderate

Trovador, Praça Sé Velha, ((039) 25475, is decorated in traditional Coimbran style and

Inexpensive

Zé Manuel, Beco do Forno N°12, ((039) 23790, is a rather trendy spot with a noisy bistro atmosphere, and **Pinto d'Ouro**, Avenida João das Regras N°68, ((039) 44123, is another favorite serving regional food, with chicken the specialty.

HOW TO GET THERE

There are three train stations in Coimbra: Coimbra A ((039/27263), Coimbra B ((039/ 24632), and Coimbra Parque (used mainly for local trains to Lousã). Coimbra A is most

The most extensive Roman remains ABOVE and OPPOSITE in Portugal, at Conimbriga south of Coimbra.

centrally positioned, but some trains stop only at Coimbra B, north of the town center, in which case you can easily pick up a connection to Coimbra A. Trains run frequently from Porto and from Lisbon's Santa Apolónia station to Coimbra B, those from Porto sometimes making a train change at Pampilhosa.

Express buses run regularly to Coimbra from Lisbon, Porto, and also from the major towns and cities, arriving at the bus station in Avenida Fernão Magalhães, ((039) 27081. The international bus service connecting Lisbon with Paris also stops here.

Partial excavation has so far uncovered houses, pools, fountains, baths, heating and cooling systems, and some exquisite mosaics. The remains of a hastily erected defensive wall cut through the city, evidence of a desperate effort by the inhabitants to fend off Suevi attack. They failed, and the city was taken in 465 AD, her citizens either killed or enslaved. Over the years that followed people gravitated towards the nearby settlement of *Aeminius*, present-day Coimbra, and Conimbriga was eventually abandoned.

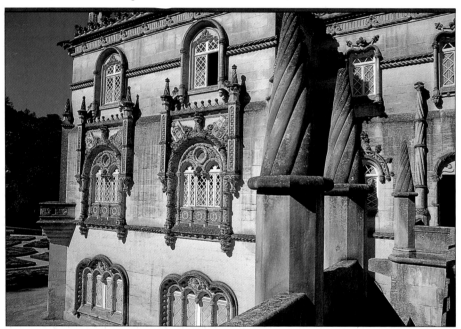

Coimbra is 196 km (122 miles) north of Lisbon and 117 km (73 miles) south of Porto, just four kilometers (two-and-a-half miles) east of the Lisbon-Porto motorway, the A1-IP1, which makes driving from either direction fairly straightforward.

AROUND COIMBRA

CONIMBRIGA

Conimbriga is Portugal's largest and most impressive Roman site, just 15 km (nine miles) southwest of Coimbra, where you can see the remains of a Roman city dating from between the first and fifth centuries AD.

A well-laid out museum houses artifacts unearthed at the site, giving a fascinating insight into how this sophisticated city functioned. Opening times on Tuesday to Saturday are from 10 am to 1 pm and from 2 pm to 5 pm (until 6 pm in peak season), call ((039) 941177 for information.

The museum has a good café, but for more substantial fare make a short detour to the town of **Condeixa-a-Nova**, just two kilometers (one mile) outside Conimbriga. Worth seeing there is its eighteenth- and nineteenth-century houses, many of them emblazoned with coats-of-arms. It's finest building is the **Solar Sotto Maior**, a baroque mansion which has hosted royal visitors in its time.

There is an infrequent bus service from Coimbra to Conimbriga, and a more frequent one running to Condeixa-a-Nova, two kilometers (one mile) away. If you take the bus to Condeixa but don't fancy the walk to the site, it won't cost much to take a taxi there.

LOUSÃ

The village of Lousã lies 25 km (15 miles) southeast of Coimbra, at the foothills of the wild and wooded **Serra da Lousã** by the River Arouce; with a *pensão* to stay at, it

hectares (250 acres) and makes a delicious escape from the heat and noise of Coimbra just 27 km (17 miles) away. If your trip to Portugal brings you anywhere near this part of the country, you must visit it. Ideally, stay at the Buçaco Palace Hotel, but if you can't afford the expensive rates try to have dinner or lunch there. Nearby Luso has plenty of reasonably priced accommodation.

Background
The forest's religious connections began in the sixth century when Benedictine monks

makes a good base for exploring the Serra. A scenic pathway leads up and out of the village to a ruined castle above the surrounding forests, and to the nearby **Sanctuary of Nossa Senhora de Piedade**. As befits such a romantic ruin it is shrouded in legends.

Trains run from Coimbra to Lousã, but for the trips into the Serra you will need either a car or walking boots.

BUÇACO AND LUSO

The **Forest of Buçaco** on the northern slopes of the Serra da Buçaco is one of Portugal's most enchanting sights. At its heart lies the magnificent **Buçaco Palace**, now one of Europe's finest hotels. The forest covers 101

made a hermitage in its depths, far from worldly distractions. In the seventeenth century Carmelite monks built a wall around it and made themselves a monastery. They then busied themselves with the planting of new and exotic trees from all over the world, among them bay trees, maples, giant ferns, laurels, and huge Mexican cypresses. In such careful and devout hands the forest became famous; papal bulls were issued threatening excommunication to anyone who damaged so much as a leaf, and, mindful of the brothers' chastity, women were prohibited. (The text of the

Set in luxuriant forests, sybaritic Buçaco Palace OPPOSITE and ABOVE has been described as "the shadiest hotel in Portugal."

papal bulls is inscribed on the Coimbra Gate).

Buçaco's perfect peace was shattered when in September 1810, an English and Portuguese army of 30,000 under Wellington defeated Napoleon's larger force under Masséna at the Battle of Buçaco, which was fought on a ridge nearby. Things were probably never the same again, or at least not for very much longer, for in 1834 a decree was issued dissolving all religious orders in Portugal. So the forest passed into the hands of laymen who continued the tradition of

introducing new varieties of trees. Towards the end of the century an Italian architect, Luigi Manini, was commissioned to build a royal hunting lodge on the site of the Carmelite monastery. The neo-Manueline palace was not finished until 1907, by which time the monarchy was in its death throes; when the last of the Braganças had sailed away from Portugal the government gave permission for the royal chef to run the Buçaco Palace as a luxury hotel.

General Information

The *Turismo* is in Luso at Rua Emidio Navarro, ((031) 939133.

What to See and Do

Despite the stream of coach parties the luxuriant forest maintains its serenity, and walking along some of its hermitage-dotted pathways is a refreshing and calming experience. The Buçaco Palace Hotel and the *Turismo* in neighboring Luso can supply maps showing the various routes. One of the most beautiful sights is the **Fonte Fria**

(Cold Fountain) where a spring pours from a cave and cascades down a long stairway into a pool lined with magnolias.

The modest **Museu da Guerra Peninsular** (Peninsular War Museum) is close by the Porta da Rainha, with a special bias toward the Battle of Buçaco. Precious little is left of the old monastery, but close to the hotel the **monastery church** still stands with the cloister and cork-lined cells, one of which was used by Wellington on the eve of the battle.

Just outside the forest the spa town of Luso nestles in a valley, with a good collection of hotels. Luso is particularly popular with the Portuguese who come here to take the waters, said to be good for rheumatism, circulatory and metabolic disorders, and skin, kidney, and urinary problems. Pamper yourself with some of the wide range of treatments available — massage, physiotherapy, mud baths, etc. — all under medical supervision and reasonably priced. There are sports facilities: a jogging track near the lake, rowing, tennis courts, and swimming facilities.

Where to Stay

Hotel Palace do Buçaco, Mata Buçaco, Buçaco, 3050 Mealhada, ((031) 930204, fax: (031) 930509. Expensive.

The Palace is an unusual example of a mixture of styles being used to good effect, a magnificent confection of arcades and neo-Manueline encrustation that reaches its highest point in the lace-like filigree stonework of the restaurant terrace, but maintaining a human scale, shown in the discreet entrance. The public areas are grand but not intimidating, and the overall effect relaxing. The smell of polished chestnut pervades the hallways; the service, proper yet charming, is enhanced by the obvious pride that everyone takes in the place. The Palace retains its Edwardian atmosphere and the tranquillity of the forest around it.

There is a variety of large, airy rooms and suites with views of the palace and forest, all at luxury prices. An extensive room refurbishment project has recently been undertaken and their character is enhanced rather than diminished – a feat the Portuguese seem rather good at. In Luso there are three hotels, and the first choice is the **Grande Hotel da Termas**, Rua dos Banhos,

Luso, 3050 Mealhada, ℂ (031) 930450, fax: (031) 930168, a very smart art deco-style place next to the spa with an Olympic-sized swimming pool and sun terrace. Prices are mid-range. There are several pensãos, most of them pretty good and all inexpensive, or there is a TURIHAB place on a hill overlooking the town, the **Via Duparchy**, Rua José Duarte Figueiredo, Luso, 3050 Mealhada, ℂ (031) 93120, a nineteenth-century house set in a garden.

Where to Eat

The dining room at the **Hotel Palace do Buçaco** is open for lunch and dinner to non-guests, though it is best to make reservations. Its carved Gothic-style ceiling and Manueline terrace are a spectacle, the food top class, and the cellar renowned. The superb Buçaco wine is made and bottled exclusively on the premises and is exclusive to this and other hotels owned by Mr. Alexandre d'Almeida.

Most of the restaurants are attached to the hotels and *pensãos*, and the only independent restaurant seems to be the inexpensive **Restaurante O Cesteiro**, Rua Dr. Lúcio Pais Abranches, ℂ (031) 939360, on the edge of town.

How to Get There

Buses from Coimbra to Luso make a detour through the forest to the Palace Hotel, and express buses run from Coimbra to Luso. Buses from Coimbra to Viseu also make a detour from Luso through the forest to the Palace Hotel.

If you are driving from Coimbra, go 23 km (14 miles) up the A1 motorway to Mealhada then along the N234 to Luso. If you have a little more time to spare, take the longer, more scenic route (38 km or 24 miles) on the N110 along the Mondego to Penacova, and the N235 through the Serra de Buçaco to Luso.

FIGUEIRA DA FOZ AND ENVIRONS

The fishing port of Figueira da Foz lies 46 km (29 miles) west of Coimbra, where the River Mondego meets the sea. A working town, it has been a seaside resort since the nineteenth century. Its two-mile stretch of sandy beach is usually crowded and people come simply to bask, surf, and visit the casino. The **Museu Municipal do Dr. Santos Rocha** in the Rua Calouste Gulbenkian, ℂ (033) 24509, has particularly good archaeological displays and sections on the decorative arts, and the **Casa do Paço**, Largo Prof. Victor Guerra N°4, ℂ (033) 22159, is a grand old building with an excellent collection of Delft tiles.

To the north of Figueira is a long stretch of quiet coastline, but before you head off with your bucket and spade, remember that the beaches are often very exposed. **Praia de**

Mira, some 41 km (25 miles) north is another traditional fishing place with a wide sandy beach. You can still see oxen pulling in the nets, and houses built on stilts above the water.

The ancient town of **Montemór-O-Velho** down in the Mondego Valley, 17 km (11 miles) east of Figueira da Foz on the Coimbra road merits a detour. Once important in the defense of Coimbra, it is overlooked by the sprawling eleventh- and fourteenth-century castle, which although in ruins remains an impressive sight.

General Information

In Figueira da Foz the *Turismo* is on the seafront at Avenida 25 de Abril, ℂ (033) 22610.

Where to Stay

In Figueira da Foz there is a choice of large modern hotels and *pensãos*, although it does get very full in the summer. The only

The Ria OPPOSITE spreads its finger-linke inlets over the eerie marshes of the Beira Litoral, creating rich deposits of salt for panning ABOVE.

four-star hotel is the **Grande Hotel da Figueira**, Avenida 25 de Abril, 3080 Figuei-ra da Foz, ((033) 22146/7/8, fax: (033) 22420, looking on to the beach. It has an Olympic-sized swimming pool and guests have free access to the Figueira Casino. Mid-range. The **Hotel Universal**, Rua Miguel Bom-barda Nº50, ((033) 26238, fax: (033) 22962, although it rates only one star, has a lighter atmosphere. Inexpensive. Alternatively, come for the day from Coimbra.

How to Get There

A frequent train service runs from Coimbra A to Figueira da Foz, and also from Lisbon via Óbidos and Leiria. A local bus service links Figueira with Praia de Mira.

The drive from Coimbra to Figueira da Foz is straightforward as Figueira lies 46 km (29 miles) west of Coimbra along the N111.

AVEIRO AND ENVIRONS

Aveiro is a city crossed by canals and sitting at the edge of a shallow, salty lagoon which gives it an unusual charm. The central canal has some fine buildings and colorful wooden bridges, but overall impression is gray, misty, busy and often a little malodorous from the gathered seaweed. But it is a starting point for day trips on the **Ria** (the Lagoon) and to explore other parts of the **Parque Natural da Ria de Aveiro**.

Background

Once a thriving seaport and trade center, Aveiro suffered a devastating blow in 1575 when, at the height of her prosperity a vio-lent storm moved the sandbanks, blocking off access to the sea and creating a huge lagoon. Business dried up, livelihoods were lost, and the town began to empty. Many years later in 1808 another dramatic storm helped to reopen the passage to the sea, and although Aveiro could not be said to have had a riches-to-rags-to-riches story, a meas-ure of prosperity has returned. Today two of Aveiro's main activities give rise to some of the its most striking features: the collection

Swan-prowed, flat-bottomed moliceiros of Phoenician ancestry trawl the Ria gathering seaweed for use as fertilizer.

of seaweed for fertilizer in the elegant swan-necked boats called *moliceiros*, and the strange geometric lines of salt pans with their white pyramidal mounds of salt.

General Information

The *Turismo* is in Rua Joaō Mendonga Nº 8, ((034) 23680 or 20760.

What to See and Do

Aveiro's major sight is the fifteenth-century **Convento de Jesus** in the Rua Santa Joana, ((034) 23297, now the regional museum.

The convent chapel, also part of the museum, is filled with gold carving, occasionally relieved by the blue of the *azulejos*. In the eighteenth century a magnificent tomb was created in the lower chancel to honor Saint Joana, a remarkably delicate work of art inlaid with pink marble, supported by stone phoenixes and angels, and topped with cherubs supporting her coat-of-arms and crown. The museum is open from 10 am to 12:30 pm and from 2 to 5 pm; it is closed on Mondays.

There are several other churches in Aveiro, though none as interesting as the convent. The other main attraction here is the lagoon, (the *Turismo* has leaflets on trips) offering a variety of sporting possibilities

such as fishing, water skiing and boating, but pollution can be a problem.

Aveiro itself doesn't have a beach, but there are several within easy reach. **Praia de Barra** at the mouth of the Vougais is the nearest, just a bus ride away but it is usually crowded and ugly developments have spoiled the look of the place. The very tall lighthouse doesn't help either: its pink and white stripes make it look like a stick of seaside rock-candy. Better go a few kilometers further south to **Costa Nova**, a smart new resort also characterized by its predi-

lection for stripes, usually so vividly painted that they remain imprinted on your retinas when you look away.

Where to Stay

Aveiro has several hotels with little to choose among them. However, the **Pomba Blanca**, Rua Luís Gomes de Carvalho Nº23, 3800 Aveiro, ((034) 22529, fax: (034) 381844, is the exception. The pretty villa has a loggia and a fountain in the courtyard, and a comfortable and well-equiped interior. Mid-range.

Of the inexpensive places, the well-located **Hotel Arcada**, Rua Viana do Castelo, ((034) 23001, fax: (034) 21885, is one of the better examples. The interior can no longer be described as grand, but its rooms have fine views of the Central Canal. **Pensão Palmeira**, Rua da Palmeira N°7-11, ((034) 22521, is centrally placed but you have to share bathroom facilities.

Outside Aveiro, some of the best accommodation is to be found at the **Pousada da Ria**, 3870 Murtosa, ((034) 48332, fax: (034) 48333, on the isthmus that separates Murtosa from São Jacinto, approximately 29 km (18 miles) north of Aveiro. This 1960s building is long and low; its ample use of glass means that one is surrounded by

although there are several good cafés. **Cozinha do Rei** in the Hotel Afonso V, ((034) 26802, is a smart restaurant with a cheaper snack bar. Both the service and food are excellent. **Telheiro**, Largo da Praça do Peixe N°20, ((034) 29473, serves local specialties close to the fish market; in the same area, **O Mercantel**, Rua de António dos Santos, is recommended for its seafood.

How to Get There

Frequent train services to Aveiro run from both Coimbra and Porto, while a less

views of the lagoon and sea, a real boon for bird lovers. Prices vary between inexpensive and mid-range depending on time of year.

The **Hotel Palácio de Águeda**, Quinta da Borralha, 3750 Águeda, ((034) 601977, fax: (034) 601976, is close to the town of Águeda, 23 km (14 miles) southeast of Aveiro, and an outstanding manor house with spacious accommodation and modern amenities. Surrounded by gardens and with plenty of sporting facilities, you probably won't want to move from it. Expensive.

Where to Eat

Seafood abounds in Aveiro, but surprisingly there is not a great choice of restaurants,

frequent service operates from Lisbon stopping at Coimbra en route. From Viseu it is necessary to take a bus as far as Sernada where you can pick up a train to Aveiro. Express buses run from Coimbra and from Porto to Águeda, 19 km (12 miles) away, where you will have to change for Aveiro, making the train journey the easiest means of public transport.

For drivers, Aveiro lies 14 km (nine miles) off the Lisbon–Porto motorway (A1), an overall distance of 47 km (29 miles) from Coimbra and 69 km (43 miles) from Porto.

Local scenes are depicted on *azulejos* OPPOSITE at Aveiro's railway station, while three canals slice through the town ABOVE.

Coimbra and the Beiras

Porto and the North

PORTO

Portugal's second city clings to the rocky slopes rising sharply from the north bank of the River Douro, 314 km (195 miles) north of Lisbon on the coast. Its heart is a fascinating and compact tumble of old buildings facing the suburb of Vila Gaia de Nova across the water, where port wine matures in the cool darkness of the lodges.

Lisbon is relaxed when Porto is busy; it frolics while Porto turns in early, it is as radical as Porto is conservative. Despite its *sang-froid*, Porto's ancient riverside quarter, its grand central square and avenue, and its seductive views across the Douro make it a fascinating town to visit.

BACKGROUND

In the days of the Roman Empire the settlements of *Cale* and *Portus* (modern-day Porto) faced each other across the main crossing point of the River Douro. Their names fused together and the region that lay between the Minho and Douro rivers became known as the earldom, later the kingdom, of Portucale. Thus Porto (or Oporto as the British persist in calling it) gave its name to the state.

The British connections go back many centuries and it was in Porto cathedral that the alliance between England and Portugal was sealed with the marriage of Philippa of Lancaster to King João I in 1387. In a nearby house, also still standing, Philippa gave birth to the Infante, Henry the Navigator, who was to pioneer Portugal's golden age.

In the fifteenth century Henry busied himself in Porto's thriving shipyards overseeing the building of the ships used to carry troops to Ceuta in North Africa, where the famous battle of 1415 was fought. As food for the journey the citizens of Porto surrendered all their cattle, leaving themselves with only the tripe, which prepared in imaginative ways remains a delicious local specialty.

English merchants had been coming to Porto since the days of the Crusades, but in the seventeenth century, when trade relations between France and England were strained it became even more attractive. The Methuen Treaty of 1703 lowered the import duty on

wines to England and on wool to Portugal, effectively allowing the British to dominate the port wine trade. In order to break their monopoly, in 1755 the Marquês de Pombal created the world's first demarcated wine region in the Upper Douro, forming the Casa do Douro to control and administer it. Thenceforth British shippers were forced to buy brandy for fortyfying port from the company, whose regulations vastly improved the quality of the wine. However, the British had assumed such a proprietorial attitude towards Porto and had become so attached to port

wine that despite these devastating changes many stayed on, adapting to and finding ways around the tight regulations imposed by the company. The British standpoint was cynically described in the words of Captain Marryat: The Portuguese and the English have always been the best of friends because we can't get no Port Wine anywhere else.

GENERAL INFORMATION

The Porto I.P.T. (Instituo de Promoção Turistica) has its offices at Rua Clube Fenianos Nº25, ((02) 312740, fax: (02) 384548. There is also a *Turismo* at Praça do General Humberto Delgado, ((02) 312740, a smaller one close by in the Praça Dom João I Nº43, ((02) 201-3957, and one at the Aeroporto de Franciso sá Carinero, ((02) 948-2141.

For specific travel inquires, the following telephone numbers may prove useful:

Porto's Old Town OPPOSITE has a medieval mien, while a daily market is held on the Ribeira water front ABOVE in the shadow of Dom Luís I double decker bridge.

Franciso sá Carinero: ((02) 948-2141; for reservations ((02) 948-2144.

General rail information: ((02) 564141.

Rodoviária Nacional (coach travel), ((02) 200-6954.

The main office of TAP Air Portugal is at Praça Mouzinho de Albuquerque N°105, ((02) 600-5555, fax: (02) 600-1966.

Contact the Automóvel Clube de Portugal (A.C.P.) at Rua Goncalo Cristóvão N°2-6, 4000 Porto, ((02) 316732, fax: (02) 316698, for motoring information.

WHAT TO SEE AND DO

The city center north of São Bento

The **Estação São Bento** is a fairly central point from which to begin your explorations, and quite a sight in its own right. The cathedral-like entrance hall is a swirl of blue and white *azulejos*, but look beyond it to the platforms: through the graceful iron and glass station building are remarkable views of the steep streets behind it, a setting worthy of a Graham Greene novel. Just to the north you can see the **Praça da Liberdade** beyond which stretches the wide **Avenida dos Aliados**, lined with grand buildings, excellent cafés, and mosaic pavements.

To get your bearings and a remarkable overview of Porto, proceed westwards to the **Torre dos Clérigos** (Clérigos Tower), ((02) 200-1729, an elaborate baroque masterpiece and once the tallest structure in Portugal. It was built between 1732 and 1750 by the Italian architect Nicolau Nasoni, who also designed the stately oval church at its base. Climb the 225 steps up the 76-m (250-ft) bell tower for some splendid views. The church and tower are open from 10:30 am to noon and from 3:00 to 6 pm Mondays to Saturdays, from 10:30 am to 1 pm and from 8 pm to 10 pm on Sundays.

Close by the tower, smart streets lined with art galleries surround the **Coardaria gardens**. At the back of the church is a network of winding lanes where the pungent smell of *bacalhau* issues from little grocery shops. To the south of the tower along the **Rua das Flores** are shops that have changed little in the last 100 years. In the same street it comes as some surprise to stumble across another of Nasoni's grand

buildings, the Baroque **Misericórdia church**. Tucked away in the depths of the adjacent **Casa de Misericórdia** is one of Portugal's renaissance jewels, an enigmatic painting dating from the sixteenth century showing King Manuel I and his family, all in vividly colored robes, gathered around the bleeding, crucified Christ. You will need to ask at the Casa de Misericórdia to be shown the painting.

Northwest of Clérigos along the Rua Dom Manuel II, Porto's most important museum, the **Soares dos Reis Museu**, ((02) 200-7110,

is installed in the eighteenth-century Carrancas Palace. It was opened in the 1930s as Portugal's first national museum and was later named in honor of one of the foremost Portuguese sculptors of the last century. Some of Soares dos Reis' major works are on display here together with early French, Italian, Flemish and Portuguese paintings. Opening hours are from 10 am to 1 pm and from 2 to 5 pm Tuesday to Sunday. Admission is free on Sunday mornings.

In the northeastern corner of the nearby **Jardim do Palácio de Cristal** (Crystal Palace Gardens), the site of a sports pavilion, a fun fair and occasionally of exhibitions, is an attractive mansion set in gardens called the **Quinta da Maceirinha**, Rua de Entre

Quintas N°220: it contains the **Solar do Vinho**, ((02) 694749, where you can enjoy a glass of port in an elegant, relaxing, atmosphere. Open from 11 am to 11 pm, Mondays to Fridays and from 5 to 11 pm on Saturdays. Another part of the *quinta* is furnished and decorated in nineteenth-century style befitting its one-time resident, King Carlos Alberto of Sardinia, who died in exile here in 1849. This comprises the quaint **Romantic Museum**, ((02) 609-1131. Open from 10 am to 12 pm and from 2 pm to 5 pm. Closed Mondays.

Between São Bento and the River

A steep walk up the hill to the south of Estação São Bento will bring you to Porto's brooding and fortress-like **Sé** (Cathedral) set on a wide flagged square; it dates from the twelfth century and there is a darkness about the interior that Baroquification seems to have accentuated rather than counteracted. The nicest part is the Chapel of the Holy Sacrament where you can see the highly-prized silver retable that was sagaciously painted over during the Peninsular Wars to escape the notice of looting

A little to the east of São Bento station is the **Rua de Santa Catarina**, Porto's most expensive shopping area. Various European shops have outlets here, as do a number of old stores such as Reis Filhos with its black Art Nouveau shop front. Make a point of visiting the **Café Majestic**, another of the street's Art Nouveau classics, where large mirrors and fading leather create a pleasing setting for lunch or a drink. Off to the west of Rua de Santa Catarina at the junction of Rua Formosa and Rua de sã da Bandeira you will find the **Bolhão Market** where local produce and flowers are on sale. It is open Monday to Friday from 7 am to 5 pm, and from 7 am to 1 pm on Saturdays.

soldiers. The delicate paintwork in the choir has the look of faded tapestry. For relief from the excesses of the high altar, turn your gaze towards the south transept and the simplicity of the Romanesque arches. Climb the steps from the fine Gothic cloister for views over the battlements. Adjoining the Cathedral is the former **Bishop's Palace**, an enormous slab of restrained baroque designed by Nasoni. One of Porto's most prominent features, it now houses municipal offices.

One of the best reasons for visiting the Cathedral is for its views. From the cathedral square overlooking the Douro and its

Oporto at the mouth of the Douro, looks across at Vila Nova de Gaia on the south bank.

graceful bridges you can see the port wine lodges across the water in Vila Gaia de Nova, with famous names emblazoned on the roofs — Crofts, Dow, Sandeman — as well as Porto's extraordinary medieval district, down the hill below the Cathedral in a labyrinth of steep, narrow streets hewn into the rock. This quarter is known as the **Barredo** in which both the houses and the standard of living have remained, for the most part, quite medieval. The Barredo is beginning to change, however, and there are plans afoot to smarten it up.

It runs south and west of the cathedral down to the **Cais de Ribeira**, a colorful quayside area where the smell of fish and perfume of flowers mingle around the market. Many of the cavernous buildings have already undergone clever restoration, where restaurants and cafés now make this a lively nightspot. Down here you are close to another great Porto landmark, the **Ponte de Dom Luís I**. This magnificent iron bridge was built in 1886 and is used by both vehicles and pedestrians. It spans the Douro on two levels, linking both the upper and lower city with Vila Nova de Gaia. Its design reflects that of the **Ponte de Maria Pia** further east, an iron railway bridge built by Eiffel in 1877.

A short walk from the riverside along the Rua do Infante Dom Henrique will take you by the **Casa do Infante**, the house where Prince Henry the Navigator is believed to have been born, now an archival museum. In the same road stands the splendid **British Factory House**, built in 1785 by the British consul in Porto for the British merchants and still owned by the British port wine firms. Beautifully painted ceilings groan under the weight of massive chandeliers. No casual sight-seers are admitted, but it is possible to arrange a visit through tour operators and wine societies.

Across from the Ferreira Borges Market stands the **Bolsa** — the Stock Exchange — an imposing nineteeth-century building. If you want to look inside you will have to join a guided tour which rattles through the minutiae of some of the building's less interesting parts before reaching the marvelous **Arab Room**. Designed in the 1860s in loose imitation of a chamber in the Alhambra Palace, it is smothered in gold and intricate geometric patterns.

However, this pales in comparison with that of its neighbor, the **Igreja de São Francisco** (Church of St. Francis), probably the most dazzling of Portugal's gilded baroque extravaganzas. This sprawling building overlooking the river contains a golden cave where gilded wood carving runs riot, a style known as *talha dourada* (golden cut). Originally a Gothic structure, the church was given an eighteenth-century refit so that archways are covered with angels, birds, flowers, garlands, animals and fruit. It is said that 500 pounds in weight of gold leaf were used on this interior, and one cannot doubt it. Opening hours are from 9 am to 5 pm. Closed on Sundays.

The **Igreja de Santa Clara** in the Largo de 1 de Dezembro has another glittering interior: once attached to the Convent of Santa Clara, it was built in 1416 and transformed with seventeenth-century ornamentation, a refit predating that of São Francisco's. The sudden wealth that landed in Portugal's lap at that time is evident in another golden grotto: if you ask nicely, you may be allowed a close look at the finely carved choir stalls behind the grilles which have, as is often the case, some singular carvings hidden away under the seats. Open from 9:30 to 11:30 am and from 3 to 6 pm; closed on Sundays.

Vila Nova de Gaia

No visit to Porto is complete without a trip across the river to the suburb of Vila Nova de Gaia for a visit to at least one of the port wine lodges, and for excellent views of Porto. Take yourself across the Ponte Dom Luís I from the Cais de Ribeira, over the upper deck if you have a head for

once the only means of transporting the port wine down the Douro to the lodges. Today the job is done by trucks, but some of the lodges keep their boats on the river for promotional purposes.

If you cross the Ponte Dom Luís I on the upper level, it will bring you to the **Monastery of Serra do Pilar**, with even more stunning views of the city. The sixteenth-century convent church is unusual in its octagonal shape and its beautiful, though sadly damaged, round cloister ringed with classical columns.

heights. Just pick a lodge that takes your fancy and join a tour of the premises, invariably rounded off with a free tasting. The coolness of the cellars is a particularly enticing prospect on a hot summer's day. You may buy some bottles after the tasting if you wish, but there is no obligation to do so. General opening hours are weekdays from 9 or 10 am to noon and from 2 to 5 pm, sometimes until later. From May to October the lodges are open on Saturdays.

Afterwards enjoy a drink (maybe a black coffee if you've done more than one tour) at a riverside café, watching the *barcos rabelos* moored along the quayside. These elegant little flat-bottomed boats, distinguished by their curved prows and square sails, were

---

BOAT TRIPS

The **Ribadouro cruise**, ((02) 324236, takes its passengers along the Port wine route to Entre-os-Rios, Peso da Régua, and Pinhão. Cruises leave the Praça da Ribeira daily from March to December and seats must be booked in advance. The 50-minute **Three Bridges Cruise** runs between May and October every hour between 10 am and 6 pm except on Saturday afternoons and Sundays. Boats depart from Dom Luís I bridge

---

Barcos Rabelos OPPOSITE once plied the Douro from the port-growing Alto Douro region to the "lodges" of Vila Nova de Gaia, where the wine lies ageing in oak casks ABOVE.

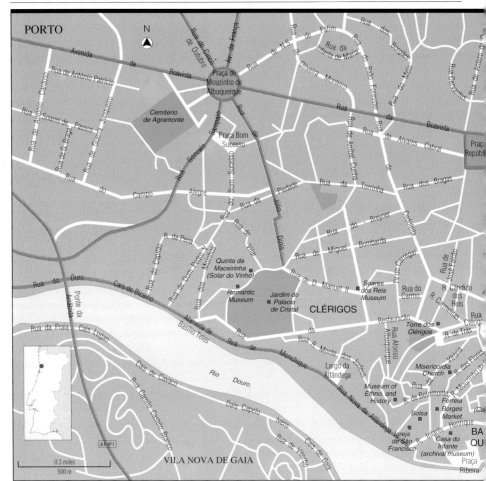

(lower roadway) in front of the Ferreira Wine Lodge. For details of longer cruises, get in touch with the *Turismo*.

GETTING AROUND

The driving is just as crazy here as in Lisbon: parking spaces are not always easy to find, and unless you revel in the challenge of congested and complicated one-way systems, don't explore the city by car. Most of the main sights are within walking distance anyway, and there are plenty of buses, trams, and taxis if the hills prove too much for you.

As in Lisbon, if you intend using buses or trams frequently it is cheaper to buy blocks of tickets or to get a tourist pass from one of the kiosks around the city, although full fares won't break the bank. Taxis are easy to find except during rush hours and

all have meters; note that there is a fixed fare for crossing over to Vila Nova de Gaia. The Praça da Liberdade in the heart of the city is the main tram and bus terminal. A City Tour leaves the Avenida dos Aliados on Monday and Thursday mornings between May and September, taking in Serra do Pilar, a visit to a port wine lodge, and several other sights.

SHOPPING

Porto, probably more than anywhere in Portugal, is the strictest observer of the sacred lunch hour: shops are rarely open between 12:30 and 2:30 pm and close at around 7 pm. On Saturdays they open between 9 am and 1 pm, and close on Sundays. The exceptions are the new shopping centers which tend to stay open seven days a week and late into the evenings.

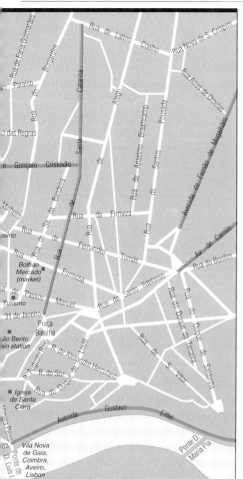

Rua de Santa Catarina is a main shopping street with numerous shoe shops and some international fashion boutiques. The particularly handsome and exclusive Reis Filhos store sells expensive tableware, antique furniture, leatherwear and more. Close to the Rua de Santa Catarina on the corner of Rua Formosa and Rua de sã da Bandeira, the colorful **Bolhão Market** has local produce on sale every day but Sunday. Near the Clérigos Tower, in **Rua Cândido dos Reis**, the famous Vista Alegre porcelain factory has its shop, while several others in the vicinity sell pottery and earthenware.

Porto is renowned for its gold and silverware, and is one of the best places to buy Portugal's famous delicate filigree work: some of the best jewelry shops are along the **Rua dos Flores**.

There are several big shopping complexes in town: two of the most central are **Clérigos**, just beside the Clérigos Tower at Praça de Lisboa, and **Brasilia** on the Rotunda de Boavista. Like Lisbon, Porto is an excellent place to shop for traditional craftwork, and the **Ribeiro Craft Center** down by the riverside at Rua da Reboleira N°37 offers a very good range.

NIGHTLIFE

Unlike Lisbon, Porto doesn't sparkle at night, and other than going to the popular clubs in the outlying suburb of Foz do Douro the best place for a little nightlife is the Ribeiro district where there is a cluster of restaurants and bars, several of them offering live entertainment. You may even catch some rogue *fado* music at **Mal Cozinhado**, Rua do Outeirinho N°13, ℂ (02) 381319, where you can eat or just have a drink. Jazz music plays at **Aniki-Bóbó**, Rua Fonte Taurina N°36, ℂ (02) 324619, and sometimes at **Luís Armastrondo**, Rua Fonte Taurina N°26, also in the Ribeiro.

Porto boasts some beautiful cafés such as the **Majestic** at Rua de Santa Catarina N°112, the **Imperial** in the Praça da Liberdade, and **A Brasileira** at Rua de Bonjardim N°116. For a more subdued but elegant atmosphere, there is the **Solar do Vinho do Porto** in the Quinta da Maceirinha, Rua de Entre Quintas N°220, where you can sip port wine.

WHERE TO STAY

Luxury
Porto's top hotel is the **Hotel Infante de Sagres**, Praça Dona Filipa de Lencastre N°62, 4000 Porto, ℂ (02) 201-9031, fax: (02) 314937, centrally located just off the Avenida dos Aliados. Built in the 1950s, its prices range from expensive to sky-high. The Hotel **Méridien Porto**, Avenida da Boavista N°1466, 4100 Porto, ℂ (02) 600-1913, fax: (02) 600-2031, offers cool, modern elegance with a French accent. A little way out of the center, this glass and concrete highrise has a health club with gym, sauna, Turkish bath and massage, as well as a first-rate restaurant, bars, and entertainment.

Nearby the Méridien, the **Hotel Porto Sheraton**, Avenida da Boavista N°1269, 4100 Porto, ((02) 606-8822, fax: (02) 609-1467, offers similarly comprehensive facilities and luxurious rooms.

Mid-range

Some of Porto's most delightful accommodation is to be found at the **Pensão Castelo de Santa Catarina**, Rua de Santa Catarina N°1347, 4000 Porto, ((02) 495599 or 497199, fax: (02) 410-6613. This small palace built on a terrace set back from the street is surrounded by gardens, palm trees, and a complex of smaller buildings. The entire structure is faced with tiles, a reminder that its original owner was the son of a major Portuguese manufacturer of tiles. In the main house a narrow staircase leads up to the guest rooms, each equipped with bathroom, telephone and television, and individually decorated with antique furniture. For something very special and for a couple of thousand escudos more, take the hotel's best suite which consists of a bedroom, dressing room, and bathroom. It is furnished in Rococo rosewood, its walls are covered in damask and wood paneling, and there are chandeliers twinkling from a ceiling painted with rosy cherubs. If you are looking for exceptional accommodation that doesn't cost the earth, this is surely it.

The **Grande Hotel do Porto**, Rua de Santa Catarina N°197, 4000 Porto, ((02) 200-8176, fax: (02) 311061, is centrally located on one of Porto's main shopping streets, across the road from the Café Majestic. Art Deco features abound in public areas, the lounge and pretty restaurant. Prices are at the lower end of mid-range. The **Hotel São João**, Rua do Bonjardim N°120, 4000 Porto, ((02) 200-1662, fax: (02) 316114, is another unusual place on the fourth floor of a conveniently positioned modern building (with elevator) where the interior exudes warmth.

Inexpensive

Residencial Pão de Acúcar, Rua do Almada N°262, 4000 Porto, ((02) 200-2425, fax: (02) 310239, is large, centrally positioned and has rooms with private bathrooms. The **Pensão Astória**, Rua Arnaldo Gama N°56, 4000 Porto, ((02) 200-3389, an old house in

a quiet location overlooking the river offers good value and is deservedly popular. **Pensão do Norte**, Rua Fernandes Tomás N°579, 4000 Porto, ((02) 200-3503, is a likable, slightly disorganized old place where some of the rooms have bathrooms and those without are as cheap as you can get.

Expensive

Portucale, Rua da Alegria N°598, ((02) 570717, perched on the top of the Albergaria Miradouro with great views of the river, serves some of Porto's best cuisine in sophisticated surroundings; *cabrito a serrana* (kid cooked in red wine) is its specialty. **Escondidinho**, Rua Passos Manuel N°144, ((02) 200-1079, is Porto's best-known restaurant. The French-run Le Méridien Hotel, Avenida da Boavista N°1466, ((02) 600-1913, has **Les Terrasses** with its smart, garden-like interior and offers French and local dishes with the option of *al fresco* dining on the terrace.

Moderate

Down by the riverside in the busy Ribeiro district restaurants abound, amongst which is **Taverna Bebobo**s, Cais da Ribeira 24-25, ((02) 313565, which has been in business for over a century. Also in the Ribeiro, **Mal Cozinhado**, Rua do Outeirinho N°13, ((02) 381319, has a traditional interior and offers *fado* music in the evenings.

Inexpensive

For Chinese food, the place to go is **Restaurante Chinês**, Avenida Vimara Peres N°38, ((02) 200-8915, close to the Ponte Dom Luís I (upper deck). **Casa Aleixo** serves regional food and is favored by the locals. The **Standard Bar**, Rua Infante Dom Henrique N°43, ((02) 200-3904, may have an uninspiring name but the excellent value, agreeable decor and palatable *bacalhau* dishes fill the tables.

The Francisco sá Carniero airport (often referred to by its former name of Pedro Rubras) is 13 km (nine miles) north of Porto and there is a shuttle bus service connecting it to the Praça de Lisboa in the city center, near Clérigos. International and domestic flights arrive here. There are numerous flights from Lisbon each day and three flights a week from Faro in the Algarve.

Trains from the south, including a frequent service from Lisbon via Coimbra B, arrive at Estação de Campanha, outside the town center. From here are frequent local connections to the centrally located São Bento Station, a journey that takes just a few minutes. Trains from Viana do Castelo, Braga, other places north of Porto and from the Douro Valley arrive at São Bento Station. Local

has a casino, a beach and a **golf** course, lots of **water sporting**, but generally lacks character.

If you wish to spend some time at a seaside resort, you would do better at Vila do Conde or Póvoa do Varzim both north of Porto.

VILA DO CONDE

Just 26 km north of Porto, Vila Conde is better for a seaside sojourn. It is also popular, but leafy, quieter, and maintains its old fishing village character along with its traditional crafts, boatbuilding and lacemaking. You will

trains come in at Trindade Station, north of the Avenida dos Aliados. Express buses run frequently to Porto from Lisbon and Coimbra, and other services connect Porto with most northern towns and Galician cities.

By road, Porto lies 314 km (195 miles) directly north of Lisbon and 118 km (73 miles) north of Coimbra. Both are connected to Porto by the A1 motorway.

find a long, wide beach, a shipyard at the mouth of the River Ave where craftsmen use traditional shipbuilding methods, a charming old town, and a noisy Friday market.

Visit Vila do Conde around St. John's Eve in June and you will be able to witness the **Festas de São João**, when there are sumptuous costumes on parade, singing and dancing around bonfires, and a candlelit procession down to the sea led by the lacemakers.

AROUND PORTO

ESPINHO

A seaside resort 19 km (12 miles) south of Porto, Espinho is popular with *Portuenses*. It

General Information

The *Turismo* is at Rua 25 de Abril, ((052) 631472/97/34/28.

Crafts women as ABOVE often display their lacework outside their homes especially in the fishing towns of northern Portugal.

Where to Stay

The best place to stay is the central **Estalagem do Brazão**, Avenida Dr. João Canavarro, 4480 Vila do Conde, ((052) 674-2016, fax: (052) 642028, which offers excellent value. The **Motel de Sant'Ana**, Monte de Sant'Ana, Azurara, ((052) 641717, fax: (052) 642693, is a country club-style place on the River Ave with one-, two- or three-person apartments and leisure facilities. Inexpensively priced, it makes an ideal choice for families.

Where to Eat

Vila do Conde has several restaurants along the seafront. Among them, **Pioneiro**, Avenida Manuel Barros, ((052) 632912, serves regional dishes and seafood at moderate prices. For something more intimate, try the family-run **Restaurante Ramon**, Rua 5 de Outubro, ((052) 631334, where the food is traditional and inexpensive.

How to Get There

Trains from Porto's Trindade Station to Póvoa de Varzim stop at Vila do Conde en route. There is a regular bus service from Porto.

Drivers should take the N13 out of Porto leaving the N13 about three kilometers (two miles) after Modivas.

PÓVOA DE VARZIM

Póvoa, 30 km north of Porto, is dominated by the stern **Mosteiro de Santa Clara** (Convent of Santa Clara), ((052) 631016, now a reformatory for boys. Founded in 1318 and virtually rebuilt in the eighteenth century, the convent's origins are only evident today in its church, which contains the renaissance tombs of the founders Dom Afonso Sanches (an illegitimate son of King Dinis) and his wife, Dona Teresa Martins. Church hours are 9 am to noon and 2 to 5 pm.

In the town center is a sixteenth-century Manueline **Igreja Matriz**, richly carved both inside and out, the work of Basque craftsmen. Visit the **lacemaking school** at Rua Joaquim Maria de Melo N°70. The town centers around a busy and colorful fishing port worked by a very old, closed community who preserve the traditions of centuries

past. The excellent **Museo Etnográfico** (Ethnographic Museum) in the Solar dos Carneiros will tell you all about its history.

The beach here is the longest in the whole country and it is cleaner than at Espinho. There are some interesting places to explore in the vicinity.

General Information

In Póvoa de Varzim the *Turismo* is at Avenida Mouzinho de Albuquerque N°166, ((052) 624609.

Where to Stay

Póvoa de Varzim has several inexpensive *pensãos*, but its top hotel is the four-star **Hotel Vermar**, Rua Alto de Martim Vaz, 4490 Póvoa de Varzim, ((052) 615566 or 615976, fax: (052) 615115. This is smart and comfortable, with sport and leisure facilities. Rooms have balconies, some with sea views, and the service is excellent. Prices vary widely within the mid-range bracket.

There are a couple of tempting choices in the environs of Póvoa. One is the **Estalagem Santo André**, Agucadoura, A Ver-o-Mar, 4490 Póvoa de Varzim, ((052) 615866, a few kilometers north of Póvoa. This is a long, low complex right by the sea and a far cry from the busy town. Nearby, the **Estalagem São Félix**, Monte de São Félix, Laúndos, 4490 Póvoa de Varzim, ((052) 682176, is set on a pine-clad hill overlooking the valley and sea. It has just eight rooms and a large restaurant. Prices at both places vary from inexpensive to mid-range.

Where to Eat

Inexpensive seafood restaurants abound, most notably the very busy **Casa dos Frangos II**, Estrada Nacional N°13, ((052) 681880, specializing in fish and chicken dishes, and **O Marinheiro**, Estrada Nacional, ((052) 682151, both on the edge of town.

How to Get There

Trains leave Porto's Trindade Station for Póvoa de Varzim and there is a bus service from Porto.

Póvoa de Varzim lies 30 km (19 miles) north of Porto: drivers should take the N13 out, then turn on to the N206 to Póvoa de Varzim.

AMARANTE

Little Amarante is a town of pleasant proportions 60 km (37 miles) east of Porto in the foothills of the Serra de Marão; its tall buildings lie along the banks of the River Tâmega, traversed by a stout eighteenth-century granite bridge. The riverbanks are fringed with willows and a narrow beach, and paddleboats await hire while geese fuss around the sandy river-island. Cafés abound and a holiday atmosphere prevails.

General Information
The *Turismo* is close to the art gallery in the convent building at Rua Cândido dos Reis, ((055) 422980.

What to See and Do
Sit on one of its café terraces overlooking the river while enjoying some of the sweet pastries for which the town is famous — *foguetes, lérias, brisas do Tâmega, galhofas* — or sipping some vinho verde, but bestir yourself to look around the **Convento de São Gonçalo** which stands close by the bridge. The church was built between 1540 and 1620, and is instantly recognizable by its red-tiled dome. To the left of its elaborate renaissance portal an arcaded loggia has niches containing statues of the kings who reigned while the convent was being built, together with the image of the hermit-saint himself. The baroque interior has columns to the side of the altar wreathed in flowers and cherubs, and the organ is supported by golden mermen.

A small side chapel contains the tomb of St. Gonçalo — a matchmaking saint believed to have come here from Guimarães in the thirteenth century and to have built the first bridge across the river. His effigy is touchingly surrounded by flowers, candles, and votive offerings, in parts blackened by the kisses of women who have prayed to him for a husband.

Close by, a café faces a large, cobbled square. Beside the river, the white and green convent buildings and a second cloister have been converted into the **Albano Sardoeira Museum of Modern Art**, ((055) 423663. The extensive use of plate glass around the cloisters gives the galleries a wonderfully light airiness, without impairing their beauty. The work exhibited favors the twentieth-century Portuguese artist Amadeo de Souza Cardoso, (1887–1927) a local who was one of the earliest Portuguese Modernists. Opening from 10 am to 12:30 pm and from 2 pm to 5:30 pm; it is closed on Mondays.

During the annual **Romária de São Gonçalo**, held in June, unmarried women give phallus-like cakes to potential husbands amid the usual dancing, singing, and fireworks

displays. Should you miss this celebration, join in the **Arraiais de São Gonçalo** held between June and October on Thursday and Saturday evenings in the gardens of the impressive **Casa da Calçada** near the bridge. For the price of a meal at an inexpensive restaurant you can purchase a ticket entitling you to eat and drink to your heart's content, dance to the band music, and enjoy some traditional singing.

Where to Stay
In Amarante the modern **Hotel Residencial Navarras**, Rua António Carneiro, 4600 Ama-

Tradition head dress and chains of gold adorn villagers at folkloric festivals in the Minho.

rante, ((055) 424036/9, fax: (055) 425891, offers swimming pool, a bar, restaurant, and large, comfortable rooms, all inexpensively priced. The **Hotel Residencial Silva**, Rua Cândido dos Reis Nº53, São Gonçalo, ((055) 423110, has more character: the decor seems not to have changed since the 1930s and bathrooms still have their old fittings. Some of the high-ceilinged rooms have balconies overlooking the river. Public areas are a little gloomy, but are compensated for by the terrace overhung with flowers that looks out across the river. Inexpensive. The town's favorite restaurant, **Casa Zé da Calçada**, Rua 31 de Janeiro, Cepelos, ((055) 422023, also offers accommodation under the TURI-HAB scheme. The position is ideal — close to the bridge and overlooking the river — and it is also inexpensive.

Where to Eat

The **Casa Zé da Calçada**, Rua 31 de Janeiro, ((055) 422023, is the best and most popular restaurant in town. A few doors along the **Confeitaria da Ponte** is a terraced café serving light food and some of the delicious local cakes.

How to Get There

Trains run frequently from Porto to Livração, linked to Amarante by bus. Buses run hourly between Porto and Amarante. By car from Porto is a 60 km (37 mile) journey along the A4.

ALTO DOURO

The River Douro cuts a dramatic gorge through the province of Trás-os-Montes and Alto Douro its stony flanks ribbed with vine-growing terraces. It slices across the width of Portugal for 210 km (130 miles) between Porto and Barca d'Alva at the Spanish border, where it turns north to form the frontier for a further 110 km (69 miles).

The spectacular Douro valley is smiled upon by the elements which make it ideal for growing vines, and synonymous with

the production of port. At harvest time laborers are brought in to pick grapes, a backbreaking task because they frequently have to carry the laden baskets up steep gradients to the trucks which transport their loads to wineries.

But harvest time is also a magical season, when the night air is alive with the celebratory sounds of accordions and drums. Occasionally, after dark, pickers still link arms in time-honored fashion and tread grapes through the night, to hypnotic rhythm.

Porto is the ideal starting point for a tour of the Douro Valley, starting in its lower reaches of green undulating hills, where *vinho verde* is grown. There are four ways to see the valley: by boat, car, bus or rail. An excellent option is to ride the Douro railway from São Bento station in Porto; a daily train leaves for Pocinho at the ends of the line, while more frequent trains run as far as Peso de Régua and Tua. Initially the journey isn't inspiring, as for the first 40 km (25 miles) or so the track runs north of the valley, dropping south at Livração. Then the sweeping views begin.

Driving out of Porto on the N108 allows you to follow the river more closely from the outset of your journey, but requires you to keep your mind on the road, which gets pretty busy during the summer months. Should you want to visit any of the *quintas*, make inquires at Porto's *Turismo* before setting off as you are unlikely to be given a guided tour without prior arrangement.

If the idea of spending a night in the valley appeals, there is a *pousada* near **Alijós**, north of the river along the N322 in the depths of the port wine producing region, and the village of **São João de Pesquiera** also has a small hotel. If a trip down the Douro is the only chance you have to explore the Alto Douro province of Trás-os-Montes, be sure to make a side trip to the famous **Solar de Mateus**, one of Portugal's loveliest buildings: a detailed description is included in the section VILA REAL on page 169.

LAMEGO

Lamego, 108 km (67 miles) east of Porto, is surrounded by orchards and vineyards. This baroque town is overlooked by two

Harvest time OPPOSITE TOP in the port growing region. The grapes are carried in wicker baskets. At some Quintas, traditional treading by foot OPPOSITE BOTTOM still takes place.

hills, one of them crowned by the ruins of a twelfth-century castle and the other by the Church of Nossa Senhora dos Remédios, a place of pilgrimage. Lamego is famous for a sparkling wine called Raposeira, its delicious smoked hams, and the monumental double staircase that zig-zags up the hill to Nossa Senhora from the lower town's main avenue.

General Information

The *Turismo* is at Avenida Visconde Guedes Teixeira, ((054) 62005.

What to see and Do

Lamego has been an episcopal town since the sixth century. Its **Cathedral** is twelfth-century Romanesque in origin but the only remaining original part is a section of the tower; the rest is mainly sixteenth-century renaissance and eighteenth-century interference. Behind the Cathedral Square, the eighteenth-century episcopal palace houses the excellent **Museu Regional**, ((054) 62008. The emphasis is on religious art, including detailed sixteenth-century Brussels tapestries, some complete baroque chapels rescued from the Convent of Chagas which was demolished earlier this century, and five of the original 20 panels by Grão Vasco that once graced the cathedral's altar. The others were lost or destroyed during major rebuilding work in the eighteenth century. Open from 10 am to 12:30 pm and from 2 to 5 pm, closed on Mondays. Admission is free on Sundays.

The elaborate **baroque staircase** at the top of the Avenida Dr. A. de Sousa leads to the Sanctuary of **Nossa Senhora dos Remédios** atop the wooded hill. The eighteenth-century church itself is overwhelmed by this lavish nineteenth-century construction which resembles the earlier Bom Jesus stairway near Braga. Over 600 steps make the pilgrim's climb suitably tiring (especially when on the knees); the less devout can motor to the top. It is a structure of whitewash and granite trimmed with balustrades and *azulejos*.

At the southeastern edge of town the unprepossessing seventeenth-century exterior of the **Capela do Desterro** (Chapel of the Exile) along Rua Cardoso Avelino hides a flam-

boyant gold interior with blue *azulejo* decoration and a fine painted ceiling. Nearby is the **Barro do Fonte**, Lamego's old and poor neighborhood on the banks of the river, a sharp contrast to the prosperous town center.

Where to Stay

On the edge of Lamego, the **Albergaria do Cerrado**, Lugar do Cerrado, 5100 Lamego, ((054) 63154 and 63164, is modern and comfortable. Mid-range prices apply. With more character is the inexpensive **Pensão Solar**, Largo da Sé, ((054) 62060, beside the cathe-

dral with 25 large rooms. Up on the hill by the church, the **Hotel do Parque**, Parque Nossa Senhora dos Remédios, ((054) 62105, is in tranquil surroundings and has the best views. Once a monastery attached to the church, it now provides inexpensive rooms and a large, moderately-priced restaurant.

How to Get There

Lamego does not have a railway station. The nearest is at Peso da Régua, whence buses run hourly to Lamego's central bus station. Douro line trains run to Régua from Porto's São Bento Station and along the Corgo Line from Vila Real. Lamego is well-served by buses, and R.N. Express buses run frequently from Viseu, Coimbra and Lisbon.

By road Lamego lies 358 km (222 miles) northeast of Lisbon and 108 km (67 miles) east of Porto. Drivers from Lisbon should take the A1 to just north of Coimbra, then turn on to the N2 to Lamego via Viseu. From Porto take either the A4 motorway (becoming the N15) to just outside Vila Real, then drive along the N2 to Lamego, or take the N108 from Porto to Entre-os-Rios, crossing the Douro on the N224 to Castelo de Paiva; continue along the N222 then hive off along the N226 just north of Lamego, which leads you into the town.

The tour of the house does not take you through all the rooms, but the guides are charming. The most striking features of the interior are the beautifully carved chestnut wood ceilings and the library. Many of the furnishings are badly in need of repair, and one can wonder at how the family must regret their decision to sell the reproduction rights of the painting to Sogrape in perpetuity for a lump sum, when they could have had a royalty on every bottle of Mateus Rosé sold. Still, maybe the house wouldn't be open to the public if that had happened.

VILA REAL

Vila Real is famous for the international motorcycle races held there in the summer, but its main attraction is three kilometers (two miles) away: the eighteenth-century **Solar de Mateus**, known world-wide in its starring role on the label of the Mateus Rosé bottle. If anything, the solar looks better in reality than in the famous picture, where in place of the swan gliding across the pond in front of the house there is now a half-submerged statue of a naked woman, the work of contemporary sculptor João Cutileiro. Its realism in the setting is disturbing.

One of Mateus' greatest charms is the garden at the back of the house, an appealing mixture of formal and informal. Box hedges are neatly trimmed, and within their constraints bloom masses of butterfly-covered flowers. A mighty yew hedge has been grown to form a dark tunnel leading to another garden, beyond which lie rolling countryside and vineyards.

The Serras de Marão and Alvão frame the town, which is somewhat outshone by its setting. Apart from the cafés of the Avenida Carvalho Araújo it has few attractions for the

Port grapes are grown on neat mountain terraces OPPOSITE. The damming of the Douro ABOVE for hydro-electric power has turned the river in a series of placid, serpentine lakes.

visitor but makes a useful base from which to explore the surrounding countryside, being 82 km (51 miles) east of Porto.

General Information

At Vila Real there are *Turismos* at Avenida Carvalho Araújo, ((059) 22819, and at Avenida 1° de Maio N°70, ((059) 22819.

Where to Stay

In Vila Real, the **Hotel Mira Corgo**, Avenida 1° de Maio N°76-78, 5000 Vila Real, ((059) 25001/6, is a tall, modern building with swim-

the Douro Line to Peso da Régua and change there onto the Corgo Line bound for Vila Real. The Transmontano bus company Cabanelas is based in Vila Real and their buses link with Lisbon, Porto, Coimbra, Bragança, and Peso da Régua. R.N. buses also operate services between these cities and Vila Real.

By road Vila Real lies 82 km (51 miles) east of Porto along the A4-IP4. From Bragança it is approximately 130 km (81 miles) along the A15-IP4. The Solar de Mateus is three kilometers (two miles) out of Vila Real along the N322.

ming pool, health club, and views over the gorge. Prices are mid-range. The centrally placed **Hotel Tocaio**, Avenida Carvalho Araújo N°45, ((059) 323106/7, fax: (059) 71675, has friendly staff, inexpensive prices, and public rooms decorated in the style of a gentleman's club. **Café Encontro**, Avenida Carvalho Araújo N°78, has decent, homely rooms which are inexpensive.

How to Get There

Internal flights run from Lisbon to Vila Real every weekday, and three times a week in winter. Rail travelers from Porto need to take

Viana do Castelo's annual August *festa* ABOVE is the largest in the Minho. The cathedral OPPOSITE at Braga, ecclesiastical capital of Portugal.

THE MINHO

For many, this undulating, verdant corner of the country is most alluring. Much of it can be seen on day trips from Porto, although you may choose to stay in one of the many small towns and villages in the area. Bordered by Galicia in Spain to the north and the Atlantic to the west, the Minho forms a major part of the region known as the Costa Verde, the Green Coast, and high levels of rainfall together with a mild climate ensure that it lives up to the name. Even the wine is green.

No inch of land is wasted. Crops are snugly grown and vines grow in every pos-

sible place. Conservative in outlook, the *Minhotos* don't hold with ideas of land cooperatives: instead, the land is divided up between the children of each generation so that smallholdings are often reduced to pocket handkerchiefs, their low stone walls making a patchwork quilt of the countryside.

To say that life hasn't changed much here over the years is a gross understatement. *Minhotos* are wary of change and are often too poor to effect it. Oxen still pull squeaking carts and old traditions flourish; prehistoric

remains dot the countryside and the pace is slow. To compensate for the harsher aspects of life deep religiousness manifests itself in a rash of festivals. The traditional women's costumes worn on these occasions are renowned for their dramatic colors and by gold jewelry that often constitutes the family fortune.

BRAGA

For centuries Braga, 50 km (31 miles) north of Porto, has been the religious capital of an exceptionally religious country, and the

Archbishop of Braga still wields significant power today. In spite of a staggering number of churches — something in the region of 30 — the face of the city is changing. All industry here used to be related to ecclesiastical needs, but today leather, textiles, and engineering are feeding the city and its economy. Braga is rapidly modernizing into the largest city north of Porto and the capital of the Minho.

General Information

There is a *Turismo* at Avenida da Liberdade N°1, ((053) 22550, and another at Rua Justino Cruz N°90, ((053) 76924 or 28565.

WHAT TO SEE AND DO

Braga's historic quarter is centered on the imposing **Sé**, built in the eleventh century on the site of an earlier church. A series of restorations and modifications has left few traces of the original Romanesque structure: only the south portal and the arch over the main entrance carry scenes from the medieval story of Reynard the Fox. The cathedral acquired an eastern extension with a fancy rooftop in the sixteenth century, and a fine granite statue of the Virgin and Child graces the exterior of the chancel, possibly sculpted by Nicolas Chanterène. Baroque reigns supreme with the occasional Manueline embellishment. The upper choir is wonderfully carved and gilded, together with a pair of ornate organs covered in blasting trumpets and cherubs.

The vaulted **Capela dos Reis** contains the tomb of the founders, Henri of Burgundy, the father of Portugal, and his wife Dona Teresa. It also holds the mummified remains of Archbishop Lourenço Vicente, a veteran of Aljubarrota whose body was found undecayed many years after his death and is now permanently on view as proof of his saintliness. The **Treasury** is now a museum devoted to religious art and should not be ignored, despite its uncared-for air. Cathedral opening times are from 9 am to 1 pm and from 2 to 5 pm; it is closed on Mondays.

On Praça da República, there is the Art Deco **Café Viana**, while on the Avenida da Liberdade is the tatty, lovely **Café Astória**. Wander around the streets near the cathedral

A baroque staircase OPPOSITE leads up Monte de Bom Jesus to reach its crowning church ABOVE.

Religious festivals afford Braga the opportunity to air its spiritual supremacy. The city is chock-a-block during Holy Week when the most spectacular of Portugal's festivals takes place. Decorations smother the town as barefoot penitents bearing torches take part in the famous **Ecce Homo** procession, the climax of the week is the great procession of **Entero do Senhor** (Burial of Our Lord), in which thousands participate.

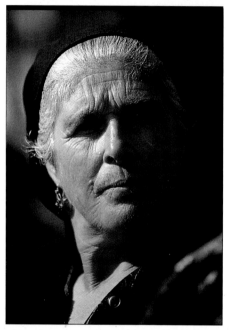

and browse through shops filled with devotional items, embroidery, rag quilts, pottery, and the Barcelos cockerel, the most widely recognized symbol of Portugal.

Braga has some splendid mansions, the most beautiful being the elegant eighteenth-century **Palácio do Raio**, with its flowing lines designed by architect André Soares; he also drew up the graceful **Câmara Municipal** (Town Hall), fronted by the unusual **Pelican Fountain**. Close by in the Rua do Raio is the oldest of Braga's sights, the **Fonte do Idilio** (Fountain of the Idol), a small Lusitanian shrine that was carved into the rock in pre-Roman times.

The **Casa dos Biscainhos**, right by the Town Hall, is a seventeenth-century aristocratic house, now housing a small museum, ((053) 27645. A passageway cuts through the facade, designed to allow horses through. Inside are collections of period furniture, pottery, glassware, silverware, textiles, jewelry, and porcelain, as well as a new section devoted to Roman artifacts turned up during recent excavations in Braga. Open from 10 am to 12:30 pm and from 1:30 to 5:30 pm; closed on Mondays.

Around Braga

The most unusual religious monument in the entire area lies just six kilometers (four miles) east of Braga: the Church of **Bom Jesus do Monte**, or, more truthfully, the stairway that leads up to it. The church stands on a wooded hill, and its eighteenth-century monumental double stairway, like the church, is a whitewash and granite Rococo affair that predates the one at Lamego. From the base, this hill of overlapping walls looks like some Disney stairway to heaven: each level is ornamented with statuary, gardens, grottoes, chapels, and fountains. That on the first landing represents the wounds of Christ while others allegorize the five senses and the three virtues. If you are not in the mood for a pilgrimage, take the funicular up to the top or drive up the roadway that, like the staircase, ascends in a series of steep hairpin bends.

Minhoto peasantry ABOVE and OPPOSITE, don rustic clothes. Widows wear black for the remainder of their lives.

On a silent hilltop 12 km (seven-and-a-half miles) east of Braga and 10 km (six miles) southeast of Bom Jesus, the ruins of an Iron Age settlement shelter behind vestiges of defensive walls. The **Citânia de Briteiros** was occupied from around 300 BC; there are the remains of roads and a water supply system; two of its circular dwellings have been reconstructed. Many of the artifacts unearthed here are on display in Guimarães at the Martins Sarmento Museu (see below).

Where to Stay

In Braga the **Hotel Turismo Braga**, Praceta João XXI, 4700 Braga, ((053) 612200, fax: (053) 612211, is a large 1950s building offering air-conditioned comfort and many amenities at mid-range prices. The **Hotel Francfort**, Avenida Central N°1-7, ((053)

22648, is an older building facing the public gardens and unmistakable because of its red-tiled facade. Rooms are simply furnished and inexpensive, while a good old-fashioned dining room adds to the friendly and pleasant atmosphere.

Some claim that the best accommodation in the area is outside the city at Bom Jesus in the **Hotel do Elevador**, Parque do Bom Jesus do Monte, 4700 Braga, ((053) 676611. This elegant villa has a good restaurant: its rooms are

light and modern and prices are mid-range. Run by the same people, the similarly priced **Hotel do Parque**, Parque do Bom Jesus do Monte, 4700 Braga, ((053) 676548, fax: (053) 676679, dates from early this century, and has a conservatory and courtyard where drinks are served; as it has no restaurant yet, you will have to eat at the Hotel do Elevador or one of the other establishments described below.

Where to Eat

Braga's top restaurant is generally held to be **Incão**, Campo das Hortas N°4, ((053) 22335 or 613235, where regional cuisine can be enjoyed in a traditional but smart setting. **Abade de Priscos**, Praça Mouzinho de Albuquerque N°7, ((053) 76750 or 76650, is a small first-floor restaurant, family-run and with a more intimate atmosphere. Among the regional dishes on offer here you will find *arroz de sarrbulho*, a variety of meats cooked with pig's blood and rice. Both restaurants are moderately priced.

In the inexpensive category is the popular **Restaurant a Ceia**, Rua do Raio; a little way out of the center, the **Restaurante Moçambicana**, Rua Andrade Corvo N°8, has African food. Remember that Braga has some delightful old cafés. At **Café Astória**, Avenida da

Liberdade, you can have a snack and some-times listen to live music; **O Brasileiro**, Rua Dom Março at the top of Rua do Souto, has a street terrace, and there is also the **Café Viana** on the Praça da República.

How to Get There

There is one flight per week from Lisbon to Braga. Trains run frequently from Barcelos and Viana, but travelers coming from north of Viana will need to change at Nine. Trains run direct from Porto but a more frequent service will take you to Nine where you have

to change. R.N. Express buses run from the main northern towns into Braga, as well as from Coimbra, Lisbon, and, less frequently, Porto.

By road Braga is 50 km (31 miles) north of Porto along the A3-IP1, and 53 km (32 miles) southeast of Viana do Castelo along the N13 and N103.

BARCELOS

The town of Barcelos lines the north bank of the River Cávado, 22 km (14 miles) to the west of Braga. Besides agriculture, this area is know for its pottery. Most typical is the brown tableware decorated with patterns of little yellow dots, but there is endless de-

mand from collectors for locally produced ceramic figurines.

The northerners relish nothing more than a miracle, one of which lies behind the most widely recognized symbol of Portugal, the Barcelos Cock. This story dates back to at least the thirteenth century and tells how a pilgrim was wrongly accused of theft and sentenced to death. His last request was to be allowed to see the judge before being hanged: he was duly taken to the judge's house where the family was sitting down to dinner. The pilgrim pointed to a roast chicken on the table and declared that his innocence would be proven when it crowed. Amid the sound of jaws dropping, the roast resur-rected itself and crowed.

The pilgrim got his reprieve and some years later returned to Barcelos to build a church to the Virgin and Santiago in thanks for the miracle. The cock was rewarded as well, commemorated today by the brightly painted ceramic cockerels produced *en masse* at Barcelos and distributed throughout the country.

General Information

The *Turismo* is at Torre de Menagem (the Keep), Largo da Porta Nova, ((053) 812135 or 811882.

What to See and Do

The **Campo da República**, a huge square shaded by trees and centered on a renais-sance fountain, bursts into life on Thursday mornings. Around it formal baroque gar-dens merge with the Campo da República into one large area with trees and fountains. Vendors bring produce and clothing to sell at the weekly market, as well as pottery. On the southwestern side stands the pretty Church of **Nosso Senhor da Cruz**, a neat octagonal building of whitewash and granite with a balustraded roof and a tiled cupola, richly decorated with gilt, *azulejos*, and some elaborate chandeliers.

Fine buildings surround the square, but the most spectacular interior belongs to the **Igreja do Terço** on the north side along the Avenida dos Combatentes da G. Guerra. Formerly the church of a Benedictine convent, it blends into the surrounding buildings with nothing to suggest its sumptuous interior. Inside, eighteenth-century *azulejos* carry scenes from the life of St. Benedict, tableaux of monastic life, *trompe l'oeil* windows, and the occasional surprise on the dado: the cockerel with a devil's tail admiring himself in a mirror, or anxious monks trying to control a prancing half-devil. Against this inky ceramic backdrop an elaborate baroque pulpit stands out, a balcony of gilt supported and surmounted by cherubs.

Southwest of the Campo da República, close to the river and the old bridge, a group of historic buildings comprise the town's oldest quarter. The ruined building with a thin chimney is the remains of the fifteenth-century **Paço dos Condes**, the Palace of the Dukes of Bragança. The ruins now form an open air archaeological **museum** covered in ancient sarcophagi and tombstones. Open from 10 am to noon and from 2 to 6 pm; closed Mondays.

Where to Stay

The **Albergaria Condes de Barcelos**, Avenida Alcaides de Faria, 4750 Barcelos, ((053) 811061/2, offers the best accommodation in town. The **Residencial Dom Nuno**, Avenida Dom Nuno Alvares Pereira N°763, ((053) 815084/5, is rather characterless with plain rooms, each with bathroom, television and telephone. Overlooking the market square, the **Pensão Bagoeira**, Avenida Dr. Sidónio Pais N°495, ((053) 811236, has a few clean rooms to offer, and a café downstairs. All are inexpensively priced.

Where to Eat

Overlooking the market square on the Avenida Dr. Sidónio Pais is **Bagoeira**, serving good food, and on Thursdays a hive of activity. There are a few restaurants along Rua Dom António Barroso, the main shopping street, and also the **Confeitaria Salvação** at N° 37, which provides an elegant setting for tea, coffee, and cakes.

How to Get There

Trains run frequently to Barcelos from Porto and Viana do Castelo; from Braga you must change at Nine. There are direct connections with all stations north of Barcelos. Buses run frequently from Braga and Viana, stopping at the southeastern edge of the square.

By road Barcelos lies 55 km (34 miles) north of Porto, and 22 km (14 miles) west of Braga. From Braga take the N103 west until the junction with the N205, two kilometers (one mile) outside Barcelos, which will bring you into town.

GUIMARÃES

In spite of the dreary industrial outskirts of Guimarães, the heart of this historic town, 21 km (13 miles) southeast of Braga, is a complex of medieval squares and cobbled

streets, overlooked both by a brooding hilltop castle close to the town center and a splendid monastery that is now one of the best *pousadas* in Portugal.

Background

Guimarães developed around a monastery, a castle, and a small settlement founded by the Countess Mumadona, a Galician noblewoman of the tenth century. In the eleventh century Henri of Burgundy and his wife held court in Guimarães castle; their son, Afonso Henriques, was born here in 1110.

The market town of Barcelos ABOVE sits on the river Cávado's north bank. Guimarães OPPOSITE was Portugal first capital.

Through persistence and ruthlessness Afonso was able to declare himself the first King of Portugal in 1139, making Guimarães (often referred to as the Cradle of the Nation) the capital of the newly formed country. Its glory was short-lived, however, as in 1143 the capital was moved to Coimbra.

General Information
The *Turismo* is at Avenida Alameda da Resistência, ((053) 412450.

What to See and Do
Start your explorations at the **Castle** that stands on a rocky hill to the north of the center. The original one was built by Countess Mumadona in the tenth century to protect the village and monastery from Norman or Mohammedan attack. Extended and strengthened by Henri of Burgundy in the twelfth century, it has undergone heavy restoration work and today its crenellated square keep, surrounded by seven smaller towers, radiates medieval ferocity. A bronze **statue** of Afonso Henriques in his battle dress stands nearby, the work of the nineteenth-century sculptor Soares dos Reis.

Just below the castle is the tiny twelfth-century **Igreja São Miguel do Castelo** (Church of St. Michael of the Castle), the simplicity of its cool and quiet interior quite breathtaking. Afonso Henriques is believed to have been baptized here, presumably in the font that is still standing. A burial ground for crusading knights, the central area of the floor is cordoned off to prevent further wear on the carved tombstones.

A little further down the hill looms the awkward hulk of the **Paço dos Duques** (the Palace of the Dukes of Bragança), ((053) 412273, built for Dom Afonso, Count of Barcelos, Duke of Bragança and illegitimate son of João I. Abandoned in the sixteenth century the palace subsequently fell into ruin, and was rebuilt at Salazar's command in the 1930s. Today it contains artifacts of varying ages: porcelain, furniture, tapestries, and paintings. Opening hours are from 10 am to 5 pm every day, and admission is free on Sundays.

To get to the old town from the palace, continue southwards past the seventeenth-century Carmo Church and walk along the

Rua de Santa Maria, one the of the oldest streets in the city. Fine houses line the way, many of them seventeenth-century with wrought-iron balconies, iron lanterns, and grills. The street brings you to the **Convent of Santa Clara**, a sixteenth-century building with a baroque facade which serves as the town hall today.

Rua de Santa Maria meets another ancient street, the **Rua da Rainha**, at the beautiful **Largo da Oliveira**, named after the Legend of the Olive Tree: in the sixth century, a deputation of Visigoths disturbed a man called Wamba while he was ploughing his field, and informed him that he had been chosen to be their king. Wamba stuck his staff into the ground declaring that the chances of his accepting the title were about

as great as of his staff sprouting olive leaves, which of course it did. This is supposed to be the spot where it happened, and a small Gothic structure of covered arches sheltering a cross marks the spot.

Behind this cross and dominating one side of the square is the **Igreja de Nossa Senhora da Oliveira** (Collegiate Church of Our Lady of the Olive Tree). A monastery was founded here in the tenth century, possibly on the site of a sixth-century temple commemorating the miracle, and in the fourteenth century King João I extended it in thanks for his victory at Aljubarrota.

The cloister and convent buildings now house the **Museu Alberto Sampaio**, ℂ (053) 42465, a striking collection of church treasures including the robe worn by King João I

during the Battle of Aljubarrota, a beautiful silver-bound Bible, and, prized above all, the delicately crafted silver-gilt triptych depicting the Visitation, Annunciation and Nativity, said to have been captured from the King of Castile's tent following his defeat at Aljubarrota. Open from 10 am to 12:30 and from 2 to 5 pm; closed Mondays. Admission is free on Sunday mornings.

Guimarães has one other important museum, the **Museu de Martins Sarmento**, ℂ (053) 42969, which occupies the Gothic cloister of the São Domingos Convent along the Rua de Paio Galvão. Named after the nineteenth-century archaeologist who devoted

Guimarães Largo da Oliveira marks the spot where a dead olive tree miraculously broke into leaf.

himself to the excavation of the Citânia de Briteiros, it contains many artifacts unearthed there and at other hilltop sites. Three items deserve mention: the ancient carved stone slab known as the Pedra Formosa which, after much debate, is now generally believed to have been used to block the entrance of a tomb; a miniature bronze votive cart pulled by men and oxen; and the mighty Colossus of Pedralva, a 3,000-year-old three meters (10 ft) high statue of a seated man with an upraised arm and uncharitably large phallus. Open from 2 to 6 pm, closed Sundays.

Overlooking the town and high up on the slopes of the Penha is the **Santa Marinha da Costa**, once an Augustinian monastery and now one of Portugal's best *pousadas*. The monastery was founded in the twelfth century by Dona Mafalda, wife of Afonso Henriques, in fulfillment of a vow to Santa Marinha: in the sixteenth century it passed to the order of São Jerónimo. The cloister is truly splendid with its rare and delicate Mozarab archway dating from the tenth century. During recent restoration work, traces of a Visigoth church were found , while other archaeological evidence suggests that this was the site of a Roman (and possibly even pre-Roman) temple. The best way of getting to see the monastery is as a resident at the *pousada*, but it is possible to come here for a meal or even a drink which will afford you the opportunity of looking around a little.

Where to Stay
From every point of view, the best places to stay in Guimarães are the two *pousadas*, one

in the center of the old town, the other about six kilometers (four miles) outside. The out-of-town one is the **Pousada de Santa Marinha**, 4800 Guimaraes, ((053) 514453, fax: (053) 514459, a carefully converted monastery on a hillside, the pride and joy of the *pousada* network. Prices range between the high end of mid-range and expensive.

Down in the town, the **Pousada de Nossa Senhora da Oliveira**, Largo da Oliveira, ((053) 514157/9, fax: (053) 514204, is completely different. Comprised of what seems to be several houses in the heart of the old town, it has 16 rooms, including a few suites, overlooking the Largo de Oliveira. Mid-range prices apply. In contrast, the **Hotel Fundador Dom Pedro**, Avenida Dom Afonso Henriques Nº760, ((053) 513781, fax: (053) 513786, is a modern high-rise block. It has comfortable rooms, good service and mid-range prices.

There are several TURIHAB options, one of which, the **Casa de Pombais**, Avenida de Londres, ((053) 412917, is an eighteenth-century house on the outskirts of town. Prices vary between inexpensive and mid-range.

Where to Eat
Both *pousadas* mentioned above have lovely dining rooms and excellent menus with international and local dishes. Each reflects its own character — at the **Pousada de Santa Marinha** a vaulted, tiled room with chandeliers and a sophisticated air, while at the **Pousada de Santa Maria da Oliveira**, a cozy, country-style room with wooden beams, dried flowers, and gleaming copper. Both are moderately priced, with the Santa Marinha maybe a little more expensive.

How to Get There
One train service from Porto runs direct to Guimarães, while others involve changing at Lousãdo. If you are traveling from Braga by train, it is necessary to change at both Nine and Lousãdo. Buses run frequently from Braga to Guimarães, and express services run from Porto, Lisbon, and Coimbra.

By road Guimarães lies 53 km (32 miles) northeast of Porto, north along the A3-IP1

The Basilica of Santa Luzia ABOVE perches high above Viana do Castelo, while the city's Praça da República OPPOSITE is adorned with flowers.

and then east onto the N105, taking you through Santo Tirso into the town. A new motorway that will link Guimarães to the A3-IP1 is nearing completion. The city is 21 km (13 miles) southeast of Braga along the N101.

VIANA DO CASTELO

The Minho's top resort is built around a lively fishing port at the mouth of the River Lima, rather different from the usual seaside holiday places. The beach is a ferry ride away from the town, and Viana itself is elegant and not too raucous, where a prosperous maritime history has endowed it with fine Manueline and renaissance buildings. Restaurants and cafés abound in the town and there are a few night clubs; the wide sandy beach nearby has breakers big enough for surfing, though not so big that you can't swim.

General Information

The *Turismo* is at Rua do Hospital Velho, ((058) 22620 or 24971.

What to See and Do

The heart of the city is the spacious **Praça da República** where sixteenth-century buildings look on to a renaissance fountain. Most striking is the **Misericórdia** (alms house), the upper tiers of which are supported by strange sixteenth-century caryatids. Adjacent to the Misericórdia is the **Antigos Paços do Concelho** (Old town Hall), its lower story an arcade of pointed arches and its facade emblazoned with Viana's coat-of-arms and a carved ship. Its setting, outdoor cafés, restaurants, and night time music are magical.

There are several fine houses in the vicinity and the *Turismo* (itself housed in a converted fifteenth-century building) has leaflets pointing out some of the more spectacular mansions. The **Rua da Bandeira** brims with them, as does the **Rua Cândido dos Reis**, where you will find the **Palácio dos Condes da Carreira**, now the Town Hall. Another houses the **Museu Municipal**, Largo de São Domingos, ((058) 24223. Its collection of decorative art is biased towards ceramics, for which Viana is famous. Open-

ing times are from 9:30 am to noon and from 2 to 5 pm; closed Mondays.

Wherever you are in the town, you can see the **Monte de Santa Luzia** with its glowering, Big-Brotherly basilica. It is worth a trip up here for the wonderful views of the town, the river, and the sea, and although there is a funicular every hour, the walk up through the woods is far more rewarding. Built earlier this century, the **basilica** is a rather cold structure. Behind it stand the grand **Hotel Santa Luzia**, and the remains of a Celto-Iberian settlement, similar to Briteiros.

Apart from the charms of the town itself, people come here for the beaches. The **Praia do Cabedelo** is a ferry ride from the Largo 5 de Outubro, while to the north of Viana is **Vila Praia de Ancora** which also has a sandy stretch. Beyond lies **Modedo**, close to the Spanish border. There are boat trips from Viana that take in the beaches and the docks, details of which are available from the *Turismo*. Viana is also a jumping-off point for trips to Spain, up the River Lima, and into the Peneda-Gerês National Park. Again, ask at the *Turismo* for details of what is available or call in on a travel agent — several have offices in the Avenida dos Combatentes.

Where to Stay

The smartest accommodation in Viana is at the **Hotel Santa Luzia**, Monte de Santa Luzia, 4900 Viana do Castelo, ((058) 828889 and 828890, fax: (058) 828892, a palatial hotel overlooking the city. This late nineteenth-century building was renovated recently in Art Deco style. There are tennis courts, a swimming pool, a good restaurant, and over 50 rooms all within the mid-range price bracket. Down in the center of town, the **Hotel Viana Sol**, Largo Vasco da Gama, ((058) 828995, has well-equipped rooms and there are good sports facilities.

In the inexpensive category, the **Residencial Vianamar**, Avenida Combatentes da Grande Guerra Nº215, ((058) 828962, is an older hotel on the main shopping street offering basic rooms that are clean and comfortable. There are also some tempting TURIHAB options under in the Viana area, details of which can be obtained from the *Turismo*, or from the TURIHAB office in Ponte de Lima, an old town 23 km east of Viana.

Where to Eat

Os 3 Potes, Beco dos Fornos Nº9, ((058) 829928, close to the Praça da República was once the city bakery and is a popular restaurant. The decor is traditional, the menu basically regional with some international dishes slipped in, and traditional entertainment such as folk dancing or singing is often laid on. **Cozinha das Malheiras**, Rua Gago Coutinho, ((058) 823680, is housed in the Malheiras Palace; its seafood is very good. Both the restaurants are moderately priced.

Seafood is also the specialty at the excellent **Três Arcos**, Largo J. Tomás da Costa Nº25, ((058) 24014. Prices are inexpensive or moderate, depending on whether you eat at the bar or in the restaurant proper. **Túnel**, Rua dos Manjovos Nº1, ((058) 822188, has inexpensive food, and **Casa de Pasto Trasmontano**, Rua Gago Coutinho Nº12, just off the Praça da República, is similarly cheap and good.

How to Get There

Trains run direct to Viana from Porto via Barcelos, and from stations north of Viana. Passengers from Braga need to change at Nine. Buses run frequently from Porto, Braga, and other main northern towns, and a less frequent service runs from Lisbon and Coimbra.

By road Viana is 67 km (42 miles) north of Porto along the N13-IC1; from Braga it is 52 km (32 miles) along the N103 and N13.

THE LIMA VALLEY

The Lima is a magical, sleepy green valley, surrounded by wooded hills and graced with noble *quintas*.

Ponte de Lima

Ponte de Lima's charms lie in its setting and its buildings rather than in any specific sights. Located 21 km (13 miles) east of Viana, it demands unhurried exploration, maybe even a stay at one of the many manor houses in its environs. It is the center from which the province's TURIHAB scheme is operated, and if you call in at the office they may be able to fix you up with some accommodation at short notice.

Two bridges cross the river here: a modern one, and the famous, much-photographed older structure which is part Roman, part medieval. There are plenty of restaurants in the town so spend an evening here if you can.

Ponte da Barca

Seventeen kilometers (11 miles) east of Ponte de Lima, at Ponte da Barca attention again focuses around a bridge, dating from the fifteenth and eighteenth centuries. There is an old belief in these parts that an expec-

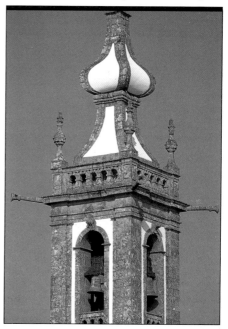

tant mother who is worried about her pregnancy should ask the first person who crosses the bridge after midnight to baptize her belly with water from the Lima, in order to safeguard her unborn child. Should you be the first person to cross it after midnight, you could well find yourself called upon to perform a baptismal rite.

The town has the same serene charm as Ponte de Lima; its riverbank is shaded by trees, and along it, next to the appropriately named **Jardim dos Poetas** (Poets' Garden), the **Bar do Rio** beckons you to lunch.

An onion-shaped church spire, typical in the Minho, soars skywards over Ponte de Lima at the heart of the province.

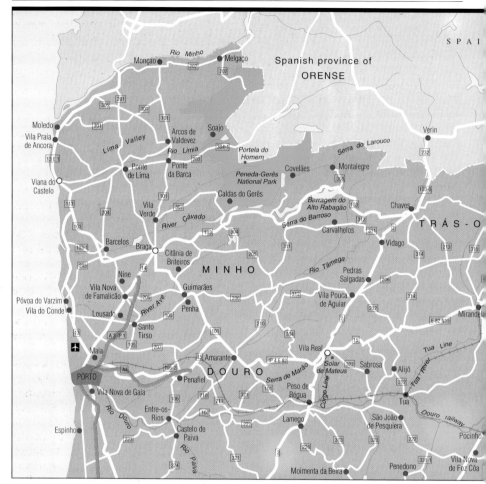

Soajo

About 15 km (nine miles) east of Ponte de Barca, the N203 enters the Peneda-Gerês National Park. A short deviation from the river road, just four kilometers (two-and-a-half miles) north along the N304 will bring you to Soajo. This remote and hardy little village in the Serra do Soajo is surrounded by cultivated land punctuated by rocky granite outcrops. On one is the sight that brings cameras to Soajo: a collection of strange, coffin-like stone granaries raised on stilts. Known as *espigueiros*, these rectangular slatted boxes have pitched roofs, and their funereal appearance is enhanced by the crosses on each of them. *Espigueiros* can be seen throughout the Minho, even in parts of Galicia, but it is rare to find such a large grouping as this, evidence that communal farming is still practiced.

General Information

In Ponte de Lima the *Turismo* is in the Praça da República, ((058) 942335, as is the headquarters for the Minho *Turismo de Habitação* scheme which organizes manor house and farmhouse accommodation (TURIHAB), ((058) 942729, fax: (058) 741444.

Where to Stay

This region may lack hotels, but it more than makes up for that with its glut of TURIHAB accommodation. The head office for Minho TURIHAB in Ponte de Lima (see GENERAL INFORMATION) can supply you with details, or for advance booking you can obtain a leaflet from the larger Turismos and I.P.T. offices. There are over 30 establishments in the Ponte de Lima district alone with prices from inexpensive to mid-range. The **Paço de Calheiros**, Calheiros, 4990 Ponte de Lima,

THE NORTH

N

18 miles
30 km

Parque Nacional de Montesinho

M O N T E S

Bragança

Quintanilha

Vimioso

Morais

Miranda do Douro

Mogadouro

Serra do Mogadouro

Rio Sabor

rca
Alva

PARQUE NACIONAL PENEDA-GERÊS

Portugal's largest reserve encompasses some 72,000 hectares (177,916 acres), including four mountain ranges — Peneda, Gerês, Soajo, and Amarela — cut by deep river valleys. The park is a crescent-shaped area taking in parts of both the Minho and Trás-os-Montes, skirting around an intruding chunk of the Spanish province of Orense. It encompasses a system of dams and reservoirs of interest to water sports enthusiasts and over a hundred villages; quiet spots can always be found, especially at the less-visited northern section. The hub of the park is the pretty spa town of **Caldas do Gerês**, where most of the accommodation is. It is a sedate, rather Victorian spa, good for sipping herbal teas, taking the waters, and using it as a base for excursions. but nightlife lovers will find the evenings quiet. It tends to fill up on summer weekends.

With deep wooded valleys, rocky summits, streams, and cascades, this place invites the use of your hiking boots, providing you come armed with a map of the park. Driving through it is also a possibility, if you and your car can cope with large potholes and roads that disintegrate into rough tracks. Mountaineers, trout fishermen, campers, and pony trekkers will all find fulfillment in the the park, which gets the highest rainfall in the country. The result is dense forests of cork oak, silver birch, pines, ferns and sycamores, together with Gerês fern and the Gerês iris, unique to the area. Wild ponies and cats, deer, and wolves roam free, while the bird population includes golden eagles and barn owls. Prehistoric man has left us his dolmens, some of them 5,000 years old, while many Roman milestones recall a less-distant past, especially at **Portela do Homem** near the border where part of the Roman road which once linked Braga to what is now Spain can still be seen.

((058) 947164, is approximately seven kilometers (four miles) outside Ponte de Lima, and possibly the most desirable of all TURI-HAB accommodation, a noble eighteenth-century house set in gardens with views of the Lima.

How to Get There
The Lima Valley is not served by rail. A bus service runs frequently from Viana do Castelo to Ponte de Lima, and four buses a day run to Ponte de Barca. They also run from Braga to Ponte da Barca and Ponte de Lima.

By road, Ponte de Lima lies 21 km (13 miles) east of Viana de Castelo. Two roads run inland from Viana along the Lima Valley: the N202 on the north bank and the N203 on the south bank. The N202 has the best views.

General Information
The *Turismo* in Caldas do Gerês is at Avenida Manuel Ferreira, ((053) 39133. The park's head office is in Braga at Rua de São Geraldo Nº19.

Where to Stay

Most of the accommodations in Caldas do Gerês are *pensãos* but there are a handful of hotels. The **Hotel do Parque**, Avenida Manuel Francisco da Costa, 4845 Caldas do Gerês, ((053) 676548, is a charming turn-of-the-century place with an outdoor pool. Prices are inexpensive. The **Hotel das Termas**, Avenida Manuel Francisco da Cost, ((053) 391143, is another old-fashioned spa hotel with similar facilities and mid-range prices.

Outside the town the best place to stay is the **Pousada de São Bento**, 4850 Caniçada, ((053) 391106, fax: (053) 391117, near Caniçada 10 km (six miles) south of Gerês. Prices are mid-range.

How to Get There

The northern section of the park can be approached from Arcos de Valdevez and from Melgaço on the River Minho. Other points of entry are the more central Caldas do Gerês and Covelães in the province of Trás-os-Montes. It is best to travel there by car, but there are six buses a day running between Braga and Caldas do Gerês.

TRÁS-OS-MONTES

Trás-os-Montes is curtained off from the neighboring Minho by the Marão and Gerês mountain ranges and bordered by Spain to the north and west; this northeastern extremity of Portugal stands aloof and very much apart from the rest of Portugal. Named with customary Portuguese directness, Trás-os-Montes means Behind the Mountains. There are two faces to this land beyond the mountains, simply referred to as *Terra Quente* (Warm Land) and *Terra Fria* (Cold Land). *Terra Quente* is the southern area that encompasses the cultivated sections of the Tua and Corgo rivers, and the upper reaches of the Douro Valley where port wine grapes are grown. *Terra Fria* lies to the north, a rugged plateau cut by deep valleys where the land is poorer, and the bitterness of winter and cruel heat of summer — nine months of winter and three months of hell — combine with poor communications to enforce the isolation and independence of many villages.

In such an atmosphere ancient traditions flourish, strange dialects are spoken, superstition holds sway; the local *bruxa* or witch is consulted on matters of health, and religious belief is at its strongest though often in unorthodox form. Small, almost medieval communities exist in a time warp, where a tough, peasant existence is eked out, educational standards are often at rock bottom, and there is a high instance of emigration because life here is simply too hard.

Roads to the main cities — Bragança, Chaves, Miranda do Douro, — are improving all the time and making the province more accessible. But if you want to delve into the remote villages that comprise some of Europe's most backward corners, you will need a car, an adventurous spirit, and time. Even where roads are good, they are often winding; with the constant possibility of carts and oxen around the corner, travel takes more time than the distances seem to merit. Still, with such majestic scenery to enjoy, it would be a shame to hurry anyway.

CHAVES

Chaves lies in a wide, fertile valley, a mere 11 km (seven miles) away from the Spanish border. Once a key point of attack for invading armies (hence the name Chaves meaning keys), these days the town has an extraordinarily peaceful air. Riding and golf facilities, a tennis club, a spa, and trout fishing in the river all contribute to a a restful ambience. Chaves should be visited for the sum of its parts: architecture, its setting, and superb smoked hams, which many believe to be the best in Portugal.

General Information

There is a *Turismo* is at Rua de Santo António Nº213, ((076) 21029, another at the Spa, ((076) 21445, and one at Terreiro de Cavalaria, ((076) 21029.

What to See and Do

The Romans particularly liked Chaves, or *Aquae Flaviae* as they knew it, for its hot springs. Their legacy was the bridge over the Tâmega, now almost 1900 years old and still bearing up well, although over the centuries it has lost a few arches and some masonry.

Posts at the southern end bear Roman inscriptions and were once used as milestones.

The center of the old quarter is the handsome **Praça de Camões** where there is a seventeenth-century **Misericórdia Church** ornamented with twisted columns. Before it stands an elegant Manueline **pillory**. Also in the square, the one-time palace of the Dukes of Bragança now houses the **Museu de Região Flaviense** (Municipal Museum), ((076) 21965, with archaeological and ethnographic displays on the region. Opening times are from 9:30 am to 12:30 pm and from 2 to 5 pm; closed Mondays and on Saturday and Sunday mornings. Admission is free on Sundays.

Behind it, the fourteenth-century keep contains the **Military Museum**, part of the Municipal Museum, the entry fee covering admission to both. There are displays of ancient weaponry and armor, but the museum deals most thoroughly with the Portuguese role in World War I and the twentieth-century colonial wars. The keep itself is all that remains of King Dinis' castle, a square, chunky tower affording views over the valley. Opening hours are the same as for the Municipal Museum.

Beyond the keep and below the old walls a very ordinary modern complex houses the **spa** where you can try out the effects of the warm spring water on your rheumatism, hypertension, or gout. Better still, stop at a café to try some of that wonderful ham (presunto) and maybe a glass or so of the local red wine.

Around Chaves

Southwest of Chaves along the N2-IP3 are two popular spa towns, both surrounded by trees and hills. The first is **Vidago**, 17 km (10 miles) from Chaves, where there are tennis courts, a nine-hole golf course, horseback riding, and good walks. The spa itself is an Art Nouveau building in the grounds of the Hotel Palace, the most impressive sight in Vidago. Twelve kilometers (seven-and-a-half miles) further south along the N2-IP3, **Pedras Salgadas** has a similar character.

Where to Stay

In Chaves the **Hotel Aquae Flaviae**, Praça do Brasil, 5400 Chaves, ((076) 26711, fax:

(076) 26497, is a slick new establishment with a pool and solarium. Mid-range prices. The modern **Hotel Trajano**, Travessa Cândido dos Reis, 5400 Chaves, ((076) 22415/6, has an agreeable terrace overlooking the old town. Inexpensive to mid-range. For character, though, go to the **Hotel de Chaves**, Rua 25 de Abril N°25, 5400 Chaves, ((076) 21118, a rambling old building with high ceilings. Rooms are available with or without bathrooms. Inexpensively priced.

There are several hotels and *pensãos* in Vidago, but the best choice is the turn-of-the-century **Hotel Palace de Vidago**, Parque, 5425 Vidago, ((076) 97356, fax: (076) 97359, in its stylish garden setting. Rooms vary in size and decor. The hotel's modern extension is actually more expensive, but has less charm. Try the excellent restaurant and wine list. Mid-range prices.

Where to Eat

In Chaves, the **Hotel Trajano** (see WHERE TO STAY above) has a basement restaurant serving good regional food, as does the popular **Restaurante Arado**, Ribeira do Pinheiro, ((076) 21996. Prices at both are inexpensive to moderate. In Vidago, go to the restaurant at the **Hotel Palace de Vidago** (see WHERE TO STAY above).

How to Get There

The old Tua narrow-gauge railway used to run to Chaves from Peso da Régua, but sadly has been pruned back as far as Vila Real, nowadays the nearest train station to Chaves. Passengers traveling from Porto must take the Douro Line as far as Peso da Régua, change to the Corgo Line for Vila Real, then complete their journey by bus. It should be said, however, that short as it is now, the Corgo is still one of the great train journeys of Europe. Buses run to Chaves from Bragança and Braga, and there are express buses from Lisbon, Coimbra, Porto, and Vila Real. On Thursdays and Sundays the Internorte bus links Chaves with Vérin and Orense in Spain.

About 120 km (75 miles) west of Chaves a collection of villages centers around the large lake at the **Barragem do Alto Rabagão** — Sapiãos, Boticas, Vilarinho, Sendim,

Pardornelos, Seara Velha, Montalegre to name a few — sheltering in the Serra do Barroso and the foothills of the Serra do Larouco. Monsanto has a café and a *pensão* or two, but you won't find many restaurants or hotels elsewhere in these parts; it may be better to base yourself at Chaves, Vidago, or the spa town of Carvalhelos.

For many years Portugal's narrow-gauge railways were a source of delight for train enthusiasts, but sadly they were casualties of the modernization programs. There are two left, however: the Tua Line that runs

industry and university is keen to exploit its proximity to various Spanish cities and its direct road link to Porto. New roads are eroding Bragança's image of isolation, but one suspects it may take much longer to rid the city of its deep-seated self-sufficiency and independence.

General Information

The main *Turismo* is at Avenida Cidade de Zamora, ((073) 22273, and another can be found at Largo Principal, ((073) 23078. For leaflets and information on the Parque

from Tua on the River Douro to Bragança, and the Corgo line that runs from Peso de Régua to Vila Real. They make a delightful way to see some beautiful countryside, so catch them while you can.

Nacional de Montesinho drop in at the park headquarters in Bragança, Rua Alexandre Herculano.

What to See and Do

A cluster of public buildings and white-washed houses huddle within stout walls fortified by 18 towers, above which rises above a tall keep. In this medieval **citadela** a community still keeps livestock and grow a few small crops. Most extraordinary of all the buildings is the **Domus Municipalis** (Municipal Hall), a twelfth-century Roman-esque meeting-place where respected members of the community once gathered to discuss public matters and settle disputes. Built over a cistern, which is visible through a

BRAGANÇA

When you reach this hilltop citadel what you will find there is truly extraordinary: a complete rustic, medieval village, domi-nated by its ancient castle, a symbol of Bragança's isolation.

Bragança's other persona is as the administrative capital of Trás-os-Montes, a new town changing rapidly. This agricul-tural center with an expanding textile

grille in the floor, it is a pentagonal structure lit by arched windows around the entire building and topped with a pitched tiled roof. The meeting room has a simple stone bench along the walls and a carved frieze running above the arches. If you want to look inside you may have to ask around in the village for the keyholder.

Stone vines climb the twisted columns that flank the Manueline doorway of the sixteenth-century **Church of Santa Maria** next to the Domus Municipalis. Facing the church, a twelfth-century **keep** rises above

the castle towers to challenge Spain. It now houses a **Military Museum**, open Friday to Wednesday, 9 am to 12:30 pm and 2 to 5 pm. Below the castle walls near the keep, a **pillory** curiously rises out of a prehistoric sculpture of a pig, rather unpleasantly skewering the creature. There are several of these lumpy prehistoric pigs, known as *berrões* or *porcos*, throughout Trás-os-Montes, the most famous being the one that stands in the main square of the town of Murça. (It may be that they were fertility symbols or offerings to the gods.)

Outside the walls in front of the castle, the churches of **São Bento** and **São Francisco** stand close together. The renaissance-style São Bento is the most interesting church

in Bragança. In the nave the eighteenth-century barrel vaulted ceiling is painted with stunning colors, while the magnificent chancel ceiling is inlaid with a Moorish-style geometric pattern.

A stone's throw from here along Rua Abilio Beça, the former episcopal palace houses the **Museu do Abade de Baçal**. It is named after Francisco Manuel Alves (1865-1947), Abbot of Baçal, a campaigner for religious tolerance who studied the history of Bragança in depth with particular attention to the history of its Jewish community. The museum has a fascinating collection of exhibits that include traditional costumes, furniture, coins, illuminated manuscripts, religious art, and paintings of Transmontano landscapes by Alberto Souza. Open from 10 am to 12:30 pm and from 2 to 5 pm; closed Mondays.

When the Jews of Spain were expelled by Ferdinand and Isabella in 1492, many of them sought refuge in Portugal. However, Manuel I had them forcibly baptized in 1497, thus compelling them to practice their religion in secret while outwardly adhering to the Christian faith. Many of these New Christians, as they became known, chose remote corners of the country in which to live in peace. Bragança's isolation was ideal for them. They have left their mark on the local culture, the specialty on sale at the **Market** next to the city's unexceptional cathedral, alheiras, cunning sausages made with chicken or turkey rather than pork and designed to fool the Inquisition.

Where to Stay

Just outside Bragança the **Pousada de São Bartolomeu**, Estrada de Turismo, 5300 Bragança, ((073) 22493/4, fax: (073) 23453, is a 1950s building on the heights of Serra da Nogueira. Its balconied rooms and pleasant terrace afford superb views of the citadel and surrounding hills. The **Hotel Bragança**, Avenida Sá Carneiro, ((073) 22578, another modern building with similar views over the citadel, is in the city itself. It has comfortable rooms with picture

Fortified Bragança was once at a strategic crossroads crucial to the defense of Portugal. Today, the city is important as an agricultural hub.

windows, a restaurant, and a bar. Both have mid-range prices.

In the inexpensive category the **Pensão Rucha**, Rua Almirante dos Reis Nº42, ((073) 22672, exudes Transmontano hospitality and friendliness, and produces excellent meals in its huge, old-fashioned kitchen. The **Pensão São Roque**, Zona da Estacada, Lote Nº26-27, ((073) 23481, has simply-furnished rooms with private bathrooms and views of the castle.

Where to Eat

The **Pousada de São Bartolomeu** (see WHERE TO STAY above) has a restaurant serving mainly Transmontano dishes at moderate prices. At **Plantório**, Estrada Cantarias, ((073) 22426, the views are as good as the delicious regional cooking, and prices are inexpensive to moderate. **Arca de Noé**, Avenida do Savor, ((073) 22759, is essentially a wine cellar serving good, inexpensive food. For something a little more up-market try the **Solar Brangançano**, Praça da Sé Nº34, ((073) 23875, an old townhouse now housing a restaurant with a bar.

How to Get There

By road Chaves lies 61 km (38 miles) from Vila Real along the N2-IP3, the route that drivers from Porto will take. Bragança is 99 km (61 miles) east of Chaves along the N103, and Braga is 119 km (74 miles) further west along the N103.

Internal flights run on weekdays from Lisbon to Bragança. Cabanelas buses run daily on weekdays to the Spanish border town of Quintanilha, and twice daily on weekdays from Lisbon to Bragança, stopping at Coimbra and Vila Real en route. The Internorte express runs from Porto to Quintanilha and Zamora via Bragança once a day from Tuesday to Saturday.

If you are traveling by train from Porto, you will need to change at Tua to join the old Tua Line that nowadays only runs as far as Mirandela. From Mirandela there is a bus connection to Bragança.

By road Bragança is approximately 130 km (81 miles) from Vila Real along the N15–1P4, while Porto lies a further 82 km (51 miles) from Vila Real along the same road.

MIRANDA DO DOURO

High on a hill, 160 km (99 miles) northeast of Vila Real, Miranda do Douro overlooks the Douro Gorge, which is dammed to form a lake and the frontier with Spain at this point. Despite numerous attacks over the centuries, Miranda's old walled town remains relatively intact. There is a local dialect, *Mirandês*, quite unlike any other, and the town is famous for its traditional dances: the Pingacho, the Geribaila, and in particular the dance of the Pauliteiros, possibly derived from an ancient war dance.

General Information

There is a *Turismo* at Largo Menino Jesus da Cartolinha, ((073) 42132.

What to See and Do

Miranda's greatest coup was to be made a diocese in 1545, thus the province's religious capital until the eighteenth century when the bishopric was moved to Bragança. The sober **renaissance cathedral** overlooking the gorge has a lavish interior: its gilded altarpieces are a mass of intricate carving, and there is an elaborate organ. The most endearing feature there is Menino Jesus da Cartolinha — the Child Jesus in a Silk Hat. This porcelain statue of the child Jesus is kept in glass case in the south transept, and his clothes are regularly changed. He has a substantial wardrobe of specially made costumes.

There is a story that at a crucial point during the 1711 battle with the Spanish in Miranda, a little boy filled the Portuguese with courage and led them into attack. After they had won, he could not be found and it was naturally assumed that it was the child Jesus who had come to help them in their hour of need. The statue commemorates the incident and is one of Miranda's most cherished possessions.

Around the cathedral are some medieval dwellings, especially in the **Rua da Castanilha** where carved windows and coats-of-arms adorn some of the grander houses. The **castle** stands in ruins, a reminder of the gunpowder store explosion during the siege of

1762. To find out about the history of the region and of the Transmontano lifestyle, go along to the **Terra de Miranda Museum**. There are ancient stones with Latin inscriptions, artifacts from Celtic, Roman, and Moorish times, and often curious implements for things you never knew needed doing. The museum's hours are from 9 am to noon and from 2 to 4:45 pm; it is closed Mondays.

Of the traditional *Mirandês* dances the most famous is the **Dance of the Pauliteiros**, performed during the **Festas da Santa** prices. If you'd like to stay in the old town, then it has to be the **Pensão Santa Cruz**, Rua Abade de Baçal N°61-61A, ((073) 42474, the only accommodation there. Luckily it is a family-run place and rooms are available with or without bath. Inexpensive.

How to Get There

Trains run twice daily from Porto to Pocinho, the nearest train station to Miranda do Douro. From Pocinho you must continue the journey by bus. Bus services also link Bragança and Guarda with Miranda.

Bárbara held in mid-August by young men wearing strange, rather feminine costumes: white skirts, embroidered shirts, hats festooned with flowers, striped socks, and a pair of incongruously heavy boots. The banging of sticks and thudding of boots has lead some to believe that the dance originated from an ancient war dance. If the dance ever does die out, blame it on the clothes.

Where to Stay

The modern **Pousada de Santa Catarina**, Estrada da Barragem, 5210 Miranda do Douro, ((073) 42255 and 42755, fax: (073) 42665, overlooks the gorge and dam, offering 12 rooms and one suite at mid-range

The Spanish border crossing to Zamora is just across the dam, but only cars can use this road. By road Miranda lies 83 km (52 miles) east of Bragança along the N218. It is 160 km (99 miles) northeast of Vila Real along the N15-IP4 and the N317 which connects with the N218 into Miranda.

Bragança's medieval aura lives on amid the cobbled streets and tumbledown cottages squatting at the foot an austere castle keep.

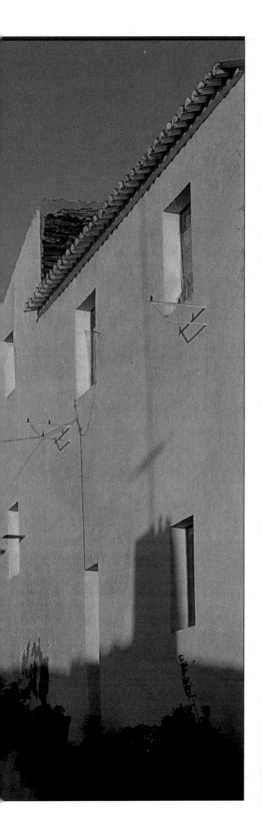

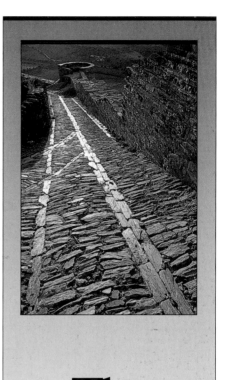

The Alentejo

THE PROVINCES OF Alto (Upper) and Baixo (Lower) Alentejo stretch from the coast to the Spanish border and together cover roughly a third of the country. Wide, sweeping plains of wheat fields are dotted with olive trees and cork oaks, with a thin scattering of whitewashed settlements huddled around castle-topped hills. In the blistering summer heat, the wheat, the red soil, and the strangely naked-looking cork trees stripped of their bark turn the plain into a palette of reds and golds, intensified by the bright blue of the sky. Some prefer spring to explore the Alentejo, when the days are cool and wild flowers cover the plain.

In sharp contrast to the smallholdings of the north, in the Alentejo land is gathered into huge estates known as *latifúndios*. These were formed in Roman times and worked by the landless peasantry, a system that has continued into the twentieth century. In the early days of the 1974 revolution locals led by communists seized the lands to form cooperatives, with predictably catastrophic results. For a time agrarian reform banned the holding of large estates by individuals, but lack of know-how on the part of the usurpers, recognized by increasingly practical governments has in most cases ensured the return of estates to their rightful owners, or simply allowed the cooperatives to disintegrate. Despite its size and although the world's largest producer of cork, the Alentejo remains very poor, inhabited by only 12 percent of the country's population.

This is a little-visited region, with most of the heavy traffic pounding along the Lisbon to Algarve road. It is not well-served by public transport, though there is consolation for drivers in that the roads here are generally straight and relatively quiet. The Alentejo has much to offer its visitors, dreamy villages with old castle walls, some good wines, and a jewel of a city called Évora.

ÉVORA

Évora is Portugal's most consistently beautiful city: visit it even if you see nothing else in this country. Easily accessible, being only 150 km (93 miles) east of the capital, its ancient walls embrace Moorish alleyways,

renaissance squares, sixteenth-century palácios, and monuments ranging from the Roman to the Rococo. Such wonderfully preserved architecture has brought Évora's old town under the protection of UNESCO through its World Patrimony scheme, making the restoration and preservation of Évora an international concern. More than just a museum town, its lively squares, cafés, and university life make the town an immensely enjoyable place to visit. Stay here if you can: there is some tempting accommodation and much to see.

BACKGROUND

Évora flowered during the Middle Ages, when, under the House of Avis, it became a center of power where the King often held court. Such patronage inevitably brought in its wake the artistic and literary elite of the time, the construction of palaces, and in 1559 a university. Things took a downward turn during the years of Spanish rule, from which time onwards Lisbon was the favored royal seat. Évora's decline was helped along by the Marquês de Pombal, whose campaign to rid the country of Jesuits led to the closure of the university. During the following years Évora redefined itself as a market center, and only regained its high profile after the 1974 revolution when, as the capital of the Upper Alentejo, it became the center for sweeping agrarian reform.

Marvão OPPOSITE and Monsaraz ABOVE are two of the Alentejo's most medieval-feeling fortified hilltop towns.

GENERAL INFORMATION

The *Turismo* is in the Praça do Giraldo, ((066) 22671.

WHAT TO SEE AND DO

The **Praça do Giraldo** at the center of the town is a good place to begin a tour of the city as it has car parking; the *Turismo* is located here, and is a popular meeting place, particularly on Tuesdays when the market comes

to town. Outdoor cafés make it an ideal spot in which to soak up some of Évora's atmosphere. The **Rua 5 de Outubro** leading off the eastern side of the square will bring you to Évora's most important cluster of monuments, where you will find the **Temple of Diana**, the best-preserved Roman remains in the country, dating from the second or third century. It is raised on a stone platform, and the close proximity of buildings some 1200 years younger emphasizes its antiquity. Corinthian columns of granite topped and tailed with Estremoz marble still stand on three sides, probably because the temple

Évora Cathedral ABOVE is part fortress part place of worship while the city OPPOSITE as a whole has been declared a UNESCO world heritage site.

was bricked up and adapted for various uses over the centuries. It served as a fortress, a store, and, somewhat ignominiously, as a slaughterhouse until 1870.

Facing the temple is the **Lóios Convent and Church**, built in the late fifteenth century by Dom Rodrigo Afonso de Melo on the site of Évora castle. The convent buildings now house a magnificent *pousada*, but if you can't afford the luxury prices, ask for permission to look at the Moorish-inspired Manueline cloister and some of the elegantly frescoed public rooms.

Be sure to visit the **Museu de Évora**, ((066) 22604, housed in the former episcopal palace. The museum's highlights are the collection of sixteenth-century paintings and a thirteen-paneled *Life of the Virgin* by Flemish artists, which was once on the cathedral's altar. Amongst its sculptural treasures is the bas-relief of a vestal virgin, the fine classical tomb carved by Nicholas Chanterène, and a collection of modern work including some strange figures by João Cutileiro, sculptor of the naked figure in the lake of the Solar de Mateus. Hours are 10 am to noon and 2 to 5 pm; closed Mondays. Admission is free on Sundays.

Behind the museum looms the battlemented **Sé**, a redoubtable twelfth- and thirteenth-century building that has been added to over the years. Its twin square towers are topped with sixteenth-century cones, and Apostles join with animals and strange creatures in ornamenting the elaborate Gothic doorway. The somber interior has one of the longest naves in the country, measuring 70 m (230 ft). The stalls of the upper choir carry some wonderful sixteenth-century carvings.

A small entrance fee entitles you to wander around the spacious fourteenth-century cloister and go into the treasury, housing some unusual works of art. Most notable is the small thirteenth-century ivory of the Virgin whose abdomen opens to reveal intricately carved scenes from her life. Get your bearings by climbing up to the roof for views over Évora. Open from 9 am to noon and from 2 to 5 pm; closed Monday.

A short stroll from the Sé is the **Igreja de São Francisco**, a sixteenth-century Gothic church with Manueline and

Moorish flourishes, and the macabre **Capela dos Ossos** (Chapel of Bones). A chirpy inscription at the entrance to the chapel reads in translation: We bones here are waiting for your bones. Inside, the pebble-like decoration around the walls turns out to be human bones stacked with horrible neatness. Open from 8 am to 1 pm (to 11:30 am on Sundays).

A short walk south of here along the Rua da República to just outside the city walls will bring you to what looks like an old Hollywood version of a medieval castle. It is the **Ermita de São Brás**, an extraordinary

in the form of a white marble orb. From here the Rua Conde da Serra da Tourega will bring you to the **Universidade de Évora**, with its elegant renaissance courtyard.

Throughout the old town you can trace the remains of fortifications that date from the first to the seventeenth centuries. Almost every inch of old Évora has something captivating: numerous convents, mansion houses, winding streets crossed by Moorish arches. With the major monuments illuminated, and the lights and chatter of the cafés, evenings here are a delight.

fifteenth-century building with chunky round buttresses tipped with cones, large battlements, and gargoyles. Going back north up the Rua da República and turning right after passing São Francisco will bring you to the **church of Nossa Senhora da Graça**, which like São Brás has an exterior of considerably more interest than its interior. Built in Italianate renaissance style, it has four strange giant figures sitting on its side pillars bearing flaming spheres.

To the east of Graça and slightly south of the cathedral is the **Largo das Portas de Moura**, centered on a renaissance fountain

The most robust Roman ruin in Portugal is Évora's Temple of Diana. Flood lit, it makes a romantic spectacle.

WHERE TO STAY

The most sought-after accommodation in town is the **Pousada dos Lóios**, Largo Conde de Vila Flor, 7000 Évora, ((066) 24051, fax: (066) 27248, installed in the old fifteenth-century monastery overlooking the Temple of Diana. High vaulted ceilings, archways, frescoes, and antique furniture create a memorable interior. Prices rise to the luxury category in the summer and drop to mid-range out of season.

If you can't afford the *pousada*, you won't feel hard done by if you stay instead at the **Pensão O Eborense**, Largo da Misericórdia N°1, ((066) 22031, fax: (066) 742367. This is a lovely sixteenth-century mansion located in a leafy corner of Évora, and after passing through the entrance, it comes as no surprise to find guestrooms furnished in a style that would do a *pousada* proud. There is an arcaded loggia for breakfast or drinks in the warm weather. All rooms have private bath, television, and telephone, and are inexpensively priced. Book to avoid disappointment.

Pensão Policarpo, Rua da Freiria de Baixo N°16, ((066) 22424, is an equally ancient place with a warm, friendly atmosphere, cheerful decor, and inexpensive prices. Another interesting option is the **Casa Conde da Serra**, Rua Conde da Serra da Tourega N°1, ((066) 22313 or 31257, operating under the TURIHAB scheme. It is built into one of the towers of the Largo das Portas de Moura, once part of the gateway into the walled town.

WHERE TO EAT

For the surroundings alone the **Pousada dos Lóios** (see WHERE TO STAY for its address) is a real treat. You dine under the vaulted ceiling of the cloister glassed-in when the weather is cold. The cuisine is both regional and international, and prices are moderate. **Cozinha de Santo Humberto**, Rua da Moeda N°39, ((066) 24251, is tucked away in a narrow street. They serve good regional food and prices are moderate. **Guiao**, Rua da República N°81, ((066) 23071, offers excellent Alentejan food. It is inexpensive to moderate. **Fialho**, Travessa das Mascarenhas N° 16, ((066) 23079, has a high profile, being an award-winner and famous for its exceptionally good appetizers. Moderately priced.

HOW TO GET THERE

Trains run to Évora station (about one kilometers southeast of the center) from Lisbon, Faro, and Beja. Travelers from Lisbon need to take the Sul Line from the Barreiro station, and some of the trains require a change at Casa Branca. R.N. Express buses run from Lisbon, Beja, less frequently from Porto, and from other towns in the Alentejo (Elvas, Estremoz, Vila Viçosa, Évoramonte, Portalegre). One bus a day runs from Faro in the Algarve.

By road Évora lies 150 km (93 miles) east of Lisbon. If you are driving, leave the city from the south along the A2-IP1 becoming the N10-IP1 at Setúbal; turn left at Marateca on to the N10-IP11, then on to the N4 to Montemor-o-Novo, and continue along the N114-IP7 to Évora.

AROUND ÉVORA

ARRAIOLOS

Twenty-one kilometers (13 miles) northwest of Évora, this village of white and blue houses is shadowed by the walls around its hilltop castle and ancient parish church. Arraiolos is famous for its handmade rugs, and throughout the village factories or homes and workshops, workers beaver away with brightly colored wools to produce them.

The inspiration came from Persian carpets in the Middle Ages; in the seventeenth century the village began to make its own of hemp or linen and embroidered with wool. Patterns imitating Persian ones were used at first; later the characteristic, simple designs of animals or flowers emerged. They are not cheap, as the work involved is extremely time-consuming: still, the prices are lower here than in Lisbon.

PAVIA

The Alentejo, particularly around Évora, is rich in prehistoric structures called **dolmens**, consisting of two or more upright slabs of stone supporting a horizontal one. The *Turismos* provide details of where to find them, but the most obvious example lies in the middle of the otherwise unremarkable village of Pavia, 20 km (12 miles) north of Arraiolos. This 5,000-year-old monument was enterprisingly turned into a tiny chapel in the sixteenth century, and today stands in a diminutive square, crowned with a small belfry and cross.

ÉVORAMONTE

The name of Évoramonte came to the fore when in 1834 the Convention of Évoramonte was signed there, marking the end of the civil war. The old walled village, some distance away from the newer settlement, is very much a one-donkey, one-street kind of place but worth the side trip from Évora (28 km or 17 miles) or Estremoz for the views from its castle battlements across miles of sun-baked plains.

MONSARAZ

The fortified border town of Monsaraz, 52 km (32 miles) southeast of Évora, has an eagle's eye view of the Alentejan plain and the Guadiana Valley. Its location and stout walls that protected it against enemy attack seem also to have kept the twentieth century at bay. Monsaraz's military days are over, and it has sunk back into sleepy village life. King Dinis' castle, once a Templars' fort, is now a bull ring. A town of great charm, Monsaraz is slowly adapting to visitors: a few shops and cafés have mushroomed and a few rooms are to let.

HOW TO GET THERE

Buses run from both Évora and Estremoz to Arraiolos. Arraiolos is 21 km (13 miles) north of Évora along the N114-4 and the N370. Continue along the N370 for a further 20 km (12 miles) to reach Pavia.

The Évora-Estremoz bus stops at Évoramonte. By car Évoramonte is 28 km (17 miles) from Évora on the N18.

Évora is the nearest railway station to Monsaraz and a bus service connects the two. R.N. buses run infrequently from Lisbon to Évora and Reguengos de Monsaraz, also connected infrequently by bus to Monsaraz. By car (the best way to travel here) Monsaraz lies 52 km (32 miles) southeast of Évora. Drivers should leave Évora on the N18-IP2, after 16 km (10 miles) turn on to the N256 to Reguengos de Monsaraz, then follow the signs to Monsaraz.

NORTHEASTERN ALENTEJO

ESTREMOZ AND ENVIRONS

Gleaming white and stoutly fortified, Estremoz stands on a hilltop in the heart of the province's marble-producing region, 194 km (120 miles) east of Lisbon. It was once a strategically important town, and has retained its Vaubanesque fortifications, its battlemented marble keep, and a garrison. Its size and importance have shrunk over the years, and Estremoz seems to have settled as an agricultural center with a large **Saturday market**, its reputation resting on pottery rather than military strength.

The streets of the old town snake around the ruins of King Dinis's hilltop castle, which together with the palace was largely destroyed in the seventeenth century when the gunpowder store blew up. Part of the **palace** has been restored to create an exceptional *pousada*. In what remains of the castle is a seventeenth-century chapel dedicated to Queen Isabel, built in the room in which she is said to have died in 1336. It is decorated with *azulejos* showing the miracle in which the alms she was smuggling out to the poor turned into roses. Behind the altar a small chamber is set aside for votive offerings.

The hub of the lower town is the large **Rossio Marquês de Pombal**, a busy tree-shaded square fringed with bars and cafés. It is the scene of the Saturday morning **market**, an enjoyable opportunity to buy pottery or the excellent local cheeses.

Vila Viçosa

Thirteen kilometers south of Estremoz, Vila Viçosa was the seat of the Dukes of Bragança, Portugal's royal family from 1442 to 1910, and their vast **Paço Ducal** (Ducal Palace) overwhelms the town. Its severe marble facade occupies one entire side of the Terreiro de Paço (Palace Square), and before it stands a statue of João IV on horseback, the eighth Duke of Bragança but first to be King. Jaime, the fourth duke, killed his young wife and her page here in front of his entire court in a misplaced fit of jealousy. There is a long string of indifferent rooms, some beautiful tapestries, and huge kitchens glowing with hundreds of copper pans. The private rooms are scattered with the personal possessions of the last two kings

Estremoz OPPOSITE TOP rises out of the Alentejo's expansive plains, while further east Monsaraz OPPOSITE BOTTOM crowns a craggy hill top.

and their wives. Open from 9 am to 1 pm and from 2 to 6 pm; closed Mondays, ((068) 98659.

Vila Viçosa's other famous feature is the **Porta dos Nós** (Knot Gate), a much-vaunted gateway set in the sixteenth-century town walls. In a Manueline conceit, unwieldy ropes and knots carved in stone grotesquely lash together the components of the archway. Close by the palace is the **old castle**, the original residence of the Braganças built by King Dinis.

General Information
In Estremoz the *Turismo* is at Largo da Re-

old house with guestrooms, while the **Residencial Alentejano**, Rossio 15, ((068) 22834 or 22343, is above the busy Café Alentejano in the market square, a lively spot offering basic, inexpensive accommodation.

Where to Eat
Under the vaulted and chandeliered ceilings of Estremoz's **Pousada da Rainha Santa Isabel** (see *Where to Stay*), the cuisine is exceptional even by *pousada* standards. Located in a rather grand house on Estremoz's main square, **Aguias d'Ouro** in Rossio

pública Nº26, ((068) 22538, near the Rossio, and there is also a kiosk in the Rossio Marquês de Pombal. At Vila Viçosa the *Turismo* is on the Praça da República, ((068) 98305.

WHERE TO STAY

At Estremoz the best accommodation is at the **Pousada da Rainha Santa Isabel**, 7100 Estremoz, ((068) 22618 or 22655, fax: (068) 23982, housed in the restored palace overlooking the town and the plain below. It is one of the best *pousadas* in the country, with rich fabrics in both public and guest rooms. Luxury prices apply.

Moving downmarket, **Casa Miguel José**, Travessa de Levada Nº8, ((068) 22326, is an

Marquês de Pombal 27, ((068) 22196, has good regional food and wines. Both are moderately priced. The cheery **Arlequim Restaurant**, Rua Dr. Gomes de Resende Jr Nº15, ((068) 23726, is a favorite with both locals and visitors and has some first-rate dishes just a little out of the ordinary.

How to Get There
The nearest railway station to Estremoz is at Évora, where trains run from Lisbon's Barreiro station connecting with buses to Estremoz. R.N. Express buses run infrequently to Estremoz from Lisbon, from Elvas, and from Arraiolos. By road Estremoz is 44 km (27 miles) northeast of Évora along the N18, which becomes the N4 just before reaching town.

Buses run from Évora to Vila Viçosa, and the express from Lisbon passes through Vila Viçosa en route for Elvas. By road Vila Viçosa is 18 km (11 miles) southeast of Estremoz along the N4-IP7 and the N255.

ELVAS

Just 12 km (seven-and-a-half miles) from the border, Elvas is the stoutest fortress on the whole peninsula, possibly even in Europe, and still maintains a garrison. Its Roman and Moorish defenses were reinforced against Spanish attack, and were further extended during the Spanish Wars of Succession. From these well-preserved ramparts are views across the countryside and of the ungainly **Aqueduct of Amoreira** that stretches a total of seven-and-a-half kilometers (five miles) across the plain. Elvas also has a softer side to its character: it is famous for its sugared plums.

Within the walls there are cobbled streets overhung with iron lanterns and wrought-iron balconies brimming with flowers. Overlooking the **Praça da República**, a square paved with diamond-shaped mosaic patterns, is the sixteenth-century Sé (Cathedral) whose fortress-like design and ferocious gargoyles reflect the military aspect of the town. Of more interest is the **Igreja Nossa Senhora da Consolaçao** on the steeply sloping Largo Santa Clara. Unremarkable from the outside, it has an octagonal interior with a distinctly Arab flavor. Blue and yellow *azulejos* line the walls, delicately painted columns support a cupola, and dim lighting creates an air of mystery.

General Information
In Elvas the *Turismo* is also on the Praça da República, ((068) 622236.

Where to Stay and Where to Eat
The **Pousada de Santa Luzia**, Avenida da Badajoz, 7350 Elvas, ((068) 622194 or 622128, fax: (068) 622127, is one of the less attractive modern *pousadas* at mid-range prices, but it has a bar and courtyard. The **Estalagem Dom Sancho II**, Praça da República N°20, ((068) 622684/6, fax: (068) 624717, has more character, with small but pleasant rooms, and a good restaurant. Inexpensive.

How to Get There
The nearest train station to Elvas is at Fontainhas, four kilometers (two-and-a-half miles) north of the city, where trains arrive from Lisbon, Évora, and Badajoz in Spain. A bus service links Fontainhas with Elvas. R.N. Express buses run to Elvas from Lisbon but involve one or two changes, and also run from Évora and Estremoz. By road Elvas is 44 km (28 miles) east of Estremoz along the N4-IP7.

UPPER ALENTEJO

PORTALEGRE
As the capital of the Upper Alentejo, the bustling city of Portalegre is well served by transport and conveniently positioned for exploring Marvão, Castelo de Vide, and the towns of Crato and Alter do Chão. Lying 57 km (35 miles) north of Estremoz, it has an older quarter within the castle walls, a world apart from the so-called new town. Many fine buildings are the legacy of the sixteenth and seventeenth century years of affluence when Portalegre gained fame and revenue from its tapestries and silk mills.

You may enjoy a visit to the **Tapestry Factory**, ((045) 23283, within the old Jesuit seminary where you can see how the expensive business of translating pictures into tapestries is done. Tours operate Monday to Friday 9:30 to 11 am and 2:30 to 4 pm. Nearby on the Avenida George Robinson (he was the founder of town's cork factory) stands the **Church and Convent of São Bernardo**, now used by the infantry although a polite request may gain you admittance to the church. The main reason for doing so is to see the wonderfully pompous tomb of the founder, Bishop Jorge de Melo, the work (at least in part) of Nicolas Chanterène.

From here move along into the old town, making sure to stroll along the **Rua 19 de Junho**, where fantastic wrought-iron work bedecks the houses. This street bring you to the somber **Sé** (Cathedral) next door to the old seminary which houses the **Museu Municipal**. Here archaeological finds and

Montemor-o-Novo's medieval castle OPPOSITE is seen from afar, high above the Alentejan flatness.

sacred art are exhibited with a more eccentric mix of objects. Open from 9:30 to 12:30 and from 2 to 6 pm; closed Tuesdays.

MARVÃO

Twenty-five kilometers (15 miles) northeast of Portalegre, the well-preserved medieval village of Marvão nests some 865 m (2,838 ft) up in the Serra de São Mamede at the foot of a thirteenth-century **castle**. Its sturdy keep offers the best views in the village: you can see across to Spain and, on a good day, the Serra da Estrêla to the north. Such views made Marvão a crucial military point in the past and have made it worthy of its charming *pousada* (see WHERE TO STAY, below).

Visit the **Museu Municipal** in the **Church of Santa Maria** close by the castle to see displays on local costume and culture.

CASTELO DE VIDE

Castelo de Vide is a small, mainly sixteenth-century spa town on the slopes of a wooded hill.

The interesting part of the town is the **Judiaria** (Ghetto) which has remained relatively unchanged since the Middle Ages. There is a small thirteenth-century **synagogue** in the Rua da Judiaria which contains some Hebrew stone inscriptions. Traces of fourteenth century doorways that closed the area off from the Christian parts of town can still be seen and down the hill at the town center, noble buildings surround the **Praça Dom Pedro V**. Among them are the **Paços do Concelho** before which stands a pillory, the eighteenth-century **Church of Santa Maria**, and the **Torre Palace**, now the hospital.

GENERAL INFORMATION

In Portalegre the *Turismo* is at Estrada de Santana Nº25, ℂ (045) 21815; in Marvão there is one at Rua Dr. Matos Magalhães, ℂ (045) 93226; in Castelo de Vide it is at Rua de Bartolomeu Alvares da Santa Nº81, ℂ (045) 91361.

WHERE TO STAY

In Portalegre the **Hotel Dom João III**, Avenida da Liberdade, 7300 Portalegre, ℂ (045) 21192/5, is modern with the bonus of a swimming pool, but rather dull. Prices are mid-range. The **Pensão Alto Alentejo**, Rua 19 de Junho Nº59-63, ℂ (045) 21605, close to the cathedral, has inexpensive rooms and more atmosphere.

Marvão has the **Pousada de Santa Maria**, Rua 24 de Janeiro Nº7, 7330 Marvão, ℂ (045) 93201/2, fax: (045) 93202, made up of three converted old houses in the old town with traditional Alentejan furnishings. It has magnificent views and mid-range prices. Several places offer private accommodation of varying quality within the town walls: ask at the Turismo for details.

In Castelo de Vide the modern **Hotel Sol e Serra**, Estrada de São Vicente, 7320 Castelo de Vide, ℂ (045) 91301, fax: (045) 91337, overlooks a public garden and has a swimming pool, bar and restaurant. Mid-range. Overlooking the same garden, the inexpensive **Albergaria Jardim**, Rua Sequeira Sameiro Nº6, ℂ (045) 91217 or 91577, has less uniformity and more character. The **Pensão Casa do Parque**, Avenida da Arameha 37, ℂ (045) 91250 or 91228, is homely and old-fashioned with low prices.

WHERE TO EAT

In Portalegre, **O Abrigo**, Rua de Elvas Nº74, ℂ (045) 22778, is a centrally placed, inexpensive restaurant and serves regional cuisine. **O Cortico**, Rua Dom Nuno Alvares Pereira Nº17, ℂ (045) 22176, is quite lively at night. Moving upmarket, **O Tarro**, Avenida Movimento das Forças Armadas, ℂ (045) 24345, combines a café and restaurant, and has a more formal atmosphere. Moderate.

In Marvão, the **Pousada de Santa Maria** has a restaurant (see Where to Stay) serving excellent local dishes at moderate prices. In Castelo de Vide some of the best dining to be found is in the hotels and *pensãos*.

HOW TO GET THERE

Trains run from Lisbon, Évora, and Estremoz to the Estação de Portalegre, 12 km (seven-and-a-half miles) south of the city, with a bus shuttle service between the station and Portalegre proper. Several R.N. Express buses run into the center daily

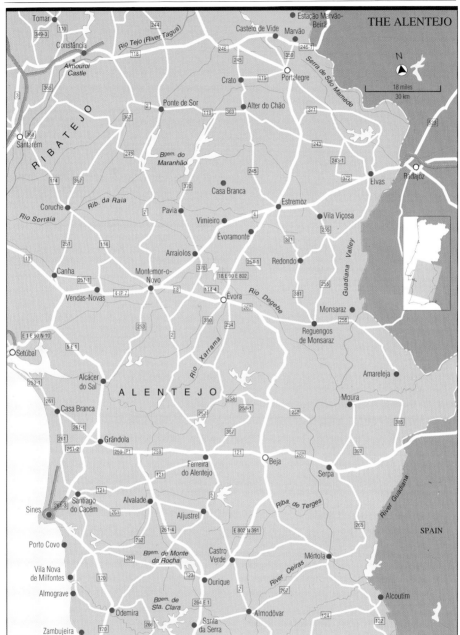

THE ALENTEJO

from Lisbon. By road, Portalegre is 57 km (35 miles) north of Estremoz along the N18-IP2.

Lisbon–Madrid trains stop at the Estação Marvão-Beirâ on the border, about nine kilometers (five miles) north of Marvão and linked to it by bus. Buses also run to the village from Elvas and Portalegre, a quicker option than traveling by train. By car Mar-

vão is 25 km (15 miles) northeast of Portalegre. Drivers should leave Portalegre along the N359 then follow the signs for Marvão.

The nearest train station to Castelo de Vide is also the Estação Marvão-Beirâ, and buses again link the station with the town. By road, Castelo de Vide lies 25 km (15 miles) from Portalegre along the N359 and the N246-1.

LOWER ALENTEJO

BEJA

The capital of the Lower Alentejo stands surrounded by wheat fields, and is the hottest spot in the whole country. Being 177 km (110 miles) from Lisbon, it could serve as a useful base from which to explore the Lower Alentejo, although accommodation here is limited to *pensãos*.

The Convent houses the **Museu Regional**, ((084) 23351, exhibiting coins and mosaics from Roman and Visigoth eras, Spanish, Portuguese and Flemish paintings and the usual church treasures.

SERPA

Serene and white, Serpa lies 27 km (17 miles) west of Beja, set amid fertile land famous for its ewes' milk cheese, and if you are lucky (or unlucky) you may have your ear bent by the mournful songs of the traditional Alentejan male choir which sometimes puts in an appearance in town. On the main square, the **Café Alentejano** makes a convenient place to stop for lunch.

Entering the town by the **Porta de Beja**, the first sight of Serpa is impressive: an eleventh-century **aqueduct** runs along part of the castle walls, its slender arches more graceful than those of the stodgier Elvas construction. The walls themselves remain largely intact, but as you enter the courtyard you will see a great slab of masonry menacingly poised overhead. No need to worry: it has been like that since 1707 when the Spanish blew up part of the fortifications! The castle's **museum** has some prehistoric, Roman, Visigoth and Moorish remains, as well as a rather alarming life-sized tableau of the Last Supper.

MÉRTOLA

The sleepy little town of Mértola lies 50 km (31 miles) southeast of Beja, overlooking the River Guadiana at its confluence with the River Oeiras. A steep, winding road leads up to the ruined **castle** overlooking the small streets and modern town. Down the

hill a converted thirteenth-century mosque is now a unique **Igreja Matriz.** Inside this whitewashed building the ceiling is low and vaulted, and a niche known as a mihrab, which indicates the direction of Mecca, is a reminder of its former use.

GENERAL INFORMATION

In Beja the *Turismo* is at Rua Capitão J.F. de Sousa Nº25, ((084) 23693, south of the central square; in Serpa at Largo Dom Jorge de Melo Nº2, ((084) 90335; in Mértola it is on the the Rua da República.

HOW TO GET THERE

Trains from Lisbon's Barreiro station, from Évora, and less frequently from Faro run to Beja. R.N. Express buses run to Beja from Lisbon and Faro. By road, Beja lies 177 km (110 miles) from Lisbon. Drivers should follow the IP1 out of Lisbon and 20 km (12 miles) beyond Grandola turn on to the IP8 to Beja. From Évora Beja is 77 km (48 miles) along the N18-IP2.

Serpa is served by bus only. The nearest train station is at Beja which is linked to the town by bus. One R.N. Express bus runs daily from Lisbon to Serpa. By road Serpa is 27 km (17 miles) from Beja along the N260-IP8.

The R.N express from Lisbon also serves Mértola. By road, Mértola is 50 km (31 miles) southeast of Beja on the N122.

THE COAST

One of the greatest surprises that the Alentejo has is its lovely (and as yet unspoiled) coastline, a combination of cliffs and coves. The waters here are colder and rougher than in the Algarve and it can be windy, but if you like rugged seascapes and don't mind the scarcity of tourist amenities, this could suit you well.

PORTO COVO DA BANDEIRA

In this clean and orderly village 173 km (128 miles) south of Lisbon, neat white cottages with blue trim are laid out along a grid plan, the handiwork of the Marquês de Pombal who gave instructions to rebuild the village after the 1755 earthquake. It has the sea on its doorstep, a few cafés, bars, restaurants and a *pensão*. Just one kilometer offshore is the Ilha do Pessegueiro, (Peach Tree Island), fortified during the seventeenth century to protect the village from pirate attack, containing the remains of a Roman harbor and a sixteenth-century church. The real attraction is the onshore **beach** facing the island, with a campsite, washing facilities, and restaurant.

VILA NOVA DE MILFONTES

This is probably the most popular place on the Alentejan coastline, 17 km (10 miles) south of Porto Covo and a favorite *Lisboetan* holiday spot at the mouth of the River Mira. The fishing town itself is typically Alentejan in style, surrounded by rolling hills, sandy beaches, and overlooked by a small medieval castle now restored to provide some some of the most exclusive accommodation on the coast. Its few hotels and pensãos, tend to fill up fast during summer months.

ON THE WAY SOUTH

Twelve kilometers (seven-and-a-half miles) south of Vila Nova de Milfontes the coastline becomes more dramatic and rockier at **Almograve**. The beach here is quiet and has a nudist section at the southern end. The village has a smattering of bars and cafés, but little else. Further south, **Zambujeira** offers a similarly dramatic prospect, perched on a cliff above the beach; its lack of accommodation means that you will probably have to limit yourself to a daytrip.

A better possibility for accommodation is the inland town of **Odemira**, an oasis of green in the typically sunburnt Alentejan landscape. Overlooking the River Mira it is not quite geared to a tourist inflow, but can cope with a few visitors.

WHERE TO STAY

In Porto Cova there are a couple of reasonable *pensãos* that are basic, while Vila Nova

de Milfontes has a wider range. Top of the list is the **Castelo de Milfontes**, ((083) 96108, housed within the old fort. It offers some exclusive accommodation and food, but bookings should be made well in advance. Prices are high. Other private accommodation is on offer under the *Turismo de Habitação* scheme at the **Quinta do Moinho de Vento**, Milfontes, 7645 Vila Nova de Milfontes, ((083) 96383, fax: (083) 96383, a modern villa close to the beach. In addition there are a few *pensãos* and a modern complex outside the town itself.

Zambujeira has a some basic *pensãos*, but Odemira has more. The **Residencial Rita**, Largo do Poco Novo, 7630 Odemira, ((083) 22423, and the **Pensão Paisagem**, Avenida das Escolas de São Teotónio, ((083) 95406, fax: (083) 95442, are inexpensively priced.

HOW TO GET THERE

An express bus runs twice daily from Lisbon to Vila Nova de Milfontes, Almograve, and Zambujeira. A local service links Odemira to Zambujeira and there is a more frequent service between Odemira, Almograve, and Vila Nova de Milfontes. A car is by far the best way of getting around the coast.

By road Vila Nova de Milfontes lies 190 km (118 miles) south of Lisbon. Drivers should leave Lisbon along the IP1, turn off shortly before Grandola on to the IP8 and continue along it until just outside Sines, then take the N120 to Vila Nova de Milfontes. To continue on to Almograve, 12 km (seven miles) further south, take the N393 out of Vila Nova then follow the signs. Zambujeira lies 18 km (11 miles) further south along the coastal road while Odemira lies 19 km (12 miles) inland. Porto Cova is 28 km south of Sines, best accessed along the coastal road south of the town.

The Algarve

WITH ITS WARM winters, brilliant summers, and beautiful beaches, it was inevitable that this southernmost strip of Portugal should attract tourists from around the world. In fact, it has for centuries: the Phoenicians, the Carthaginians, the Romans, and the Moors — who clung to it doggedly until they were prised out in 1249 — all arrived. Their legacy lives on in the local place names, (Algarve itself is derived from *Al Gharb* meaning the West), in the cuisine, and the design of the houses, traditionally low with roof terraces and crowned with the latticed chimney tops that have become a symbol of the province.

Unfortunately, the tourist boom of the 1970s resulted in unchecked development, overcrowded beaches, and the spoiling of many of the very elements that the tourist industry sought to exploit. Villas are still going up in the Algarve, though this time with a view to attracting quality tourists, the kind prepared to spend more money than those on cheap package holidays. Crowds have colonized the coastline between Faro and Lagos but there are still corners where one can enjoy the superb climate in relative peace.

Spring is a particularly good time to visit when there are fewer people around. Visitors in January and February may get to see one of the Algarve's most famous spectacles: the almond trees in blossom.

The quieter parts of the province are to be found east of Faro, west of Lagos, and inland where the Monchique and Caldeirão mountains separate the province from the Alentejo. However, there is no doubt that if you are looking for glorious weather, beaches, sporting opportunities — including some of Europe's top golf courses — and good tourist facilities, you will find plenty of choice in the resort-filled Faro-Lagos strip.

EASTERN ALGARVE

ALCOUTIM AND CASTRO MARIM

One of the most enchanting corners of the Algarve is its eastern edge beside the Spanish border. The road meanders through the hills along the Guadiana River, passing border towns and villages such as the little river port of **Alcoutim**, where whitewashed houses

and sleeping dogs lie at the foot of a ruined fourteenth-century castle facing the larger Spanish fortress across the river in Sanlucar. Unwind a little, rest on one of the benches at the quayside, and just watch the river flow.

Migratory and wading birds proliferate around **Castro Marim**, some 40 km (25 miles) south of Alcoutim, where the fertile marshland as far as Vila Real de Santo António is a nature reserve. Castro Marim was the headquarters of the Order of Christ from 1321 until 1334, when it was moved to Tomar. Their castle, along with a fortress

built by King João IV on a facing hill, was reduced to ruins by the 1755 earthquake. If you are interested in a hike through the nature reserve, look in at the castle where the *Turismo* can furnish you with details of walks and wildlife.

VILA REAL DE SANTO ANÓTNIO

Just four kilometers (two-and-a-half miles) south of Castro Marim is Vila Real de Santo António, a major border crossing point. The proximity of the popular seaside resort of **Monte Gordo**, three kilometers (two miles)

Silves OPPOSITE was the Moorish capital of "Al Gharb," whose coastline ABOVE has all the ingredients of the modern beach holiday.

to the west, together with the through traffic makes this a busy place geared to tourism. Its center was built at the command of the Marquês de Pombal, with the same rigid geometry as he applied to Pombaline Lisbon, but here the effect is somewhat soulless. One of the main reasons to visit Vila Real is to take a **boat trip** up the River Guadiana or to make a quick foray into Spain (ask at the *Turismo* for details of trips).

It is a surprise to find a little oasis of peace 14 km (nine miles) west of Vila Real at the tiny village of **Cacela Velha**, centered around a fortress and church high on a clifftop and with views looking over the sandspit.

TAVIRA

Tavira is perhaps the prettiest town in the Algarve, unspoiled despite catering to tourists. A mixture of holiday town and tuna fishing port, it is cut off from the sea by the sandy spit. The town occupies both banks of the River Séquia, which is crossed by two bridges, one of them a seven-arched Roman structure. A garden stretches along one bank, complete with bandstand, palm trees, and an ornamental building that houses the morning **market** where fish, local produce, and handicrafts are sold. Behind the gardens there is a long row of seafood restaurants while elsewhere in the town there are cafés to cater more for the fishermen's needs.

Tavira seems overendowed with churches. The hilltop **Church of Santa Maria do Castelo**, contains the tombs of crusading knights including that of Dom Paio Peres Correia, who captured Tavira from the Moors in 1242, but views of the town are best from the ruined castle nearby. The **Carmo Church** with its baroque interior is worth a visit, as is the fine renaissance **Misericórdia Church**. You may have to ask around for keys to both these places.

The sandbar, known as the **Ilha de Tavira**, has a stretch of beach along its eastern side. A bus from Tavira will take you to the Praia de Tavira, two kilometers (one mile) out of town, where boats leave frequently for the stretch throughout the summer months. It tends to get quite crowded in the high season.

GENERAL INFORMATION

Vila Real de Santo António's *Turismo* is on the Praça Marquês de Pombal, ((081) 43272; Tavira's on the Praça da República, ((081) 22511.

WHERE TO STAY

Tavira's **Hotel Apartamento Eurotel**, Quinta das Oliveiras, 8800 Tavira, ((081) 324324, fax: (081) 325571, is a large and luxu-

rious tourist development by the sea a few kilometers east of Tavira with good leisure facilities. Self-catering apartments and hotel rooms are available, and prices vary from inexpensive to mid-range. In Tavira itself, the **Pensão do Castelo**, Rua da Liberdade N°4, ((081) 23942, has large rooms, and the **Pensão Princesa do Gilão**, Rua Borda d'Agua de Aguiar, 8800 Tavira, ((081) 22665, overlooking the river, is particularly popular with youngsters. Both are inexpensive.

The Algarve's eastern flank is still relatively unscathed by the excesses of tourist developments. It's jewel is Tavira OPPOSITE TOP and ABOVE near an off-shore sand bar OPPOSITE BOTTOM.

WHERE TO EAT

Something worth sampling during a stay in the Algarve is one of the delicious seafood dishes prepared in a *cataplana*, a Moorish precursor of the modern-day pressure cooker, comprising two hemispherical copper halves that fit tightly together. *Cataplana* dishes are usually ordered as a main course to be shared by two people.

In Tavira the quayside restaurants offer an excellent range of seafood. **O Caneção**,

Rua José Pires Padinha N°162, ℂ (081) 819211, and **Cad'Oro** at number 148, ℂ (081) 325746, both offer excellent food and wine with good service. Prices vary between inexpensive and moderate. Slightly back from the quayside, the **Restaurante Imperial**, Rua do Cais N°22, ℂ (081) 22234, has some of the best seafood in town.

HOW TO GET THERE

The Algarve Line links Lagos with Vila Real de Santo António, calling at Portimão, Silves, Tunes, Faro, and Tavira. Lisbon trains link with the Algarve line at Tunes. There are also plenty of buses linking Tavira with Vila Real de Santo António, Faro, and other towns in the eastern Algarve. At Vila Real ferries run to the Spanish town of Ayamonte, en route for Huelva and Sevilla.

By road Vila Real de Santo António lies 51 km (32 miles) from Faro and 23 km (14 miles) from Tavira, along the N125 which follows the coast. The N122 runs north of Vila Real shadowing the path of the River Guadiana,

going through Castro Marim, four kilometers (two-and-a-half miles) north of Vila Real, and continuing northwards into the Alentejo, passing close by Alcoutim, 40 km (25 miles) north of Castro Marim.

OLHÃO AND THE ILHAS

The town of Olhão, eight kilometers (five miles) east of Faro, is one of the Algarve's major fishing ports, and beyond its seedy outskirts the old section is a maze of Moroccan-style houses. Unlike the lacey designs most commonly seen in the Algarve, these square, flat-roofed buildings with stairways on the outside and simple angular chimneys, makes the town distinctive and drew the attention of artists when they explored Cubist themes.

GENERAL INFORMATION

The *Turismo* is on the Rua do Comércio, ℂ (089) 713936.

WHAT TO SEE AND DO

The main attraction is the ferry service to two nearby islands where (surprising for these parts) it is possible to find enough sand to lie on without finding your toe lodged in a fellow sunbather's ear. Ferries run every hour or so to **Ilha da Armona** (less frequently after September), which has swimming, a few restaurants, beach huts and a lot of sand, all preferable to the other option, the **Ilha da Culatra**.

Much of the Olhão's daily life centers around the extensive indoor **fish market**, one of the best in the country. Nearby the public park next to the river affords views of the **Reserva Natural da Ria Formosa**, a wildlife reserve some five kilometers (three miles) long that encompasses islands and a sandspit and contains large oyster and clam beds that are a drawcard for those who like fresh molluscs.

The bell tower of the baroque **Church of Nossa Senhora de Rosário** on the main street offers good views of the unusual townscape, and at the back of it, the **Capela dos Aflitos** is open all hours for women who come to pray for those in danger on the sea.

WHERE TO STAY

The **Hotel Ria Sol**, Rua General Humberto Delgado N°37, 8700 Olhão, ((089) 705267, has inexpensive rooms, all with telephones and private baths. Apart from this there are half a dozen or so *pensãos*, the best of which are the **Pensão Bela Vista**, Rua Teófilo Braga N°65-67, ((089) 702538, and the **Pensão Helena**, Rua Dr. Miguel Bombarda, N°42, ((089) 702634. Both are inexpensive.

decayed; its clock has stopped at ten to three, and although plans are afoot for restoration it will take a long time to return it to its former glory. The gardens are still carefully tended, possibly by the man who is followed through the grounds by an entourage of 20 or so very friendly dogs.

Because of its dilapidation access to the palace itself is prohibited, but the views of it from the garden, where statues rise above palm trees, orange groves, magnolias, and rare plants, make this a very rewarding side trip. The centerpiece is the ornamental

HOW TO GET THERE

Olhão is on the Algarve Line, so trains link it to towns in the eastern and western Algarve, as do the local bus services. By road it is eight kilometers (five miles) east of Faro and 43 km (27 miles) west of Vila Real de Santo António along the N125.

ESTÓI AND MILREU

In the little village of Estói, 11 km (seven miles) north of Faro, is the **Palácio do Visconde de Estói**, hidden behind a pink wall. This pink rococo confection is now quite

staircase, tiled, balustraded and topped with statuary. At its foot an iron grille protects a vaulted and columned chamber containing statues of goddesses, surrounded by greenery. If you strain your eyes you will see that the interior walls are decorated with Roman mosaics appropriated from nearby Milreu. While walking through the gardens look out for the elegant wrought-iron bandstand surrounded by greenery and palms. Its canopy is edged with lace-like ironwork, and the dogs sometimes doze in the shadow of its music stand.

Frescoes OPPOSITE in the Palácio do Visconde de Estói. The brilliantly white Moorish fishing port ABOVE of Olhão.

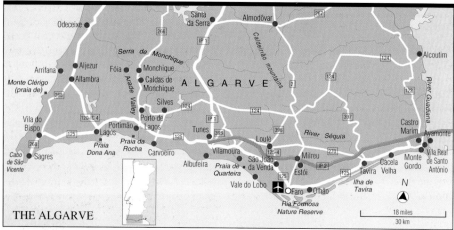

THE ALGARVE

Roughly one kilometers west of Estói and just off the road at Milreu are the remains of the Roman town of *Ossonoba*, built between the first and third centuries and occupied until about the sixth century. A ruined apse stands in a field, once a temple, later used as a church. There are the remains of baths, columns and delicate mosaics of dolphins, prawns, and other forms of sea life. Excavation here is still at a relatively early stage.

WHERE TO STAY

The nearest accommodation is to be found eight kilometers (five miles) to the north of Estói and 17 km (10 miles) north of Faro at the town of São Brás de Alportel. There are rooms to rent here, but many choose to stay at the **Pousada de São Brás**, Estrada de Lisboa, N2, 8150 São Brás de Alportel, ((089) 842306, fax: (089) 842305, an attractive 1940s villa with views of the Serra de Caldeirão. Its swimming pool and pleasant sun terrace make it a good and comfortable base from which to explore the eastern Algarve. Mid-range prices apply.

HOW TO GET THERE

Buses run frequently to Estói from Faro and also to São Brás de Alportel from both Faro and Loulé. By road from Olhão, Estói lies 10 km (six miles) northwest of Olhão along the N2-6; from Faro it is 11 km (seven miles) north along the N2.

FARO

The old walled town and harbor (now a yacht marina) surrounded by street cafés and squares is a setting of great charm, an affliction that has caused the Algarve's capital to swell almost unchecked with huge apartments and holidaymakers basking on the beach just nine kilometers (six miles) from the city center.

BACKGROUND

The Moors founded the city of Faro early in the eighth century, and by the time the Christians captured it in 1249, Faro had grown into a prosperous and important port. Following the re-conquest, the city was rebuilt and in 1577 became a bishopric. Its new pride was short-lived, for in 1596, during the period of Spanish rule, English troops under the Earl of Essex sacked and burnt the city after removing 200 valuable books from the Bishop's Palace, which became an important asset of the Bodleian Library in Oxford. Further disaster befell Faro in the guise of the great earthquake of 1755 but it was again rebuilt under the direction of Bishop Francisco Gomes de Avelar.

GENERAL INFORMATION

The *Turismo* is at Rua de Misericórdia Nº8-12, ((089) 25404, and there is also a desk at the airport, ((089) 22582, which is located about six kilometers (four miles) out of town.

WHAT TO SEE AND DO

At the eastern end of the harbor, the eighteenth-century renaissance archway known as the **Arco da Vila** leads into the old walled town from the Jardim Manuel Bivar. The Rua do Municipio will bring you to the **Largo da Sé**, a cobbled square surrounded by elegant buildings. Amongst them stands the **Cathedral,** a baroquified structure of no great interest, other than for a rather daring but incongruous red Chinoiserie organ. Behind it, the two-storied cloister of the sixteenth-century **Convento de Nossa Senhora** is now an **Archaeological Museum,** with an excellent collection of Roman, pre-Roman, and Moorish remains. Some Roman statues on display were unearthed at nearby Milreu, and one room is set aside solely for the reconstituted Roman mosaic of Neptune uncovered in Faro itself. Open from 9 am to noon and from 2 to 5 pm; closed Saturdays.

Leaving the walled town by the Arco do Repouso, look in at the **Igreja de São Francisco** to see that very Portuguese combination of gilt-covered woodwork and blue and white azulejos. In the Praça Alexandre Herculano, the **Museu Etnográfica Regional,** ((089) 27610, provides an insight into local culture with models of houses, reconstructed interiors, paintings, and photographs of Faro before the tourist explosion of the 1970s. Open from 9:30 am to 12:30 pm and from 2 to 5:30 pm; closed Sundays.

North of the harbor in the Largo do Carmo, behind the grand baroque facade of the **Igreja do Carmo,** lurks the gruesome **Capelo dos Ossos,** a chapel whose walls are decorated with skulls and bones from the surrounding cemetery.

WHERE TO STAY

Hotel Eva, Avenida da República N°1, 8000 Faro, ((089) 803354, fax: (089) 802304, is generally held to have the best accommodation in town. There are some rooms in this modern hotel on the harborfront that overlook the sea and others that face the old town. It provides plenty of amenities: rooftop swimming pool, hairdressing salon, bar, restaurant, and disco. Prices vary from mid-range to expensive.

The English-run **Casa de Lumena**, Praça Alexandre Herculano N°27, ((089) 801990, is an old townhouse decorated with antique furniture, and has a popular bar and restaurant. Its prices are mid-range. The **Pensão Madalena**, Rua Conselheiro Bivar N°109, ((089) 805806, is inexpensive, friendly, and efficiently run.

WHERE TO EAT

Restaurante Cidade Velha, Rua Domingos Gueiro N°19, ((089) 27145, is the smartest

place in town to dine. It is located in an eighteenth-century house close to the cathedral, offering local and international cuisine. Moderate. **Dois Irmaos**, Largo do Terreiro do Bispo, ((089) 23337, is old by Faro standards, as it started life in the 1920s. It serves seafood, particularly *cataplana* dishes, and it is inexpensive.

HOW TO GET THERE

International and domestic flights from Lisbon and Porto arrive at Faro airport (see the GETTING THERE section under TRAVELERS' TIPS), six kilometers (four miles) west of the town. A bus shuttles between the airport and the town center, and taxis are plentiful. The Algarve Line links Faro by rail to Lagos in the west and Vila Real de Santo António in the east. Buses link Faro with all the main towns in the Algarve and various express services, including R.N. Express, run between Lisbon and Faro.

Faro's Capelo dos Ossos decorated with skulls and bones from foor to ceiling.

By road, Faro is 300 km (196 miles) southeast of Lisbon along the IP1, and 52 km (32 miles) from Vila Real de Santo António.

FROM FARO TO LAGOS

This stretch of coastline is jam-packed with resorts and tourist villages; it has the highest concentration of package holiday destinations in the Algarve. **Vale do Lobo**, 16 km (10 miles) west of Faro, has a huge and luxurious holiday village with its own

sports facilities including golf courses. Moving downmarket, neighboring **Praia de Quarteira** has long shed its image of a small fishing village, while nearby **Vilamoura** is one of the largest tourist developments in the Algarve, boasting two 18-hole golf courses.

Albufeira lies 36 km (22 miles) west of Faro, a one-time clifftop fishing village that seethes with holidaymakers. Its **old town**, however, has retained its charm, where the narrow streets are lined with whitewashed

houses and crossed by Moorish arches, gaily-painted boats still line the fishermen's beach, and there is a morning fish market. The main beach is framed by jagged cliffs and reached by a tunnel carved through the rock.

West of Albufeira is a sweep of rock-sheltered beaches where development is similarly intensive. The relatively small resort of **Carvoeiro** is pleasant but its beach quickly gets overcrowded during the peak season. Continuing westwards, the large fishing town of **Portimão** is notable only for its shopping opportunities and the proximity of the delightful **Praia da Rocha**. This, along with the **Praia Dona Ana** (nearer Lagos), is one of the most-photographed Algarvian beaches, unusually framed by strange yellow rock formations but spoilt by the crowds.

One of the most elegant resorts is **Lagos**, a harbor town that has retained a great deal of charm, probably more so than any other along this stretch of coastline. No visit here is complete without a look at the early eighteenth-century **Church of Santo António**, the interior of which shimmers with baroque gilt. Attached to the church is the **Regional Museum** with exhibits of a very general kind. Another curiosity is the strange **statue of King Sebastião** in the Praça Gil Eanes, commemorating the ill-fated crusade against the Moors that he led from Lagos in 1578. In an attempt to capture the essence of the messianic cult that grew up around King Sebastião (whose body was never found) the sculptor, João Cutileiro, has depicted him as a bewildered spaceman.

INLAND

LOULÉ

About 20 km (12 miles) northwest of Faro, Loulé is something of a craftwork center, with numerous shops that sell locally-produced baskets, lace, leather, and metalwork. You can see some of its craftsmen at work in the **Art Gallery and Handicraft Center** close by the castle. The restored medieval **castle** now houses the *Turismo* as well as the

---

The golf professional ABOVE and marina OPPOSITE TOP at Vilamoura. Cafés line the waterfront at Portimão OPPOSITE BOTTOM. OVERLEAF: Praiia da Rocha, "Rocky Beach" west of Faro is a favorite for the Algarves sun worshippers.

Museu Municipal which has some archaeological exhibits. The thirteenth-century
Igreja Matriz in the Largo da Matriz is
worthy of a brief visit, a Gothic-style building with a tiled interior looking on to the
evocatively-named Jardim dos Amuados —
Sulky People's Garden.

SILVES

As Xelb, the Moorish cultural and political
capital of the Algarve, this city was once
famous for its great beauty. Now a shadow
of its former self, Silves has some riverside
cafés and restaurants. There are few vestiges
of its bygone glory other than the heavily
restored Moorish castle, whose red sandstone ramparts still dominate the town.
Apart from the views from the walls, the
most interesting features in the castle are
the huge vaulted cisterns which stored
water during the sieges of the *Reconquista*
period when Moorish strongholds resisted
Christian forces.

The red sandstone Sé was founded in
1189, then rebuilt in 1242; although the
structure has undergone extensive repair
work over the years it has retained its Gothic
simplicity. In it are tombs believed to be
those of Crusaders killed during the *reconquista*. At the eastern edge of the town
along the N124 stands one of Portugal's
most prized monuments, the sixteenth-
century Cruz de Portugal (Cross of Portugal), a white sandstone cross with a lacey
outline that bears the image of the crucified
Christ on one side and his ascent on the
other.

CALDAS DE MONCHIQUE

The roads running inland from Portimão
and Silves meet at Porto de Lagos, where
N266 continues north along the Arade
valley, climbing into the wooded Serra de
Monchique. This mountain range divides
the Algarve from the Alentejo and provides a cool retreat from the busy coastline,
while remaining within easy daytripping
distance of the beaches. The road leads to
the little spa town of Caldas de Monchique,
set in a ravine some 22 km (14 miles) northwest of Silves, that apart from the advent

of a modern bottling plant and spa, has
hardly changed since the nineteenth century. It has a faded charm with some
unusual *pensãos*.

Many of the buildings date from the
nineteenth century when the town enjoyed great popularity, particularly with the
well-to-do Spanish. A remnant of this heyday is a mock-Moorish casino, now a craft
center in a shaded square alongside cafés
and restaurants. Today the thermal waters
(said to be good for rheumatism and respi-

Romantic Silves castle ABOVE stands on a hill
blanketed with almond groves and orange orchards.
Inhabitants of inland Monchique OPPOSITE and
Silves ABOVE do brisk business with tourists
through the summer months.

ratory problems) can be taken at the modern spa.

MONCHIQUE

The N266 continues to climb upwards for some seven kilometers (four miles) from Caldas de Monchique to the town of Monchique, where low whitewashed houses lie high up in the *serra*, overlooked by the ruined Franciscan monastery of **Nossa Senhora do Desterro**. Marvelous views reward those prepared to make the climb to it. The town itself has several craft shops but few buildings of individual interest other than its **Igreja Matriz**, which has a Manueline doorway surrounded by carved ropes twisted and knotted into five points above the arch.

FÓIA

One of the most spectacular panoramas in the whole country is to be had at Fóia, eight kilometers (five miles) west of Monchique. Here the highest point in the *serra* is marked by an obelisk and an unsightly television transmitter, with views from Portimão to the Cabo de São Vicente. There are a few shops, a *pensão*, and a hotel here as many organized tours of the Algarve make stops.

GENERAL INFORMATION

In Loulé the *Turismo* is in the castle, ((089) 63900.

In Silves, you can find the *Turismo* at Rua 25 de Abril, ((082) 442255.

WHERE TO STAY

Loulé has a few *pensãos* and one hotel, the **Hotel Loulé Jardim**, Praça Manuel d'Arriaga, 8100 Loulé, ((089) 413094/5, fax: (089) 63177. Its traditional building, quite luxuriously furnished, has two bars, a restaurant, and a swimming pool. Mid-range.

Silves has the modern **Albergaria Solar dos Mouros**, Horta do Pocinho Santo, 8300

Silves, ((082) 443106, fax: (082) 443108, which has an excellent restaurant, good rooms and low prices. Otherwise there are a few pensãos and the possibility of renting private rooms.

At Caldas de Monchique, the **Hospedaria Central** in the main square, ((082) 92203, has charm and a good restaurant. Inexpensive. **Albergaria do Lageado**, ((082) 92616, 8550 Monchique, has small rooms, a garden with swimming pool and patio, a restaurant and a bar. Inexpensive.

Set in woods a few kilometers outside Monchique, the **Estalagem Abrigo da Montanha**, Corte Pereiro, Estrada de Fóia, ((082) 92131, fax: (082) 93660, has views down to the coast. Mid-range.

The Algarve

WHERE TO EAT

Loulé has several bars and places to eat including a couple of French restaurants. Some of the best food is to be had at the smart **Avenida** on Avenida José da Costa Mealha, ((089) 62106. Moderate.

At Silves there are bars and cafés at the riverside with outdoor seating in the warm weather. **Marisqueira Rui**, attached to the Albergaria Solar dos Mouros, is good, inexpensive, and popular.

Caldas de Monchique has several restaurants, the best of them being the **Restaurante Central**, attached to the Hospedaria Central. Moderate.

HOW TO GET THERE

There are frequent buses between Faro and Loulé. Silves is served by the Algarve Line which links it with major towns in the province, Silves is also linked to Portimão, and Portimão has bus service to Monchique.

To reach Loulé by road from Faro, a distance of 20 km, take the N125 until São João da Venda where you turn on to the N125-4. To reach Silves from Loulé, 47 km (29 miles) away, head out of Loulé along the N270 then continue along the N125 to Lagoa, where you can follow the signs north to Silves. Caldas de Monchique lies a further 22 km (13 miles) north of Silves along the N124 as far as Porto de Lagos, then north along the N266. Monchique is a further seven kilometers (four miles) north along the N266.

ODECEIXE TO SAGRES

Along the Algarve's west coast, on the provincial border with the Alentejo, the Moorish-style village of Odeceixe lies just three kilometers (two miles) from the **Praia de Odeceixe**. This sandy cove is sheltered by high cliffs; there is good surfing because this is a quiet spot except during the peak

Prince Henry the Navigator founded his school of navigation ABOVE at Sagres. Further east at Alvor OPPOSITE, the coastline is pitted with caves.

summer months. In the village there are cafés and restaurants, and a few of the houses have rooms to rent.

Seventeen kilometers (10 miles) further south along the coastal road, the village of **Aljezur** huddles below a ruined castle, and with accommodation in the form of private rooms and a *pensão* it makes a convenient spot from which to visit the sandy beaches of **Monte Clérigo**, eight kilometers (five miles) to the northwest and **Arrifana**, 10 km (six miles) southwest, both more peaceful than Odeceixe.

A further 45 km (28 miles) south along the coast is Europe's most southwesterly point, the **Cabo de São Vicente**, a lonely exposed promontory 75 m (246 ft) above the crashing waves. For hundreds of years this was a shrine to St. Vincent, whose martyred body is said to have arrived by boat in the twelfth century, guided by ravens who continued to keep watch over his grave until he was removed to Lisbon. Now all that stands here is a powerful **lighthouse** and the ruins of a sixteenth-century **Capuchin convent**.

Six kilometers (four miles) east is **Sagres**, where Prince Henry founded the School of Navigation, the powerhouse of the Voyages of Discovery; there navigation was taught and voyages were plotted. English attack under Sir Francis Drake followed by the ravages of the 1755 earthquake, ensured that nothing remains of the school. The major point of interest is the **fortress**, believed to have been built on or near the site of the school, and itself rebuilt after the same earthquake. It has a fourteenth-century chapel which is usually locked, but most impressive of all is the **rosa de ventos** — the wind compass — made of stones set into the ground on the plateau overlooking the sea. Excavated earlier this century, it measures 43 m (141 feet) in diameter, a strange construction that seems to date from the time of Henry the Navigator. Today its radial lines are traced with moss. The fishing village of Sagres does have some accommodation and restaurants.

GENERAL INFORMATION

In Sagres the *Turismo* is in the main square in Sagres village, ((082) 64125.

WHERE TO STAY

In Sagres, the **Pousada do Infante**, 8650 Sagres, ((082) 64222/3, fax: (082) 64225, is a modern building built in Algarvian style perched on a cliff overlooking the port. It has a swimming pool and tennis courts. Mid-range prices apply. It also has an annex, the **Fortaleza do Belixe**, ((082) 64124, located in the fort and run along the same lines as the *pousada* with prices at the lower end of mid-range.

HOW TO GET THERE

There is a frequent bus service from Lagos to Sagres, and a couple-a-day run from Lagos to Aljezur via Sagres.

To reach Sagres and the Cabo de São Vicente from Faro by car, take the N125 to Lagos then follow the signs to Vila do Bispo, where you take the N268 to Sagres. For Aljezur and Odeceixe, take the N125 from Faro as far as Lagos, then continue northwards along the IC4. Drivers from Lisbon should leave the city on the IP1, branching off to the N263 to Odemira then continue south along the N120-IC4 to Odeceixe. To proceed to Sagres and São Vicente, turn off the IC4 on to the N268.

Giant sundial ABOVE at Sagres. Natural rock bridge OPPOSITE frames bathers at a beach west of Faro.

Travelers'
Tips

GETTING TO PORTUGAL

BY AIR

TAP Air Portugal, Portugal's national airline, offers a variety of saver fares and discounts, and can arrange reasonably-priced car rentals to fit in with your flight and travel plans. In New York the TAP office is at 521 Fifth Avenue, ((212) 661-0035, fax: (212) 867-3275, and in London it's at 19 Lower Regent Street, ((071) 839-1031, fax: (071) 839-3682.

In Britain both TAP and British Airways operate direct flights from London to the main Portuguese airports of Lisbon, Faro, and Porto, and TAP also runs flights from Manchester and Dublin to Lisbon, and from Birmingham to Faro. There are hosts of package holidays to Portugal and therefore numerous charter flights, mainly to Faro in the Algarve, although there are also a few to Lisbon and Porto. This makes it possible to pick up a cheap flight through a charter operator or bucket shop.

TAP flies from New York, Newark, Boston, Toronto, and Montréal to Lisbon, with connecting flights from Los Angeles; TWA flies from New York; Air Canada from Montréal and Toronto. All land in Lisbon. TAP and its subsidiary airline, LAR, operate an internal network of services linking the main Portuguese airports with regional ones.

BY TRAIN

All international rail connections run through Spain and France. Probably the most comfortable train is the Spanish *Talgo* express from Paris to Madrid, where you have to change on to the *Lisboa* Express: two trains a day depart from the Gare d'Austerlitz in Paris each evening, and two trains from Madrid–Chamartin at roughly the same times. The journey takes 12 to 15 hours, depending on the service. The *Sud Express* also runs from Paris, and goes either to Lisbon via Coimbra or to Porto. Unless you have an Interail or Eurorail card, the train fare is not significantly cheaper than an air ticket. The journey takes 24 hours from Paris to Lisbon and about two days if you start from London. The journey time from Madrid to Lisbon is 10 hours.

New rail links with Europe are currently at the planning stage, and will eventually reduce international journey times.

BY BUS

There are international coach services from London and Paris although these can be more expensive than charter flights. National Express operate services from London's Victoria Coach Station to Coimbra, Lisbon and the Algarve, and the journey spans a grueling three days. Further infor-

mation is available from Victoria Coach Station, London, ((071) 730-0202.

BY CAR

If you're bringing your own car to Portugal from England you will have the choice of the Channel Tunnel or a ferry of your choice, and drive through France and Spain. The drive from Calais to Lisbon is 2,125 km (1,320 miles), so it would be wise to plan at least two overnight stops en route. There are two possibilities for cutting down the driving time: you

Red sandstone cliffs OPPOSITE crumble onto the beaches between Albufeira and Faro. Silves castle ABOVE has been painstakingly restored to become a tourist honey pot.

could take the ferry from Plymouth to Santander in northern Spain, which still leaves you with a 970-km (600-mile) drive to Lisbon (see following section for details); or you could drive to Paris, where you can put your car on the Motorail bound for Lisbon at the Gare Austerlitz, and yourself on the Sud Express. You will be reunited with your car one day after your arrival. For details of this motorail service contact the S.N.C.F. (the French national railway company) at 179 Piccadilly, London W1V 0BA ((071) 409-3518 or, of course at any French station.

Plymouth. From Santander it is an 800-km (500-mile) journey to Porto, or a 970-km (600-mile) journey to Lisbon. For further details contact Brittany Ferries at The Brittany Centre, Wharf Road, Portsmouth PO2 8RU, ((0705) 827701 or (0752) 221321. Book well in advance.

TOURIST INFORMATION

For general information contact one of the Portuguese Tourism offices.

An increasingly popular option is to fly-drive, and some good deals are available. Motoring is undoubtedly one of the best ways of exploring Portugal, but the standard of Portuguese driving makes it a thoroughly bad idea for the nervous driver. See also the DRIVING and GETTING AROUND sections for details of car hire.

BY SEA

There are no direct ferries to Portugal from Britain or Europe, but Brittany Ferries run one that carries cars and their passengers from Plymouth to Santander. The ferry itself takes approximately 24 hours to reach Santander and currently sails twice weekly from

AUSTRIA Stubenring, 16/3, A-1010 **Vienna**, ((1) 513-2670, fax: (1) 512-8828.
BELGIUM Rue Joseph II, N°5-Boite 3, 1040 **Brussels,** ((2) 230-9625 or 230-5250, fax: (2) 231-0447.
ENGLAND 22-25a Sackville Street, **London** W1X 1DE, ((071) 494-1441, fax: (071) 494-1868.
FRANCE 7 Rue Scribe, 75009, **Paris,** ((1) 47 42 55 57, fax (1) 42 66 06 89.
GERMANY Kreuzstrasse 34-3°, 40210 **Dusseldorf,** ((21) 184912/4, fax: (21) 132-0968.
GERMANY Kaiserstrasse 66 IV, 60329 **Frankfurt am Main,** ((69) 234094, fax: (69) 231433.
ITALY Via Ganzaga, 2, 20123 **Milan,** ((2) 866678 or 866112, fax: (2) 865660.

SOUTH AFRICA 8th Floor, 68 Eloff Street, **Johannesburg** 2001, ((011) 337-4782/3, fax: (011) 337-1613.

SPAIN Gran Via 27, 1°, 28013 **Madrid**, ((1) 522-9354, Fax: (1) 522-2382.

SWITZERLAND Badenerstrasse 16, 8004 **Zurich**, ((1) 241-0300 or 241-0309, fax: (1) 241-0012.

U.S.A. 590 Fifth Avenue, 4th floor, New York, NY 10036-4704, ((212) 354-4403, fax: (212) 764-6137.

U.S.A. 1900 L Street, Suite 401, **Washington DC** 20036, ((202) 331-8222, fax: (202) 331-8236.

TRAVEL DOCUMENTS

American, Canadian, Australian, New Zealand, Japanese, and British citizens need only a valid passport to enter Portugal, while other European Union citizens need only a national identity card. Other Commonwealth citizens and British nationals living overseas need a visa. British, Irish, Americans and Canadians can then stay for up to 60 days, while Antipodeans, Japanese, and citizens of certain European countries may stay for up to 90 days. The procedure for extending your stay in Portugal is fairly straightforward (see STAYING ON section), but you are not permitted to work in Portugal while staying as a tourist.

CUSTOMS

If you're driving into Portugal, pick up a leaflet from the Portuguese Tourist Office which lists the opening hours of the various frontier crossings with Spain; opening hours vary from place to place and also according to season.

Duty-free allowances are the same as in other European Union countries. There are no restrictions on the amount of money you can bring into the country, but you are not allowed to take out more than 100,000 escudos or foreign currency to the value of 500,000 escudos unless it can be proved that you brought in at least the same amount.

WHEN TO GO

Portugal's temperate climate makes between April and November a good time to visit. The peak season runs from July to September, and for those who don't have to worry about school holiday times, lower prices and fewer holidaymakers make the spring and autumn months ideal times to visit.

The Algarve, however, has a pleasant climate throughout the winter. To convert temperatures to Fahrenheit, double the figure quoted and add 32.

WHAT TO TAKE

Traveling light is always a good idea, especially if you plan to take some souvenirs home with you. As to what clothes to pack, I recommend that you take a sweater or jacket as the evenings, even in summer, can be cool, and a few smart items if there's any possibility of being invited out or if you intend to dine in some of the upmarket

Plodding donkey OPPOSITE are still a common sight in rural backwaters. Anywhere will do for a siesta ABOVE on a lazy afternoon.

restaurants; the Portuguese dress fastidiously and it's always good to reciprocate. Sightseeing in Lisbon and the hilly north most definitely requires sensible shoes. Another important accessory if you are traveling around the north, particularly off-season, is an umbrella as there are often sudden and heavy cloudbursts.

GETTING AROUND

BY AIR

TAP operates regular services between the major Portuguese cities — Lisbon, Porto, and Faro.

BY TRAIN

Portugal has quite an extensive rail network, with services that range from the slick commuter line to a slow regional service that stops at all stations on the route. Fares are inexpensive, though the faster the service, the more it costs, and booking fees (often necessary on the express services) add substantially to the ticket price. There are discounts for pensioners, students, and children. Tickets must be bought before boarding, either from a travel agent or from the station ticket office where you may find long queues. On routes other than the main inter-city lines, trains often prove slower than buses, and this is exacerbated by the fact that stations are sometimes a bus ride away from the towns they serve.

The *regionais* network covers most of the rural areas where stations can sometimes be quite far from town; the *directos* and *semi-directos* are slightly faster trains, but still quite leisurely. More efficient express trains run the Lisbon-Coimbra-Porto and Lisbon-Faro routes, and there is a fast electric rail link from Lisbon's Cais do Sodré station to Cascais, Estoril, and other places along the Costa do Sol. The fastest and most luxurious of all the trains is the *Alfa* express that runs between Lisbon and Porto.

Other commuter lines leave from Lisbon's Cais do Sodré and Rossio stations, while trains to the north and east run from

the Santa Apólonia Station. To travel south from Lisbon or to the Alentejo, you need to get to the Barreiro Station, which involves a ferry crossing from the landing station just west of the Praça do Commércio (the rail ticket includes the cost of the ferry).

BY BUS

The national bus company, Rodoviária Nacional (R.N.), runs services throughout Portugal, and there are some smaller private companies such as Mundial de Turismo and Cabanelas Expressos do Nordeste that cover specific routes or regions. This is probably the best form of public transport for touring the country and undoubtedly the cheapest. *Turismos* can furnish you with

timetables and details of where to pick up your bus.

BY TAXI

Taxis are easily identifiable by their green roofs and black bodywork. In towns and cities the cost is metered, but elsewhere the fare is calculated by the kilometer and you should check the cost before taking the cab. Prices are very reasonable, and if there are a few of you sharing can work out as cheap as the bus. A surcharge of up to 50 percent for baggage over 30 kg is imposed, and between 10 pm and 6 am there is a 20 percent surcharge. It is usually quite easy to find a taxi except at lunchtimes, when taxi drivers, like the rest of the populace, take a long lunch break.

BY THUMB

There's no law against hitch-hiking in Portugal, but few people do it and you should be aware that Portuguese drivers may be wary of stopping for you as their insurance policies won't cover hikers.

BY CAR

Although nothing beats the freedom of traveling by car, I feel it necessary to warn visitors that there are pitfalls. Apart from the variable quality of the roads, there is the

Vilamoura in the Algarve is one of the largest tourist complexes in Europe. The marina has more than 1,000 moorings.

more serious problem of the abysmal quality of Portuguese driving, which I will whinge about in the forthcoming *Driving* section.

Note that it works out cheaper, sometimes considerably cheaper, to arrange your car rental before you get to Portugal, in which case the rates compare reasonably well with other European countries. If you're booking your flight with TAP, they can arrange good-value car rental to fit in with your travel plans. Fuel costs, however, are among the highest in Europe, even more expensive than in Britain.

located and signposted with the *Turismo* symbol: a white T on a blue background. Opening hours are generally from 9 am to 7 pm Monday to Saturday, but this can vary, and in smaller towns it is more likely to be from 10 am to 5 pm Monday to Saturday with a lunch break that could be any time between noon and 2:30 pm.

If you're after information beyond the scope of a local tourist office, try one of the main city branches. In Lisbon try the I.P.T. (Instituo de Promoção Turistica) at Rua Alexandre Herculano N°51, ((01) 681174, fax:

Lastly, be extremely wary of the coastal road between Lisbon and Cascais known as the Marginal, and the stretch between Lisbon and the Algarve. Both have notoriously high accident rates.

(01) 659782 or 693394; in Porto there's a main office at Praça Dom João N°1, N°43, ((02) 313957, and in Faro there's one at Rua Ataíde de Oliveira N°100, ((089) 803667/8/9. The office of the Director General of Tourism (Direcção-Geral do Turismo) is at Avenida António Augusto de Aguiar N°86, ((01) 575086.

GENERAL INFORMATION

Virtually every town has its tourist office or *Turismo*, an invaluable source of local and regional information. It's a good idea to make a beeline for it as soon as you reach a town as staff there can supply you with a town plan, list of hotels, advice on transport, and can help with *pousada* bookings or any queries you may have. *Turismos* are centrally

EMBASSIES AND CONSULATES

American Embassy: Avenida das Forças Armadas, 1600 Lisbon, ((01) 726-6600.
American Consulate: Rua Julio Dinis N°826-3°, 1000 Porto, ((02) 63094.
Australian Embassy: Avenida da Liberdade N°244-4°, 1200 Lisbon, ((01) 523350.

British Embassy: Rua São Domingos á Lapa Nº35-37, 1200 Lisbon, ✆ (01) 661191.
British Consulate: Avenida da Boavista Nº3072, 4100 Porto, ✆ (02) 684789.
Canadian Embassy: Avenida da Liberdade Nº144-3º, 1200 Lisbon, ✆ (01) 347-4892.
South African Embassy: Avenida Luis Bivar Nº10, 1097 Lisbon, ✆ (01) 535713.

HEALTH

Visitors do not require any inoculations to

visit Portugal, and certificates are only needed if you are traveling from a country where there is an epidemic. Medical treatment at Portuguese state hospitals is free to visitors from the United Kingdom and other countries that have a reciprocal medical agreement with Portugal, but it is nevertheless advisable to take out medical insurance cover. Visitors from the US and Canada are not entitled to free treatment. They should check if any current insurance policies cover them for medical treatment while traveling, and if not are advised to take out specific insurance cover.

For minor ailments go to the nearest pharmacy (*farmacia*). You'll find that many chemists speak English and can give you

sound advice. Certain medicines are available on prescription only. Pharmacies are open during normal shopping hours and are usually closed for lunch, but there is always one in each neighborhood which stays open around the clock, and a list of those on this special duty is displayed on the door of every pharmacy.

For more serious problems you can always ask hotel reception to call you a doctor, though this might cost you more than finding one yourself. Lists of English-speaking doctors are available from Turismos. In case of real emergency, telephone 115 or go to the nearest hospital or health clinic. All principal residential areas have one or the other that provides 24-hour emergency service. As many doctors and surgeons are trained in the United Kingdom and the United States, communicating in English is rarely a problem. The standard of treatment is generally good, though some hospitals lack complete nursing back-up.

There is a small British hospital in Lisbon at Rua Saraiva de Carvalho Nº49, 1200 Lisbon, ✆ (01) 602020/603786, manned by British-trained and English-speaking staff. It sees out-patients' but has no casualty department.

EMERGENCIES

The emergency or SOS 24-hour telephone number is 115. The main hospital in Lisbon for dealing with accidents is the São José Hospital at Rua Jos António Serrano, ✆ (01) 860131. It also has a 24-hour emergency dental service. It is difficult to get a private room in a state hospital, so if you desperately want one you will probably have to go to one of the very expensive private clinics.

MONEY

The monetary unit is the escudo, which is divided into 100 centavos. The escudo is denoted by the $ sign which appears after the number of escudos and before the number of centavos, thus 20$50 = 20 escudos and

White and black cobbles as on the Lisbon shopping precinct OPPOSITE are a feature of many Portuguese towns. On the plains, windmills such as the one ABOVE are restored for nostalgia's sake.

50 centavos. You may occasionally hear one thousand escudos referred to as a *conto*. Escudos are issued in coins of a half (50 Centavos), one, two and a half. five, 10, 20, 50, 100, and notes are issued in denominations of 100, 500, 1,000, 5,000, and 10,000 escudos (note that the metric full point is used instead of a comma to denote number of thousands).

Travelers' checks are accepted by many hotels and shops but at a poor exchange rate. For better rates go to a bank. Opening hours are 8:30 am to 3 pm and they are generally

Portugal than buying currency at home and taking it with you, and often you will get a better exchange rate if you use your credit card to get money, though not in small amounts.

ACCOMMODATION

There are quite a few different kinds of accommodation to choose from in Portugal, and some of the most delightful are far from being the most expensive. Hotels are given

closed on weekends, but you may find one open on Saturdays in the main tourist areas. In some of the smaller towns they sometimes shut at lunchtime. Airport exchange offices open until 11 pm and in Lisbon the exchange at the Santa Apolónio train station and a couple of banks around the Praça dos Restauradores are also open late.

Eurocheques supported by a Eurocheque card are widely accepted, and an ever-increasing number of places now take major credit cards. Obviously the smaller the restaurant or the smaller the town, the less likely it is that you will be able to use either, so don't rely too heavily on them if you are traveling outside the cities and larger towns. You'll be better off exchanging money in

a one- to five-star rating, based on price and type. Those in the deluxe (five star) category can hold their own with luxury hotels anywhere, and in Lisbon, Porto and the major Algarve resort hotels the prices are very much at international levels, above $160 for a standard double. Some of the best bargains and nicest surprises are to be found among the *residencials* and *pensãos* which have fewer amenities than hotels, often serving only breakfast. *Estalagems* are inns rated between four and five stars; *albergarias*, also inns, are four-star accommodations. In the tourist resorts, apartment hotels, always a good family option, are rated between two and four stars, motels are given either two or three stars, and tourist villages are divided into luxury, first class, and second class. Standards on the whole are very good and even the cheapest place is usually scrupulously clean. In terms of price, the star ratings (in the index) translate generally to one star: $30 and up, two star: $60 and up, three star $90 and up, four star: $120 and up.

The institution of a state-subsidized network of hotels known as *pousadas*, similar in kind to the Spanish *paradors*, was one of the better things that materialized during Salazar's dictatorship. These are strategically positioned throughout Portugal and provide ideal accommodation for those wishing to explore the country. Some locations have been chosen purely for their scenic beauty, some because they're in a zone of historical interest, while others are converted palaces, castles, convents or monasteries. There are 40 in all and it is possible to plan a thorough tour of the country and stay only at *pousadas*. They are classified into four groups: B, C, CH, and CHL (in ascending order of quality and price). Peak-season prices vary from $75 to $150 for a double room; while not cheap, state subsidies assure that they are excellent value. Expect a warm welcome, personalized service, and first-class traditional cuisine. You can book through the Portuguese tourist offices but beware of making last-minute cancellations as money has to be paid up-front and you will lose at least the cost of the first night.

Some other interesting accommodation can be found through what is generally known as the *Turismo de Habitação* (TURIHAB) scheme under which people open their homes to guests, offering bed and breakfast accommodation. They proliferate in the Minho province, compensating for the lack of other accommodation. There are actually three categories: TURIHAB, which are manor houses (some quite grand) or houses of recognized architectural value; *Turismo Rural*, which are houses typical of the area and situated in or near a town; and *Agroturismo*, which is farmhouse accommodation. Prices vary and although these are privately owned houses they are registered with the Direcção-Geral do Turismo which insists they conform to certain standards. In general, these need to be booked at least three or four days in advance either directly with the owners or through travel agents, *Turismos*, or the owners' associations, and a deposit is required. Breakfast is included in the price but it is possible to have main meals laid on by prior arrangement. A booklet called *Turismo No Espaço Rural Guia Oficial* is available for purchase at Portuguese tourist offices in most countries, and it has photos together with details of some of the houses.

All accommodation prices vary according to the time of year. The most expensive time is during the high season (June-September), while the cheapest period is from

November to the end of March, with the exception of Christmas and Easter holidays. If you are planning your visit in the peak season and have strong ideas about where you'd like to stay you should book in advance, and if you want to stay in any of the *pousadas*, book well ahead as they are very popular. When the time comes to check out, there should be no nasty surprises in store as most establishments display the room prices, inclusive of taxes and service charges, in the lobby and usually on the door of each room. Wherever you check in you

Guests find York House OPPOSITE has more Portuguese flavor than its name suggests. Lisbon's newest luxury hotel ABOVE is a restored palace overlooking the Tagus.

will be asked for your passport. This is usually kept long enough for reception to make out the obligatory registration form, in which case you can usually pick it up before going out in the evening. Some places prefer to hang on to it during the first night of your stay.

Breakfast, unless you're staying at one of the luxury hotels, is usually very simple — fresh bread rolls, jams, and plentiful supplies of coffee or tea — but the quality of the bread and coffee is always good.

EATING OUT

The long Portuguese lunch is a respected tradition, and as so many places — shops, museums, churches — are shut around this time so that there's little choice but to join in and do the same. Lunch is anytime between 12:30 pm and 3 pm while dinner tends to be between 8 pm and 10 pm.

At a *confeitaria*, a *pastelaria*, or *salão de chá*, you can enjoy light, inexpensive food — sandwiches, omelets, simple meals — or afternoon teas and pastries in a relaxed café atmosphere. In the cities Art Nouveau coffee houses are an institution, and are ideal places for a drink, reading a paper or meeting friends.

The *cervejaria* is more than just an English-style pub or a bar. Most serve food, some have quite extensive menus, and shellfish is often a popular snack. They tend to be busy places, good on atmosphere, easy on the pocket, and similar to the *tabernas* which are generally older drinking establishments which serve wine as well as beer. You won't find the same choice of eating places in the smaller towns and villages, but remember that where there's a *pousada* there's a good restaurant, and that you don't have to be a resident to eat there.

Food portions, especially in northern restaurants, are typically huge. It is, however, quite acceptable for three people to share two main courses, or even for two people to share one.

Bread, butter, and some tasty appetizers — olives, sardines, Russian salad, or cheeses — are placed on your table while you're perusing the menu. You will be charged for them, but may decline when they are served.

RECREATIONAL ORGANIZATIONS

Portugal's temperate climate is ideal for a raft of participative sports, and the following organizations can be provide detailed information on available facilities and opportunities:

CANOEING AND KYAKING Federação Portuguesa de Canoagem, Rua António Pinto Machado Nº 60, 4100 Porto, ((02) 697350.

FISHING Federação Portuguesa de Pesca Desportiva, Rua Sociedade Farmacêutica Nº 56-2º., 1200 Lisbon, ((01) 678257.

GOLF Federação Portuguesa de Golfe, Rua Almeida Brandão Nº 39, 1200 Lisbon.

HORSE RIDING Federação Portuguesa de Equestre Portuguesa, Avenida Duque de Avila Nº 4º., 1000 Lisbon, ((01) 797-0535.

SCUBA DIVING Federação Portuguesa de Activadades Subaquátiques, Rua Almeida Brandão Nº39, 1200 Lisbon, ((01) 600006

TENNIS Federação Portuguesa de Ténis, Estádio Nacional, Caxias, 2480 Oeiras, ((01) 419-5244.

CYCLING Federação Portuguesa de Vela, Doca de Belém, 1300 Lisbon, ((01) 647324.

ETIQUETTE

Portuguese society is quite formal and good manners are considered important. It is polite to shake hands with anyone you are introduced to. and with anyone who has been particularly helpful, whatever the service performed. In a formal situation people do not address one another by their first names but by their title and surname. For a man this is *Senhor*, for a woman *Senhora*, sometimes *Dona*, while doctors, lawyers, civil servants, and other professionals are addressed by their titles. If in doubt, elevate.

It is considered impolite to talk loudly in public, although loud music and horrendously noisy motorbikes don't seem to bother anybody. Yawning in public is

Dazzlingly bright regional costume is worn on feast days and special occasions in Viana do Castelo.

frowned on and *com licença*, is the useful equivalent of excuse me. If you want to say sorry, it's *desculpe*.

To attract a waiter's attention, *faz favor* (please) is the way to do it. It is done to say thank you for everything, even if it's a service you're paying for: if you're a man that's *obrigado* while a woman would say *obrigada*. Greet people with *bom dia, boa tarde*, or *boa noite* (according to time of day) and after bidding them goodbye, it is polite to turn to say a final goodbye before you're out of sight.

The Portuguese are fastidious about their dress and appearance. Women regularly visit the hairdresser, and everyone — no matter how poor — is pretty well turned out. If you are in doubt as to how to dress, dress up rather than down for the occasion. It will be noticed.

Which brings us neatly and lastly to the subject of undress. Topless sunbathing is quite common among the Portuguese as well as the tourists and is the fashion on many Algarve and Lisbon coast beaches. Sunbathing bottomless is another matter and is actually illegal. However, if you're in search of the all-over suntan, there are a few beaches in the Algarve where it is unofficially accepted.

DRIVING

The roads in Portugal are getting better all the time. European Union money is helping to pay for improvements and new roads keep appearing: be sure you get as up-to-date a map as possible. In the northeast, once

and whether as a driver or a pedestrian you'll soon find out why. Portuguese drivers have an absence of road sense as well as a blatant disregard for traffic law. Worse, they seem to know no fear, so beware of bends and what may come hurtling around them on the wrong side of the road. The best advice I can give is to drive defensively and not to get involved in a war of nerves with a Portuguese driver. On that note, if you need emergency services call 115.

You'll need an international driving license, and, if you're driving your own car, nationality plates and a green card from your insurers as third-party insurance is compulsory. You are required to carry in your car a red warning triangle which, in the case of an accident or breakdown, is to be placed at least 50 m (164 ft) before the site. British and American automobile clubs cooperate in a reciprocal assistance scheme with the Portuguese Automobile Club — Automóvel Clube de Portugal (ACP). The head office is at Rua Rosa Araújo Nº24, 1200 Lisbon, ((01) 736121, fax: (01) 574732, and there are branches in Porto, Aveiro, Braga, Coimbra, and Faro.

Driving is on the right, continental rules of the road apply, and the international sign system is used. On motorways (freeways) the speed limits are 120 kph (74 mph); in towns and other built-up areas it's normally 60 kph (37 mph) unless otherwise marked; out of town except on motorways it's 90 kph (56 mph). Be especially careful in towns and villages, as children often play at the edge of the road and some of Portugal's large canine population choose to sleep on it. In rural areas beware of suddenly coming upon ox- or horse-drawn carts or one of the many slow and unroadworthy vehicles.

The wearing of seat belts is compulsory. The legal alcohol limit is below 5 ml per liter; penalties for driving while over the limit include heavy fines on the spot and confiscation of license. At a road junction where both roads are of equal size, traffic approaching from the right has priority; at roundabouts proceed anti-clockwise. Be especially careful at roundabouts: at some you must

renowned for its isolation and rough tracks, some of the roads are now better and smoother than those around the more heavily populated areas or the much-visited Algarve. However, in the mountainous areas there are lots of blind bends and getting stuck behind a slow-moving farm vehicle can greatly slow you down. If you're traveling through this kind of country remember that a journey may easily take you twice as long as the distance involved would normally require. For an idea of journey times, look at some of the leaflets published on *pousada* holidays, as they sometimes have charts showing distances and estimated driving times between various *pousadas*.

The really bad news is that Portugal has Europe's worst record for road accidents,

Port grapes are grown along the valley of the river Douro, which meanders from the Spanish border to its mouth at Oporto.

give way to traffic on the roundabout, while on others incoming traffic has the right of way. Pedestrians have priority at zebra crossings, but if they depend on that rule being observed they risk their lives. If you are driving it's wise to indicate your intention to the driver behind in good time because it may not cross his mind that you will be stopping, with crunching consequences.

Parking in the cities can be difficult, especially in Lisbon. You have to park facing the same direction as the traffic flow on that side of the road, but the main problem is actually finding somewhere to park legally. Vehicles do get towed away, so if you want to play safe, go to a multi-storey car park. However, if you leave your car there overnight these prove very expensive: this is when hotels with private parking come into their own.

MAIL

Post office (*correio*) opening hours vary from place to place, but in general they are open from Monday to Friday, from 8:30 or 9 am to 6 pm, and some of the smaller ones shut for lunch (12:30 pm to 2 pm). In the major cities some stay open until late evening and a few are open on Saturdays until midday. A variety of transactions take place in the post office but if you only want to buy stamps, look out for a counter signed *selos*, (stamps) which will cut down on queuing time. Alternatively, if you know what you need, try to find a tobacconist that sells them.

Mail within Portugal takes between one and three days to reach its destination and deliveries are from Monday to Friday with a second delivery only in the main cities. Mail to other European countries takes roughly one week, and to other countries between one week and 10 days. Main post offices have telex and fax services available to the public.

If you want mail sent to you during your stay in Portugal and don't know in advance where you will be staying, you can have it sent to any post office if it is marked *Posta Restante* and has the address of the branch you wish to collect it from. You need your passport for identification when you go to pick up the mail, and a small charge is made for each item collected.

TELEPHONES

The difficulty in trying to place a simple phone call in Portugal can be a major source of frustration. The system is being modernized and is improving, but for the present getting a connection is often a deeply annoying business, with local calls often proving more difficult than international ones. If you get a continually engaged tone, before cursing your friends and relatives for being gasbags remember

that it's quite likely to be the exchange that's at fault.

Telephoning from your hotel room or from a bar usually incurs a substantial surcharge, so unless money's not a problem, check what the surcharge is before using this facility. Public telephones usually take 2$5, 5$, and 25$ coins and some take phonecards. Follow the instructions on the phone carefully, as some of the older booths demand weird and wonderful procedures. You'll be better off seeking out the newer ones, from which you can make international calls (this is not always possible from the older ones). To use these you insert money while holding the receiver, wait for the tone, then dial the number you want. Once you're connected, the coins will drop and after your call any unused coins are returned. A warning tone will alert you if you need more coins in the course of your call.

You can also telephone from the post offices, a lot easier if you don't like carrying around heaps of loose change. Queue at the cashier's window, and wait to be directed to a booth. After making your call, return to the window to pay for it. Lisbon and Porto both have a telephone office open from 9 am to 11 pm. In Lisbon it's near the Rossio, and at Porto it's at the Praça da Liberdade. When phoning other European countries, dial 00 followed by the country code, area code (dropping the initial 0 if there is one), then the number. For other countries dial 097 followed by the country code, area code and the number you want. For the international operator dial 099 for outside Europe dial 098.

BASICS

TIME

On the last Sunday in March the clocks are put one hour ahead of Greenwich Mean Time and on the last Sunday in October the clocks are put back an hour. This means there is no time difference between Portugal and Great Britain and Ireland. To calculate the time in the US and Canada, subtract five to eight hours (Eastern Standard to Pacific time). Australia is eight to 10 hours ahead of Portuguese time; New Zealand is 12 hours ahead.

ELECTRICITY

The local current is 220 volts (a few remote areas still have 110 volts). The outlets take standard European plugs with two round prongs. Visitors from Britain will need an adapter, while Americans will also need a voltage converter for their appliances.

WATER

The water is safe to drink except, possibly, in the more remote areas. However, if you are prone to minor stomach upsets from change of bacteria, it's a good idea to stick to bottled water, which you can buy anywhere.

WEIGHTS AND MEASURES

Like most countries, Portugal uses the metric system. If you are used to pounds and ounces, feet and inches, pints and quarts, you may need to make some quick calculations. Rather than a list of the exact conversion formulae, there follows some rough sums that you can do in your head rather than with a calculator.

First, measurements: there are two and a half centimeters to one inch, so to convert

inches to cm you multiply by 2.5; one meter is just over a yard; one kilometer is 0.6 of a mile, so a mile is a little over 1.5 km. When it comes to buying food and drink you may find it useful to know that 125 g is approximately a quarter of a pound, that 500 g is roughly one pound and that one kg is 2.2 lbs. With regard to liquid measures, a liter is just under two English pints and just over two American pints. In reverse, an English pint is just over half a liter and an American pint just under.

To convert temperatures from Celsius to Fahrenheit, double the Celsius temperature and add 32.

CRIME

The crime rate in Portugal is relatively low, the major problems being tax evasion and drug trafficking. However, as in any country

News to peruse on Lisbon's waterfront Praça do Comércio OPPOSITE. Fishermen ABOVE amend their nets on the Beira coast.

where there is poverty, there is some theft, mostly in the cities and in places popular with tourists. So, don't leave belongings in your car for all to see, observe the usual rule about keeping your travelers' checks and slips separately, and hang on to your handbag, especially in crowded places.

Police here are armed with pistols, which rarely get used; should you wish to attract a policeman's attention you should address him as *Senhor Guarda*. The Guarda Nacional Repúblicana patrol the highways and their main occupation seems to be stopping vehicles (particularly lorries) to inspect documents.

RADIO AND TELEVISION

Radio broadcasts can be heard in English, French, and German during the summer on Program One, while Program Two, which is predominantly a classical music station, has English broadcasts for tourists in the morning and evening. Radio Algarve is an English-language station that has the news in English in the morning and early evening. The BBC World Service can be picked up while Radio Canada International and the Voice of America can be heard at various times of day. Signals are often best in the early morning and in the evening.

There are two government-run television channels: RTP 1, which goes on the air at 9 am, and RTP 2, which doesn't start up until 3 pm. They serve up a real hotch-potch of programs, with Brazilian soaps being the national favorite, and American, British, and Australian series brought in and subtitled. Satellite dishes are a growing trend and so televisions in some of the higher grade hotels can now pick up Sky, the BBC, CNN, etc.

NEWSPAPERS AND MAGAZINES

Among the most widely-read local dailies is *Diário de Notícias*, which has an entertainments guide that is particularly useful for tourists, whether or not they understand Portuguese. Also good for entertainments listings is *Sete*, a weekly that comes out Wednesday afternoons and also carries a television and radio guide.

Major European newspapers and the Paris edition of the *International Herald Tribune* are usually available on the day of publication from newsstands, hotels, and bookstalls in the cities and tourist resorts, as are European editions of *Time* and *Newsweek*. There are locally-produced English language magazines which primarily serve the expatriate community, such as the *Algarve Gazette* and the fortnightly *Algarve News*. The I.P.T. publishes the useful *What's On in Lisbon*.

OPENING HOURS

Beware the lunch break. If you're planning a tour of the country don't forget that everything — shops, churches, museums, tourist offices, and sometimes the banks — shut for lunch, otherwise you may disrupt your schedule and let yourself in for disappointments.

If you're visiting some of the more out-of-the-way churches and other historical buildings, remember that some are kept permanently closed and you may have to ask someone living nearby for the key. In general — but this is very general — churches are open from 7 am to 1 pm and again from 4 to 7 pm. Museums and galleries are closed on Mondays and public holidays, while palaces and some other buildings shut on Tuesdays. Opening hours for weekdays and weekends are roughly from 10 am to 5 pm but often closing between 12:30 and 2pm for lunch, so always try to check in advance. Government offices are usually open from 9 am to midday and from 2:30 to 5:30 pm.

Shops are usually open from 9 am to 1 pm and from 3 pm to 7 pm. Monday to Friday, from 9 am to 1 pm only on Saturdays, and are closed on Sundays. However, in the big towns and cities there are now shopping centers and supermarkets that stay open from 10 am to midnight seven days a week.

TOILETS

Toilets can be found in museums, railway and metro stations, and generally in the town centers. Look out for the sign *Senhoras* which means Ladies or *Homens* which means Gentlemen. If an attendant is on duty you should leave a tip, and in some places there is a charge of a few escudos. As usual, it can save you possible anguish if you carry a small supply of toilet paper or tissue around with you.

FADO HOUSES

Fado music is not only for the tourists: it has a serious Portuguese following. If you'd like to hear some you should take yourself along to one of the many fado houses of Lisbon, which are to be found in old neighborhoods such as the Alfama and in the Bairro Alto district. There is a cover charge or entrance fee, and you can either arrive early for a meal — which can be excellent — or go along later to drink. See DREAM TO FADO page 11.

In the early evening many of these places are filled with coach parties of tourists who come to eat and listen to a little music, so it is a good idea to book if you want a meal. However, after about 11 o'clock the big parties tend to leave, tables are cleared, and the atmosphere changes from that of restaurant to drinking club. The music then gets going in earnest and plays on often until dawn. Aficionados take their fado very seriously, so talking during the performances is not a good idea.

SPAS

Portugal has an amazing number of spas — about 45 in all — which are said to have therapeutic properties for a wide range of ailments that include liver, kidney, allergic, gastric, circulatory, and respiratory problems. The spas are well-patronized, and the better-known ones tend to have excellent treatment rooms and hotels set in restful surroundings with plenty of leisure facilities.

Most are open from May to October, some for longer. Brochures are available from tourist offices and further information is also available through the Associacão Nacional dos Industriais de Aguas Mineromedicinais e de Mesa, Rua de S. José Nº93, 1100 Lisbon, ((01) 347-5632.

TIPPING

A service charge of 15 percent is included in restaurant bills but a tip of around 10 percent will be appreciated, and generally speaking, will have been well-earned. In hotels the service charge is also included in the price but it is the done thing to tip for particular services. The porter who carries your luggage should be tipped about 100-200 escudos per bag, and it is usual to leave a tip of about 100$ (70¢) per day for the

chambermaid. In clubs, tip the the waiters about 10 percent and cloakroom attendants about 100 escudos.

Taxi drivers should get about 10 percent of the fare, maybe more if it's a short journey, while tour guides should be tipped nearer 15 percent. Few fuel stations are self-service, so if you get an attendant he should be given a few coins too, about 50$ (35¢). Cloakroom attendants get about the same, as do the ushers in theaters and cinemas. Barbers and hairdressers are normally tipped about 10 percent.

A fado singer ABOVE touches the soul of the nation with soul-wrenching themes of fatalism and lost love.

It may all sound like a bit of a pain, but these services are usually well performed and the tips are considered part of the wage packet.

STAYING ON

If you decide to stay on in Portugal for more than your allocated 60 or 90 days, apply for a permit at the local police station or contact the Serviço de Extrangeiros (Foreigner's Service) a few days before your time is up,

in case of bureaucratic delay. If you are within easy reach of the Spanish border you could consider taking a short trip into Spain: when you re-enter Portugal your entry stamp will be renewed. In Lisbon the Serviço de Extrangeiros is at Rua Consilheiro José Silvestre Ribeiro 1° N°22, 1600 Lisbon. ((01) 714-1027 or 714-1179.

PORTUGUESE FOR TRAVELERS

If you have a knowledge of Spanish, or even French or Italian, you will find it a great help in reading Portuguese. It will be of little use, however, in understanding the spoken word, for the pronunciation of Portuguese is very different. A phrase book is always a useful piece of travel equipment, but the best way to prepare yourself for your visit (other than by taking Portuguese lessons) is to get hold of a rudimentary Portuguese course book that is backed up by audio cassettes; there's no substitute for hearing the spoken language. I can recommend the BBC's *Get By In*

Portuguese booklet and accompanying cassettes, which give you just about enough language to get by. A little goes a long way, and there'll be times when it will come in handy. If you do get totally stuck, French can sometimes prove useful as it is taught in the schools. Many can understand Spanish, but they don't particularly like doing so.

PRONUNCIATION

A friend once told me, You'll know you're pronouncing Portuguese properly when you start foaming at the mouth. This is something of an exaggeration, but it is true that the Portuguese tend to speak quickly and elliptically, and that the language has an abundance of *sh* sounds. While the spelling and grammatical structure is quite similar to Spanish, there are major differences in pronunciation. Here are a few pointers.

When a word ends in *a, e, o, m, n*, or *s*, the stress falls on the last but one syllable; other words carry the stress on the last syllable. The exception to this rule is when an acute accent is placed on the syllable to be stressed — e.g., *está, rápido*.

Some vowels are pronounced nasally — that is, through the nose and mouth simultaneously as if they were followed by an ng as in *cunning*. These include vowels with a tilde (~) over them, or those that are followed by *m* or *n*. Thus:

ão is pronounced somwhere inbetween aw and owrg

on sounds like ong in *long*

un or *um* is like oo in *mood* followed by ng

in or *im* sounds like the e in *me* and is nasalized

Most consonants are similar to English, but there are exceptions:

c is pronounced s as in sit before *e* and *i* but hard before *a, o*, and *u* unless it has a cedilla, in which case (as in French) it is soft.

ch is pronounced sh, as in *push*

h is always silent

j is soft, like the s in *pleasure*

lh is pronounced ly, as in *slowly*

nh is pronounced ni

s is **soft** at the beginning of a word or **after a consonant**, but when it occurs between two vowels it is pronounced "z" — as in *zoo*, and at the end of a word or before *c, f, p, q* and *t* it is sh

x is sh, but before a vowel it is pronounced z — when between two vowels it is pronounced s

z at the end of a word is pronounced sh

VOCABULARY

Numbers

1	*um*
2	*dois*
3	*três*

21	*vinte e um*
30	*trinta*
40	*quarenta*
50	*cinquenta*
60	*sessenta*
70	*setenta*
80	*oitenta*
90	*noventa*
100	*cem*
200	*duzentos*
500	*quinhentos*
1,000	*mil*
2,000	*dois mil*

4	*quatro*
5	*cinco*
6	*seis*
7	*sete*
8	*oito*
9	*nove*
10	*dez*
11	*onze*
12	*doze*
13	*treze*
14	*catorze*
15	*quinze*
16	*dizasseis*
17	*dezassete*
18	*dezoito*
19	*dezanove*
20	*vinte*

100,000	*cem mil*
1,000,000	*um milhão*
2,000.000	*dois milhões*

Calendar

Sunday	*Domingo*
Monday	*Segunda-feira*
Tuesday	*Terça-feira*
Wednesday	*Quarta-feira*
Thursday	*Quinta-feira*
Friday	*Sexta-feira*
Saturday	*Sábado*
January	*Janeiro*
February	*Fevereiro*

The eerie marches OPPOSITE of the Aveiro ria. Regional costume LEFT at Barqueiros folkloric festival. A black-clad widow RIGHT sells flowers.

March   *Março*
April   *Abril*
May   *Maio*
June   *Junho*
July   *Julho*
August   *Agosto*
September   *Setembro*
October   *Outubro*
November   *Novembro*
December   *Dezembro*
Spring   *Primavera*
Summer   *Verão*
Autumn   *Outono*
Winter   *Inverno*
day   *dia*
week   *semana*
month   *mês*
year   *ano*

Clock

morning   *manhã*
noon   *meio-dia*
afternoon/evening   *tarde*
night   *noite*
today   *hoje*
yesterday   *ontem*
tomorrow   *amanhã*
what time is it?   *que horas são?*
now   *agora*
later   *mais tarde*

Key words and phrases

yes   *sim*
no   *não*
none   *nenhum(a)*
much, very, a lot (of)   *muito/a*
please   *por favor(se) faz favor*
thank you   *obrigado* (if said by a man)
    obrigada (if said by a woman)
thank you very much   *muito obrigado(a)*
don't mention it   *de nada*
OK/that's fine/it's good   *ésta bem*
hello   *olá*
good morning   *bom dia*
good afternoon/evening   *boa tarde*
good night   *boa noite*
goodbye   *adeus*
welcome   *seja benvindo*
excuse me   *com licença*
I'm sorry   *desculpe*
see you later   *até logo*
well/good   *bem*
beautiful   *belo/a*

how?   *como?*
how are you?   *Como ésta?*
how many?   *quantos/as?*
what?   *que?*
when?   *quando?*
who?   *quem?*
why?   *porquê?*
where?   *onde*
where is?   *onde é*
how much is it?   *quanto custa?*
I understand   *comprendo*
I don't understand   *não comprendo*
I don't know   *não sei*
can/may I...?   *posso...?*
I want/I would like   *quero*
do you have?   *tem ?*
do you sell…?   *vende…?*
I don't speak Portuguese   *não falo Português*
do you speak English?   *fala Inglês?*
he/she/it is/you are   *ésta*
there is/there are   *há*
this/this one   *éste(a)*
that   *esse(a)*
here   *aqui*
there   *ali*
near   *perto*
far   *longe*
left   *esquerda*
right   *direita*
straight on   *em frente*
hot   *quente*
cold   *frio*
big   *grande*
small   *pequeno*
open   *aberto*
closed   *fechado*
new   *novo/a*
old   *velho*
cheap   *barato*
expensive   *caro*
money   *dinheiro*

Places and things

bakery   *padaria*
beach   *praia*
boarding house   *pensão*
bookshop   *livraria*
bridge   *ponte*
bus station   *estação de autocarros*
bus or tram stop   *paragem*
butcher   *talho*
cake shop   *pastelaria*

cathedral   *catedral/sé*
church   *igreja*
cigarette   *cigarro*
cigar   *charuto*
city   *cidade*
convent   *convento*
dry cleaner   *limpeza a seco*
grocer   *mercearia*
harbor   *porto*
lane or alley   *travessa*
market   *mercado*
monastery   *mosteiro*
mountain   *serra*
palace   *paço*
pharmacy   *farmacia*
police station   *esquadra*
post office   *correio*
restaurant   *restaurante*
river   *rio*
street   *rua*
square   *largo/praça/campo*
tourist office   *Turismo*
tower or keep   *torre*
train station   *estação de comboios*
viewpoint   *miradouro*

On the road
bus   *autocarro*
two-star   *gasolina normal*
super   *gasolina super*
fill it up, please   *encha ó depósito, por favor*
oil   *óleo*
diesel   *gasóleo*
water   *água*
petrol station   *bomba de gasolina*
tire   *pneu*
lights   *luzes*
brakes   *travões*
spark plugs   *velas*
accident   *acidente*
DIVERSION   *DESVIO*
STOP   *ALTO*
SLOW DOWN   *DEVAGAR*

In the Hotel
room   *quarto*
single room   *um quarto simples*
double room (twin beds)   *um quarto com duas camas*
with a double bed   *com cama de casal*
with a bathroom   *com banho*
without a bathroom   *sem banho*
shower   *chuveiro*

soap   *sabonete*
towel   *toalha*
toilet paper   *papel higiénico*
laundry   *lavandaria*
key   *chave*
registration form   *ficha*

In the Post Office
stamp   *selo*
letter   *carta*
postcard   *postal*
parcel   *encomenda*
air mail   *via aérea*
general delivery/poste restante   *posta restante*

In Emergencies
doctor   *médico*
nurse   *enfermeira/o*
sick,ill   *doente*
pain, ache   *dor*
fever   *febre*
I am allergic to   *sou alérgico à*
I have toothache   *doem-me os dentes*
help   *ajuda*
I am diabetic   *sou diabético*

In Restaurants
breakfast   *pequeno almoço*
lunch   *almoço*
tea   *lanche*
dinner   *jantar*
menu   *lista/ementa/carta*
fixed-price menu   *preço fixo*
wine list   *lista dos vinhos*
(to summon waiter: *faz favor!*)
bill, check   *conta*
glass   *copo*
pepper   *pimenta*
salt *sal*
sugar   *açúcar*
bread   *pão*
butter   *manteiga*
sandwich   *sandes*
mineral water   *água mineral*
carbonated water   *água com gás*
still water   *água sem gás*
fruit juice   *sumo de fruta*
milk   *leite*
ice   *gelo*
coffee with milk   *café com leite*
tea   *chá*
beer   *cerveja*

draught beer	*imperial*	garlic	*alho*
red wine	*vinho tinto*	rice	*arroz*
white wine	*vinho branco*	fruit	*fruta*
rosé wine	*vinho rosado*	apple	*maca*
cheese	*queijo*	orange	*laranja*
olives	*azeitonas*	peach	*pêssego*
mixed vegetable salad	*salada mista*	pineapple	*ananás*
green salad	*salada verde*	plum	*ameixa*
meat	*carne*	figs	*figos*
beef	*carne de vaca*	watermelon	*melancia*
lamb	*cordeiro*	strawberries	*morangos*
mutton	*carneiro*	apricots	*alperces*
ham	*fiambre*	almonds	*amendoas*
veal	*vitela*	pears	*pêras*
chicken	*frango*	dessert	*sobremesa*
turkey	*peru*	ice cream	*gelado*
rabbit	*coelho*	cake	*bolo*
liver	*iscas/fígado*	rice pudding	*arroz doce*
kid	*cabrito*	caramel custard	*pudim flan*

goat *cabra*
kidney *rim*
tripe *tripa*
beef steak *bife*
rare *mal passado*
medium *normal*
well done *bem passado*
fried *frito*
roasted *assado*
stewed *estufado*
boiled *cozido*
baked *no forno*
grilled *grelhado*
smoked *fumado*
fish *peixe*
crayfish *lagostim*
sardines *sardinhas*
prawns *gambas*
clams *ameijoas*
red mullet *salmonetes*
tuna *atum*
lobster *lavagante*
sole *linguado*
swordfish *peixe espada*
crab *santola*
squid *lula*
octopus *polvo*
vegetables *legumes*
beans *feijões*
peas *ervilhas*
cabbage *couve*
potatoes *batatas*
mushroom *cogumelo*
onion *cebola*

Recommended Reading

ANDERSON, JEAN. *The Food of Portugal*. Robert Hale, London 1987.

BIRMINGHAM, DAVID. *A Concise History of Portugal*. Cambridge University Press, Cambridge 1993.

BOXER, C.R. The *Portuguese Seaborne Empire* 1415-1825. Hutchinson, London 1977.

BRIDGE, ANN and LOWNDES, SUSAN. *The Selective Traveller in Portugal*. Chatto & Windus, London 1963.

CAMIIES, LUS DE. *The Lusiads*. Penguin, London 1985.

FIGUEIREDO, ANTONIO DE. *Portugal: Fifty Years of Dictatorship*. Penguin, London 1975.

GARRETT, ALMEIDA. *Travels in My Homeland*. Peter Owen, London 1987.

GIL, JULIO (text) and CABRITA, AUGUSTO (photographs). *The Loveliest Towns and Villages in Portugal*. Verbo, Lisbon 1991.

GIL, JULIO (text) and CABRITA, AUGUSTO (photographs). *The Finest Castles in Portugal*. Verbo, Lisbon 1988.

GIL, JULIO (text) and CALVET, NINO (photos). *The Finest Churches in Portugal*. Verbo, Lisbon 1988.

INSIGHT TEAM OF THE SUNDAY TIMES. *Insight on Portugal — The Year of the Captains*. André Deutsch, London 1975.

KAPLAN, MARION. *The Portuguese*. Penguin, London 1991.

MACAULAY, ROSE. *They Went to Portugal*. Penguin, London 1985.

MARQUES, A.H.OLIVEIRA. *History of Portugal*. Columbia University Press, New York 1972.

Michelin Green Guide to Portugal and Madeira, Michelin 1989.

MODESTO, MARIA DE LOURDES. *Traditional Portuguese Cookery*. Verbo, Lisbon.

PESSOA, FERNANDO (translated and edited by Edwin Honig and Susan M. Brown). *Poems of Fernando Pessoa*. Ecco Press, New York 1986 and Penguin Books, Canada 1986.

READ, JAN. *The Wines of Portugal*. Faber, London 1987.

ROBERTSON, IAN. *Blue Guide to Portugal*. A & C Black, London 1988.

SMITH, ROBERT C. *The Art of Portugal 1500 1800*. Weidenfeld & Nicolson, London 1968.

Quick Reference A–Z Guide to Places and Topics of Interest with Listed Accommodation, Restaurants and Useful Telephone Numbers